Facing Fascism

From the time of the Abyssinian crisis through to the outbreak of the Second World War in western Europe, the British government was marked by very diverse attitudes with regard to, and adopted diverse policies towards, the fascist dictators of Europe. *Facing Fascism* by N. J. Crowson provides a complete examination of how the Conservative party responded to the problems of fascism from 1935 to 1940.

Facing Fascism provides the historical context for the foreign policy of the period and examines the historiography of the Conservative party. The author also includes a chronological outline of the international situation between Hitler's rise to power in 1933 and the outbreak of war.

Drawing on neglected sources, including little-known diaries, memoirs and minutes, *Facing Fascism* gives a new perspective on the Party's policies, focusing on members of the government aside from just Chamberlain and highlights important aspects such as the controversy over national service. By exploiting new evidence and archives, N .J. Crowson provides alternative and original interpretations of the reactions of various elements of the Conservative party to the deepening international crisis.

Nick Crowson is Director of Research, Institute of Contemporary British History, London.

Routledge Studies in Modern European History

Facing Fascism
The Conservative Party and the European Dictators 1935–1940
N. J. Crowson

Facing Fascism

The Conservative Party and the European Dictators, 1935–1940

N. J. Crowson

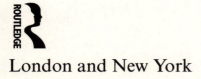

London and New York

First published 1997
by Routledge
11 New Fetter Lane, London EC4P 4EE

Simultaneously published in the USA and Canada
by Routledge
29 West 35th Street, New York, NY 10001

Typeset in Times by Routledge
Printed and bound in Great Britain by TJ International Ltd,
Padstow, Cornwall

British Library Cataloguing in Publication Data
A catalogue record for this book is available from the British Library

Library of Congress Cataloguing in Publication Data
Facing Fascism
1. Europe – Foreign relations – Great Britain.
2. Great Britain – Foreign relations – Europe. 3. Conservative Party
(Great Britain) – History. 4. Fascism – Europe.
5. Munich Four–Power Agreement (1938)
6. Europe – Politics and government –1918–1945.
7. World War, 1939–1945 –
Causes.
D727.F33 1998   97–8496
327.4104 – dc21   CIP

ISBN 0–415–15315–8

To my parents, Neville and Valerie.

Thank you for your support.

Contents

Illustrations

Acknowledgements

This book has derived from a doctoral thesis undertaken with the help of an Archival Studentship at Southampton University's history department. A further two years at the Queen's University of Belfast as a post-doctoral research fellow in the department of politics enabled me to expand the chronology of the book and to reflect upon themes and issues raised by the thesis. To my colleagues in both departments, and the students I had the pleasure to teach, I owe a debt of gratitude for providing both intellectual stimulation and friendship. In the course of my research I have incurred numerous debts from friends, fellow academics, librarians, archivists and officers of Conservative associations. Although there are too many to thank individually I must acknowledge that without your help this book would never have been written. To my colleagues at the Institute of Contemporary British History I must thank you for your patience with me as I brooded over this script during the past six months. From the days of my thesis I must thank my supervisors Tony Kushner and Martin Alexander. They kept my nose to the grindstone and provided the essential working lunches necessary to replenish a malnourished graduate researcher. Both men were, and have since, been more than generous with their time and minds. Martin must bear the responsibility of first interesting me in this period when I took his final year special subject as an undergraduate. I have incurred a debt to Stuart Ball from the very beginning of my research. His encyclopaedic knowledge of the location of Conservative association records has been an enormous benefit. Richard Aldous, Peter Catterall, Robert Walsha, Roger Eglin and Alison Kemp, all of who have read and commented upon various drafts of this book, and tolerated my poor spelling and grammar, have incurred my gratitude. Needless to say the views expressed and any mistakes made are those of the author alone.

I would like to thank the following for access to and permission to quote from copyright material: Lord Boyd of Merton; Lord Caldecote; Captain Headlam and Durham Record Office; the Trustees of the Avon papers; Sir Edward Cazalet; Vivian Brooks; Elizabeth Crookshank; Birmingham University Library for the Chamberlain papers; the late Lord Sherfield; Davina Howell; the Parliamentary History Year Book Trust; Lord Braborne and the Trustees of the Broadlands Archives; The Trustees of the Mass-Observation Archive at the University of Sussex, reproduced by the permission of the Curtis Brown Group Ltd, London; Lady Warner; Mr Dave Turnow; the Earl Winterton; the Earl of Derby; and the Earl of Selborne. I must also thank the following archives for permission to cite collections in their possession: Lincolnshire Archives (Heneage MSS); Berkshire Record Office (Glyn MSS); Trinity College Library, Cambridge (Butler MSS); Carmarthenshire Archive Service (Cilcennin MSS). The material from the Conservative Party Archive, Bodleian Library, is quoted with the permission of the Conservative party; in this respect I am also grateful to the Scottish Conservative Central Office and to the local associations, who have given similar permission. Every effort has been made to trace the copyright holders of unpublished documents from which quotations have been made; I hope that those whom it has not been possible to locate will accept my apologies.

I must acknowledge the support of my parents to whom I dedicate this book. At last they will have something tangible to show for all the years of study. Finally I must thank my wife, Charlotte, who has borne the full brunt of this project in recent months. Your daily tales of Sway reception class have helped keep this academic firmly in the real world.

N. J. Crowson
Southampton
February 1997

Introduction

On 3 September 1939 Britain declared war upon Germany for the second time in twenty-five years. Neville Chamberlain, who had been Prime Minister since May 1937, presided over the British declaration. For him the commencement of war was a bitter personal blow, after his attempts to negotiate and conciliate with the European dictators. When he spoke to the House of Commons about the declaration, he made no attempt to disguise his feelings: 'Everything that I have worked for, everything that I have hoped for, everything that I have believed in during my public life, has crashed into ruins'.[1] The fact that Chamberlain persisted as Prime Minister and was determined to see the war through says much for his tenacity. But he hated war and it took its toll. Nevertheless, he did draw some comfort from the morality of Britain's position. As he explained to the Archbishop of Canterbury,

> It was of course a grievous disappointment that peace could not be saved, but I know that my persistent efforts have convinced the world that no part of blame can lie here. That consciousness of moral right, which it is impossible for the Germans to feel, must be a tremendous force on our side.[2]

However, it became apparent that elements within the Conservative party were less than satisfied with the National government's prosecution of the war effort, and were inclined to suggest that had an alternative foreign policy been adopted in the last years of peace then war might have been avoided altogether. Eight months into the war effort, after a parliamentary revolt following reverses in Finland and Norway, Chamberlain resigned. The following day the Second World War in western Europe began in earnest when German forces invaded the Low Countries and France. Before commencing with the opening chapter it will be necessary to place this book in context: to examine the historiography of the foreign policy and of the Conservative party; to justify the necessity for this study; and to provide a brief chronological outline of the international situation between Hitler's rise to power in 1933 and the outbreak of war.[3]

THE HISTORIOGRAPHY

For a student coming afresh to study the subject of 'appeasement' there is a bewildering array of literature.[4] The topic has generated its own scholastic mini-industry, with clear lines of debate established, all generating much controversy. For the Conservative party which propagated appeasement its legacy has been considerable and the stigma, particularly the infamous 1938 Munich settlement, still rests heavily upon the leadership of today's party.[5] That the legacy of appeasement should still haunt Conservative leaders over fifty years later is testimony to the deep wounds the issue wreaked upon the party. The early historiography condemned the 'guilty men'.[6] Only by the late 1960s were historians at last beginning to study the subject more objectively but to this day it remains an emotive subject. Despite being such a widely examined issue there still remains some doubt over defining appeasement.

Professor W. N. Medlicott has suggested that the term 'appeasement' has become so generalised in meaning that the historian should avoid using it.[7] Indeed, under the collective generalisation of 'appeasement' one is confronted with a series of interlinking sub-themes – economic, political, military and imperial. Some historians have argued that appeasement had been 'traditional' British foreign policy since at least the mid-nineteenth century. They argue that successive Foreign Secretaries proclaimed British policy to be the preservation of peace, revealing the willingness to compromise to secure it.[8] Others have argued that appeasement was a phenomenon of the 1930s that sought peace by the redress of German grievances and was specifically a policy of the 1937–9 Chamberlain ministry, based upon 'a fusion of moral values, political constraints, economic necessities and military exigencies' all of which necessitated some form of understanding with the fascist powers, Italy and Germany.[9] In other words, appeasement could be advocated for apparently sound strategical reasons. Yet whilst it is common to speak of appeasement as a policy, it is evident on closer scrutiny that individuals who thought of themselves as appeasers could advocate different specific policies. For example John

McEwen, the MP for Berwick and Haddington, was willing for there to be negotiations with the Italians but he could not accept the necessity for such talks with Germany. The popular view of appeasement is that it was a policy of surrender for which Munich and appeasement have become synonymous. However, such a definition is no longer accepted by academic opinion.[10] For the former American diplomat Henry Kissinger, appeasement was 'a state of mind and the nearly inevitable outgrowth of the democracies' efforts to sustain a geopolitically flawed [Versailles] settlement with rhetoric about collective security and self-determination'.[11] Yet all these are retrospective definitions. It is necessary to consider the phrase in its contemporary context. There is a distinction that must be drawn between those who advocated appeasement. On the one hand there were those Conservatives like Neville Chamberlain who favoured such a foreign policy for strategic reasons, believing that a war with Germany would cause the demise of the British Empire and allow Europe to become dominated by bolshevism. On the other, it is apparent that there were those who supported negotiations with the dictators because of Germanophile, pro-fascist sentiments or because of pacifist ideals. Equally, appeasement appears to have been a mentality. Sir Nevile Henderson, British ambassador to Berlin from 1937 to 1939, and a leading protagonist of appeasement, described it in his memoirs as 'the search for just solutions by negotiation in the light of higher reason instead of by the resort to force'.[12] It is in this sense that one ought to conceive 'appeasement' as an underlying attitude of mind which aimed to anticipate and avoid conflict by concession and negotiation, which is why 'realism' and 'appeasement' were practically synonymous for Conservatives in the 1930s.

The 'guilty men' indictment was neither helped by the selective release in 1945 of official government papers from the period (despite the fifty-year rule), nor by the contemporary leaders of the Conservative party attempting to disassociate themselves from appeasement for reasons of their own political expediency.[13] The force of this analysis was compounded by the work of John Wheeler-Bennett and Martin Gilbert with Richard Gott (and more recently articulated by Richard Lamb).[14] Since the mid-1960s, the revisionists have argued that the British inability to resist Hitler was the inevitable result of various restraints: military and economic weakness, dominion and public opinion, and a global perspective that meant war with Germany would enable Italy, Japan and the USA to benefit at the expense of the Empire.[15] The revisionism and future direction of research was moulded by two significant changes. First, a modification of the 1958 Public Records Act lowered the closed period of public archives to thirty years; and second, a new generation of younger historians, products of the 1944 Education Act, was anxious to demythologise the 1930s. These new historians were working in the climate of the Cold War of the 1960s and in the aftermath of the 1956 Suez fiasco. Suez had revealed Britain's decline as a great power. It had revived interest in appeasement because of the Eden government's 'anti-appeasement' rhetoric and methods. That these failed, and the Egyptian dictator Nasser survived, posed questions about whether the alternative options for the 1930s might also have not been practicable. In addition Czechoslovakia was again threatened with subjugation to another power, and the events of 1968 reminded contemporaries of Munich. Against this background the new historians of the 1960s had fresh questions to ask of those who executed policy in the 1930s. These changes were to redirect the emphasis upon research, though not always in a totally beneficial way. The emergence of 'instant history', written to publishers' deadlines, and often based upon the latest release of public records without any serious collation to other sources, was the negative aspect of this redirection.[16]

The reduction in the 'closed' period for official records also encouraged a spate of biographies and edited diaries based upon private archives.[17] This has provided an additional perspective for the student of the appeasement era. Alongside these, the military, economic and other hitherto neglected aspects of appeasement came under the historians' scrutiny: George Peden and R. A. C. Parker on the economic logistics of appeasement; Robert Shay and Gaines Post Jnr on rearmament; Brian Bond, Stephen Roskill, Uri Bialer and Malcolm Smith on the military situation; Anthony Adamthwaite and Robert Young on the French perspective; and the likes of Wesley Wark and Christopher Andrew on intelligence issues.[18] All these studies, although specific in nature, have added to the complexity of the 'appeasement debate' by demonstrating that British foreign policy towards the dictators cannot be studied in isolation and that many of the above factors must be taken into consideration.

In terms of the Conservative party's relationship with appeasement, research has been approached from one of three perspectives: analysing the pursuit of peace from the ministerial angle; assessing the role of a particular individual; or examining the so-called anti-appeasers.[19] Chamberlain's fall from power has received a certain amount of analysis. From the historiography it is possible to discern several distinct approaches to the analysis. One line of enquiry has scrutinised the 'elites' of the Norway debate.[20] Others, such as

Rasmussen and Jeffreys, have placed emphasis upon the role of back-bench MPs, some of whom played a critical role in the events of May 1940.[21] Paul Addison has pointed to Chamberlain's inability to harness the extra-parliamentary dimension, in this particular instance the trade unions, which encouraged dissatisfaction with the prosecution of the war.[22] Evidently the debate about the appeasement years is still valid and unresolved. Yet this book is trying to be more than another addition to the literature on appeasement by seeking to take British foreign and defence policies between 1935 and 1940 as a case study for examining how the Conservative party functions.

It was, and still remains a widely perceived view that loyalty is the Conservative party's greatest strength. Indeed, Brian Harrison has suggested this loyalty manifests itself in silence, which makes Conservatism an elusive topic to study.[23] However, one historian has suggested that this silence may not be so advantageous because 'expectations of unity are raised so high that a minor policy debate among Conservatives occasions as much interest as a public row in the Labour party'.[24] Since 1940 historical interest concerning the appeasement era has emphasised the divisions within the party, distinguishing between appeasers and anti-appeasers. This has been a convenient explanation from the perspective of the postwar Conservative leadership keen to foster the 'myth' of rebellion. In fact, although historians accept that the overwhelming majority of the party supported Chamberlain's foreign and defence policies, the wall of silence surrounding the party has limited the scope for analysis. If silence is indeed the party's strength then it is important to understand the private attitudes of members so that a complete picture can be drawn of these crucial years. With this approach it becomes clear that from mid-1938 there was mounting private unease with Chamberlain's policies, and that in this private disquiet lie the origins of Chamberlain's fall from power in May 1940.

How does the historian circumvent this silence? The answer lies in the party's archives. Not nationally, in the collection deposited at the Bodleian, for much of the pre-1940 material and in particular the correspondence between Central Office and the constituencies has been lost, but rather in the surviving minute books of local Conservative associations themselves.[25] These are either held by local records offices or still remain in the possession of the associations. These enable the historian to hurdle the wall of silence. Until the 1970s historians appeared uncomfortable about the grassroots manifestations of Conservatism. In part this was due to source material. Before 1970 most associations retained their minute books, rarely (if ever) granting researchers access. However, Central Office, anxious to counter what it saw as a disproportionate emphasis in studies of the history on the Labour party, suggested that associations might hence-forth deposit their old minute books in county record offices. This lack of source material reinforced the image that associations were merely there for ceremonial purposes and to provide bodies for canvassing purposes at election times. It was an impression of irrelevancy rein-forced by the trend that had been taking place since the 1950s, namely the diminishing status and role an association played in the affairs of a local community. This changed with John Ramsden's *The Age of Balfour and Baldwin*, which was the first study to encompass the local perspective into the narrative.[26]

Ramsden's example was followed by Stuart Ball with his re-assessment of the creation of the 1931 National government and Baldwin's leadership during the period.[27] As these studies have shown, when national archives (such as the cabinet documents and the papers of leading Conservative figures) are combined with a comprehensive analysis of the surviving regional and constituency Conservative party records, the historian is able to provide a more balanced and nuanced appraisal than previously possible. They have shown that the influence of the rank and file can be channelled through two means: first, via the connections of leading figures in the National Union and Central Office, who always have regular and unpublicised contacts with the chairman and leadership; and second, through the reaction of associa-tions to policy initiatives. It is this methodological procedure that is being applied in this book. The importance of such an approach to Conservative politics is further justified by the trend in British political history that has emerged over the past decade which analyses parties from all levels. Such studies reveal the nature and importance of the interaction between the centre and the constituencies and enables a fuller appreciation of the dynamics of the British political system.[28]

The academic interest in Conservatism has concurrently seen a growth in our understanding and appreciation of the party machine.[29] Studies have been made of the conference system, the party's parlia-mentary committees, on policy making, finance, discipline and membership.[30] This book represents a contribution to the development of Conservative historiography by examining how the party reacted to, and influenced, the evolution of foreign and defence policy during the 1930s. The benefits of such an approach have been shown with the examinations made of the party's military and naval debates during the Edwardian period.[31] The narrative of this work removes the vacuum that exists in the current literature of appeasement by providing the first analysis of how the *whole* of the Conservative party responded to the dictators. The historiography of appeasement has been exclusively concerned with 'elite' history. In contrast, this study adopts the total approach, with an analysis of the party from its leadership to its followers in the constituencies. A premise has existed about British right-wing politics which believed that it was the domain of parliamentary elites whose contact with their grassroots followers was an infrequent and often disagreeable, if ultimately obligatory, activity. Yet during the inter-war years an MP's relationship with their association was undergoing a fundamental transformation. Ball has shown that from the end of the 1920s politicians increasingly relied upon local constituency officials and agents for analysis of public or party opinion. This replaced the role formerly dominated by the popular press (a considerable proportion of which was effectively controlled by a limited number of men, known to wield editorial control for their own ends, and who as a result were no longer considered effective barometers of voter and party morale).[32]

It is important to bear in mind the role of Conservative associations.[33] Essentially their object was to provide an organisation in a constituency which could promote the interests of the party and assist in the election of a Conservative candidate in local and national elections. A considerable portion of their time was consumed by fund-raising and providing a social focus for Conservative sympathisers. But this did not exclude them from political issues. Active discussions occurred on a wide variety of topics, and reflected a belief that the associations saw themselves as the guardians of constituency Conservative opinion. Associations supposedly had complete autonomy in the management of their own affairs: to elect officers, appoint agents and select candidates.[34] This autonomy was not absolute because the association could not control the day-to-day activities of its MP. An assumption exists that activists have only a limited role in influencing the formulation of policy. However, the necessity of the party leadership to curry favour with its activists means that they do have an indirect input. What is more, with some issues, as will become apparent in the course of this book, the activists could play a crucial role.

Figure 1.1 illustrates the party's structure and indicates how each element interlinks. Although the orthodox interpretation suggests that the party is an oligarchy with policy handed down from above by the leader, this book questions that assumption.[35] For this reason Figure 1.1 must not be interpreted as a chain-of-command structure. Rather the structure is dynamic, changing over time under pressure of circumstances, issues and personalities. Themes that will be explored during

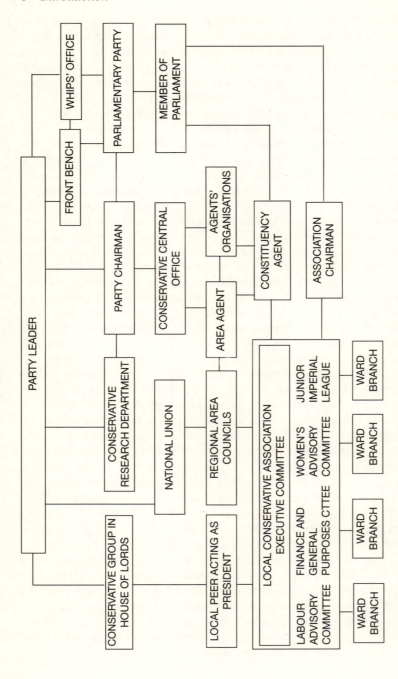

Figure 1.1 Structure of the Conservative party organisation

the course of this book include the relationship between a Conservative association and its MP, and the Conservative association and the national leadership. Before progressing further, however, it is necessary to place the debate within the context of the international situation, and to indicate the response of the British government from 1935.

NARRATIVE OF EVENTS, 1933–40

Hitler came to power in 1933, and by the end of the year had already left both the Geneva disarmament conference and the League of Nations. By 1934 German rearmament had recommenced. Feeling threatened by this action, the British government responded in March 1935 with its own full-scale rearmament programme. Within days Hitler retaliated by admitting to the existence of the German air force and announcing the reintroduction of conscription. Anglo-Italian relations were threatened when Italy invaded Abyssinia in October and once again the ineffectiveness of the League of Nations was highlighted. The invasion also destroyed the short-lived Stresa front of the previous March, when Italy, France and Britain had agreed to guarantee the borders of Austria. The response to Abyssinia was the implementation of economic sanctions against Italy. But they failed to achieve their objective of an Italian withdrawal, and Abyssinia was conquered by the beginning of May 1936. The British government eventually abandoned sanctions in June 1936, admitting their failure to succeed obliged a re-evaluation of the League of Nations' terms of reference. On the domestic front the crisis cost the Baldwin government a foreign secretary after Hoare's efforts to reach a negotiated settlement with the Hoare-Laval plan were leaked to the British press in December 1935. With attention distracted towards the Mediterranean, Hitler took the opportunity in March 1936 to flout once more the Versailles treaty by reoccupying the demilitarised Rhineland. Whilst many in Britain saw this as little more than Germany re-entering her own backyard, the crisis weakened Anglo-French relations. Within months another flashpoint occurred, this time in Spain when the militarists, supported by the Catholics, monarchists and fascists, began a Nationalist uprising against the left-wing Popular Front government. Soon, despite being signatories of the non-intervention pact, Germany and Italy were providing troops for the Nationalist cause and Russia for the Socialists.

During 1937 a realisation grew that Britain was potentially threatened not only by Germany, but also from Italy in the Mediterranean and North Africa, and Japan in the Far East. This not only re-emphasised the necessity of rearmament but gave a greater urgency to diplomacy. In January the Committee of Imperial Defence had been warned that Italy ought no longer to be considered an ally, though she was still not belligerent enough to be labelled an enemy. From May onwards Britain was simultaneously approaching Germany and Italy, believing that to separate one from the other was the means to success. Mussolini was perceived to be the more amenable of the dictators, and it was felt he could be used to pressure Hitler into peace.[36] In December the Chiefs of Staff warned that Britain was in no position militarily to sustain a simultaneous war against three aggressors, even if assisted by France and other allies. The report's conclusion was that it was of vital importance 'to reduce the numbers of our potential enemies and to gain the support of potential allies'. In other words, the chances of success in keeping peace now lay with diplomacy. It was a scenario that Lieutenant-General John Dill, commander of British forces in Palestine, had foreseen earlier in the year. He judged that the Berlin-Rome axis was 'going to cause us a lot of trouble before it breaks', since 'the two European gangsters do know what they want on their road to perdition and have the will and power to make it very uncomfortable for opulent unarmed wafflers who obtrude themselves but dare not stand directly in their way'.[37]

Baron Von Neurath, the German Foreign Minister, was due to visit London in July 1937, and the government strove to create a climate conducive to reaching an agreement.[38] In fact, the visit was cancelled at the last minute over the alleged torpedoing of a German battleship, the *Leipzig*. British attention was therefore refocused on Rome, but Mussolini proved both vacillatory and vague. In a speech at the end of October, Mussolini added his support to Hitler's colonial claims, which appeared to confirm his increasingly belligerent status. Therefore, when Lord Halifax was invited to attend a hunting convention in Germany, in his capacity as master of the Middleton Hunt, Chamberlain saw an opportunity.

The Halifax visit has often been cited as the first indication of a rift emerging between the PM and his Foreign Secretary.[39] The consequence of the visit was that it encouraged the British government to resurrect the idea of a colonial settlement, when in reality Hitler desired a revision of the central European borders. It was perhaps easy to misinterpret Hitler's intentions during this period – many Conservatives returned from visits to Germany during 1937 conscious that for the Germans the colonial issue was a topic for which there was much enthusiasm.[40] Equally, the question of returning German colonies was an issue which aroused passion amongst Conservative supporters – mostly negative.[41]

Hitler had given the issue of colonial restitution considerable prominence during his talks with Simon and Eden in March 1935 and again during the Rhineland crisis. Such overtures led the British government to believe that colonial appeasement could lead to a general settlement. Nevertheless, the Plymouth committee, which investigated the issue and reported in June 1936, concluded that colonial concessions would only be a short-term diversion and that Germany would not necessarily be diverted from pursuing her aspirations in Europe.[42] At the Imperial Conference of May–June 1937, Chamberlain gave the impression that the issue was dead – at least for the present. That month the League of Nations began an enquiry into the raw materials of mandate colonies, which when published in September invalidated the economic basis of the German claims for a return. During this period German demands were assiduously promoted by Hjalmar Schacht, the Reich Minister of Economics. That Chamberlain should decide following the Halifax visit that the issue was once more alive appears to have been denying the evidence. At Berchtesgaden Hitler had been vague on the issue whilst declaring it was the 'only direct issue' between Britain and Germany. Chamberlain had been warned by Philip Lothian that Schacht had control only over economic and not political policy.[43] Yet at the beginning of December Chamberlain made it clear to the cabinet that a colonial agreement on its own was not satisfactory: it had to be part of a general settlement.

The declared policy of the government, with regard to Europe, was the securing of a general European settlement. Although the specific details intended for such a settlement differed from time to time, the main platforms of such an agreement would involve a revision of the Versailles treaty, a series of security pacts and possibly limitations upon rearmament. The intention was that by settling the outstanding grievances of the dictators they could be brought back into the international fold. The problem for Chamberlain and Eden was that they increasingly differed over the priorities of securing a general settlement. Both men were in accord over the necessary approach towards Germany, but found themselves increasingly disputing the Italian dimension. Whilst they jointly engineered the sidelining of Robert Vansittart during December 1937 by promoting him to the position of chief diplomatic adviser in the Foreign Office, relations between the two men were to deteriorate rapidly during the opening weeks of 1938. Their conflict was initially over the Roosevelt initiative (whereby the American President offered to mediate with the dictators) and then finally concerned Anglo-Italian negotiations. The outcome was Eden's resignation on 21 February 1938 and Halifax's appointment as successor.[44]

To add further humiliation to Chamberlain, within weeks of the Eden resignation German troops marched into Austria and announced the *Anschluss*. Although condemning the means by which Hitler secured the union with Austria, Chamberlain resisted demands from the opposition and elements of his own backbenches to respond immediately to the threat by guaranteeing Czechoslovakia. Instead he waited until 24 March before explaining to the House of Commons the government's revised rearmament plans and foreign policy. He pointed out that Britain had no treaty obligations *vis-à-vis* Czechoslovakia and warned France that Britain would only assist if she were attacked by Germany. He concluded with a veiled threat that

> where peace and war are concerned, legal obligations are not alone involved, and if war broke out, it would be unlikely to be confined to those who have assumed such obligations . . . it would be quite impossible to say where it might end and what governments might be involved.[45]

For the next twelve months Czechoslovakia was to become the focus of foreign policy attention. The *Anschluss* left her, as the Chiefs of Staff commented, like a bone in the jaws of a dog.[46] With a vocal German minority population in the Sudetenland being actively stirred up by Nazi propaganda, it was perhaps only a matter of time before confrontation occured. From the British government's perspective the aim was to place pressure upon Prague to try and cajole them into concessions and better treatment of the German minority, whilst simultaneously trying to improve relations between London and Berlin and London and Rome. Equally, the British wished to discourage the French government from honouring her obligations to the Franco-Czech mutual assistance treaty, by suggesting that Britain would not come to France's assistance until alien forces had entered her territory. By August 1938, after an initial scare during May, it appeared increasingly likely that Germany intended to annex the Sudetenland. Having adopted a policy of 'realism' in March, which was intended as isolation, Britain had found herself being drawn deeper into the crisis. As William Strang, from the Foreign Office's central desk, reported after visits to Berlin and Prague in late May, 'we are naturally regarded as having committed ourselves morally at any rate to intervene if there is a European war, and nothing that we are likely to say will remove that impression'.[47] The despatching of Lord Runciman to the region during August effectively signalled Britain's active participation.

Despite concern that the situation was sliding towards war, Chamberlain remained confident that a personal appeal to Hitler would sway the dictator from any rash move. He had therefore secretly devised a diplomatic coup of last resort, Plan Z. This involved Chamberlain flying to Germany to negotiate personally with Hitler. Initially hatched on 28 August between Chamberlain and Horace Wilson, a civil servant and confidant of the Prime Minister, Foreign Office officials and most senior members of the cabinet were not told about the idea until 8 September, whilst the full cabinet was not party to the plan until the day before Chamberlain departed. Robert Vansittart, a noted Germanophobe, was opposed, whilst Inskip, the Minister for the Coordination of Defence, felt 'a little trepid[ation] about the proposal'. Other cabinet members reacted similarly. Oliver Stanley admitted to Edward Winterton that he was 'apprehensive'. For his part, Winterton, along with De La Warr, was 'a little doubtful of the ultimate result' of such a mission. Nevertheless, despite these doubts there were no overall objections from the cabinet.[48]

Plan Z resulted in Chamberlain flying to Germany three times. First to Berchtesgaden, then Bad Godesberg, and finally Munich, from where he returned to Britain on 1 October to wave his piece of paper at Heston airport and infamously claim 'peace in our time'. The Czechs, who had not been invited to the four-power conference at Munich, were persuaded by Britain and France to cede the Sudetenland to Germany. For the Czechs to have resisted would have meant fighting Germany alone. Reluctantly and amid recriminations the Czech government complied.

If Chamberlain had hoped Munich would have persuaded Hitler to become a 'good citizen' then he was to be disappointed. The German leader continued to display his old traits of unreliability, and in November the British public was to be morally outraged at the reports of mass arrest, the burning of synagogues and loss of life during *Kristallnacht* – the Nazi pogrom against German Jews. In the end, with no likely prospect of further advances with Germany, the government once again turned its attention towards Italy. The Anglo-Italian agreement was the result of approaches Chamberlain had made to Mussolini at the beginning of the year and the talks whose proposal finally provoked Eden's resignation in February. In exchange for *de jure* recognition of Mussolini's annexation of Abyssinia, the Italian dictator affirmed his friendship towards Britain and promised to withdraw Italian 'volunteers' from Spain. The agreement was initially presented to the House of Commons on 4 April 1938 and easily secured a majority. In the wake of Munich Mussolini urged Chamberlain for an

immediate ratification. And so the Anglo-Italian treaty was formally
ratified in early November, although Italy had only partially withdrawn
her 'volunteers' from Spain. In January 1939 Chamberlain and Halifax
visited Rome to demonstrate the newfound Anglo-Italian friendship.
One Conservative cynically wrote that Chamberlain was wasting his
time, since Mussolini 'has ceased to count (if he ever did count) except
as an irritant. The centre of gravity is in Berlin'.[49]

In March 1939 German troops crossed the Sudeten border and
marched into Prague, violating the Munich agreement. Unable to
justify Hitler's behaviour, Chamberlain was forced through a combination of parliamentary and public opinion to abandon his policy of
appeasement. The Territorial Army was doubled in size and shortly
peacetime conscription was introduced. On 31 March Chamberlain
broke with the traditions of recent foreign policy and offered a guarantee to the Polish nation.[50] Formally ratifying the guarantee
nevertheless proved more problematic. The Anglo-Polish negotiations
began in April 1939 when Jozef Beck, the Polish Foreign Minister,
visited London. Beck was only too conscious of the awkward position
Poland was in, having a resurgent nationalist Germany to the west
anxious to secure the Polish corridor and the implacable Soviet Empire
to the east still smarting at the loss of territory from the 1919 Polish-
Soviet conflict. Beck had no wish to antagonise either party.
Eventually the British guarantee of Poland was reciprocated with a
Polish declaration of mutual defence. These were ratified days before
war occurred. The British and French governments were also involved
in negotiations with the Soviet Union in an effort to secure a second
potential front in the east. Soviet Russia was less than enamoured with
the British-Polish guarantee, since its wording implied that Britain
would support Poland from either western or eastern attack.
Throughout the negotiations with both Poland and Russia a continuing stumbling block was the mutual suspicion between the two
countries. Russia argued that she would not agree to any pact unless
Poland agreed also and granted the Soviets concessions. Ultimately,
Hitler secured a dramatic diplomatic coup when the Ribbentrop-
Molotov pact was officially announced on 23 August 1939. With the
eastern front secured, Hitler was free to turn his attention towards
Poland without the risk of a war on two fronts. Within a week Europe
was once again plunged into war. There were few, if any, Conservatives
in May 1937 who would have desired to fight another war against
Germany, but by September 1939 the majority of the party grimly
accepted the necessity. As the MP for Lewes, T. P. H. Beamish,
observed: 'I see heavy hearts, clear minds and grim determination. . . .

No one can foresee the duration of this conflict, the Germans are confident, highly trained, unscrupulous; all the talk of quick decisions is the refuge of unpractical minds.'[51] The following chapters will illustrate how and why Conservative assessments of Germany altered during the last years of peace.

Part I

1   Facing the dictators
Attitudes and perceptions

It is said that knowledge is power. Evidently if one is in possession of the facts then deciding upon a particular course of action can be made easier. For Conservatives in the 1930s, resident in a parliamentary democracy with the benefits of security derived from Britain's island status, understanding and appreciating the transformation that was taking place on the continent was not necessarily an easy task. How did they acquire knowledge of the dictators? As the international situation deteriorated one would expect the emergence of a general distrust of the dictators. Other factors were operating that played upon the prejudices, fears and expectations of the party. Although many of these influences are difficult to quantify, it has nevertheless been possible to identify a number of potential factors such as religion, personal experience, history and culture. The importance of understanding these motivations rests with enabling a greater appreciation of how and why foreign and defence policy evolved in the late 1930s. With a greater knowledge of European affairs came a determination either to conciliate the dictators, or to oppose with every means possible.

THE CONSERVATIVE TOURIST

Personal visits to the dictator countries played a significant role in formulating assessments of the threat posed. It was a feature of the period, rather reminiscent of the eighteenth- and nineteenth-century 'grand tours', for Conservatives to travel the continent over a period of weeks, with Germany and Italy considered to be fashionable destinations. The summer of 1933 saw Duff Cooper and his wife motoring through Germany *en route* for Austria, whilst 'Chips' and Honor Channon toured Germany, Austria and Yugoslavia during August and September 1936, ensuring that they were in Berlin for the Olympics.

The young Somerset de Chair, shortly to become MP for Norfolk South East, toured Europe in 1929, taking in a visit to Italy and an audience with Mussolini. Not all who intended to travel actually made it. The Scottish Junior Unionist League had planned a two-week trip to Germany for mid-1938 but abandoned it 'in view of the recent changes in the political situation' that arose because of the *Anschluss*.[1] These visits by Conservatives to the continent were undoubtedly important in shaping many of their future responses to the threat posed by the European dictators. At the same time impressions created from such visits were mixed. Following a business trip to Germany in early 1937, a constituent of Eden's wrote:

> they are a queer lot over there, they look at things from an entirely different viewpoint to ours and they appear to see no difficulty in holding opinions which on the face of them are mutually contradictory.[2]

For a Chippenham activist returning in July 1937, the 'vigour and efficiency' of the Nazi state left 'little doubt' that the European dictators were contemptuous of British policy because of her military weakness.[3] Leo Amery visited Rome in 1938 shortly after the Anglo-Italian agreement. His talks with Italians and their leaders left him with the impression that Italy 'was wholeheartedly delighted and relieved to be free of too exclusive a dependence on Germany'. For Amery such reports confirmed his own prejudices about the need for Anglo-Italian rapprochement and the creation of a new Stresa front.[4]

Cuthbert Headlam visited Germany in September 1937. He went expecting to hear a lot and possibly 'get some new ideas about the German point of view, and where the world is going' and returned believing 'more clear[ly]' that trouble was brewing. Although such visits reinforced to tourists the threat posed, they did not necessarily discourage them from supporting the government's policy of negotiation and concession.[5] Headlam, at least until after the Munich crisis, believed

> that the only policy now is for us to try and get on friendly terms with the Nazi government: express our willingness to discuss the whole economic position with them directly – and then, if it is possible to let them have some territory, to make certain that we get a good return for what we give

– whilst pushing on with rearmament if all else failed.[6] This was equally demonstrated by Chippenham's MP Victor Cazalet, who visited

Germany in April 1936 with his sister Thelma, Irene Ward and Hamilton Kerr, who were MPs for Islington, Wallsend-on-Tyne and Oldham respectively. The Cazalet party returned gloomy at the prospect of Hitler's determination to reunite the German-speaking people, and at the corrupt and brutal nature of the regime. The 'trip did not alter our views, but merely endorsed those which we already had', Victor Cazalet wrote.[7] Nevertheless, he continued to keep faith in appeasement: 'personally I take the view that whatever you may feel and think about dictators – it is good to talk, always be willing to talk and listen and then by chance you may be able to influence them'.[8] This view would remain with Cazalet even after Munich, although from then onwards he, as with Headlam, felt increasingly pessimistic about the possibilities of avoiding war.[9] Cazalet and Headlam were representative of mainstream Conservative opinion. Despite differences in age and perspective, both had used their knowledge of European affairs to conclude the necessity for rapprochement. Public displays of rebellion over foreign policy were extremely rare, but in private they were expressing doubts which they ensured became known to the leadership. There might appear to be a contradiction of terms with Conservatives recognising the brutality of a dictatorship and yet finding no qualms about conciliating and negotiating with such a system. In fact, it stemmed from a sense of realism. Regarding Germany, critics of appeasement have retrospectively argued that if Britain had stood more firmly against Hitler then dissident elements within the country might have overthrown the regime. Some have even suggested that the British government ignored the pleas from these elements for assistance.[10] Yet there was a firmly held belief amongst Conservatives that no matter how repellent a dictatorship may appear, it was essentially a system for governing, chosen and accepted by its nation's population. In other words, the internal politics of foreign nations were none of Britain's business. It was a view accepted by contemporary Conservatives – both supporters and critics of appeasement.[11]

It is clear that the Italian and German propaganda machines recognised the importance of personal visits. They were seen as one of the chief ways in which sympathy for the dictator countries could be fostered.[12] The Germans were especially careful to cultivate those Conservatives they perceived to be sympathetic or influential. Ronald Tree, visiting Berlin in May 1934 with the Liberal (soon to be National Liberal) MP Robert Bernays, found that only he was granted an audience with Hitler. Bernays' exclusion owed much to him having recently published a book which was critical of the Nazi regime. He observed that 'the Nazis are becoming more eclectic in their choice of "reliable"

MPs. Arnold Wilson is taken everywhere. All who support the [India] white paper are regarded as degenerates. It is extraordinary how they worship strength'.[13] These reliable 'fraternisers' encompassed many from the right and centre of the party. Most were capable of expressing approval about the nature of nazism. A few of those with a diehard background, such as Thomas Moore, had associated themselves during the early 1930s with the emerging, and at that time respectable British Union of Fascists.[14] However, these links were soon severed after the violence of the 1934 Olympia meeting and the withdrawal of support by the Rothermere press empire. This flirting with fascism may have been due to a sense of frustration with the existing political situation in Britain. The National governments of the early 1930s, despite their huge Conservative majorities, appeared unable to deal with the problems in foreign policy, defence and the economy; problems which the fascist dictatorships seemed so readily to overcome. It encouraged some to question the effectiveness of British institutions and to ask whether they were sustainable. Evidently, personal visits to the fascist states reinforced these doubts. Numerous Conservatives visited Germany at the invitation of the regime, and frequently attended rallies at Nuremberg to hear Hitler speak. For example, Lord Apsley, Frank Sanderson, Thomas Moore, Arnold Wilson and Murray Sueter were guests of Ribbentrop in September 1936. For these visitors a trip to a Nuremberg rally could prove profoundly influential. The considerable space given to the experience by visitors in their private journals and letters illustrates the impact.[15] The sight of massed youth, the banners and militaristic style could be overwhelming. For some it was evidence of the revival of the German spirit; to others its was proof of the threat of impending war.[16] For someone like Arnold Wilson the sight of the Hitler Youth and SA illustrated the benefits that British youth would receive if it undertook compulsory military training.[17]

But the extent to which each dictator succeeded in cultivating the desired image is more questionable. When Conservatives compared their German experiences with visits to Italy, the latter received a more favourable review. The legitimacy of the Italian regime was more generally accepted because of the longevity of Mussolini's rule. Visitors tended to believe that the Italian nation retained a healthy, if ultimately loyal, scepticism about its leaders and was less regulated than its German counterparts. This interpretation was clearly visible in Arnold Wilson's account to the 1922 Committee in early 1936. Wilson reported that he had noticed 'some bitterness' in official Italian circles about the imposition of sanctions, but explained that 'he had been treated with great courtesy by all Italians. There was no atmosphere of repression and fear as in Germany and the people were strongly behind their government'.[18] Similar interpretations had been reached by Duff Cooper in 1934 following visits to the two countries.[19] Furthermore, in the aftermath of Munich the fraternisers were increasingly able to recognise Hitler's hegemonic ambitions and the brutality of which his regime was capable. By the time Hitler annexed Prague the vast majority of fraternisers had realised that Hitler posed a serious threat to British interests which required his being challenged, and some would be called upon to give their lives fighting nazism from September 1939.[20] In contrast Mussolini had become little more than an irritant.

BRIEFINGS, LOBBYING AND PROPAGANDA

The desire of the dictator states to welcome visits from leading Conservatives rested on the assumption that they would act as unofficial ambassadors, enabling the dictators to discern the interests of the British whilst ensuring that their concerns were communicated to the British decision-making elites. This process took place on two levels. One involved those who visited the continent reporting to their fellow party members and Whitehall officials their impressions of the visit.[21] For example, the 1922 Committee regularly had guest speakers lecturing on their experiences abroad. The mix of speakers in 1935 and 1936 suggested that for foreign affairs at least, those MPs attending the committee were being briefed by both admirers and detractors of the dictators. Lord Rennell, a career diplomat who had briefly been a Conservative MP, spoke in June 1935 on disarmament and the deteriorating situation in Abyssinia. He was followed the next month by Horace Rumbold, the British Ambassador to Berlin, who gave a very negative assessment of the German regime. In February 1936 Arnold Wilson told the committee of his impressions of Italy and Germany, and was followed in April by a lecture on Russia delivered by Sir Bernard Pares, professor of Russian language, literature and history at University College London. The talks for May and June were given by the retired diplomat Francis Lindley and Lord Londonderry respectively. The latter recounted his impressions of a recent visit to Germany.[22] The desire of visitors to report on their impressions was evident. Lord Mount-Temple, who was the president of the Anglo-German fellowship, following his meeting with Hitler in mid-1937, cabled London ahead of his return to request an immediate briefing with Neville Chamberlain; whilst Ronald Tree was asked by the

Foreign Secretary to report on his impressions of Germany and the Saar plebiscite.[23]

The second level required enrolling the services of the fraternisers in organisations that sought to promote conciliation between the nations. This also had the consequence of providing a conduit for officials from the dictator regimes to deliver propaganda about their causes direct to the British population. Such organisations were the Anglo-German Fellowship and the Scoto-Italian Society. In reality it was those organisations seeking to promote Anglo-German rapprochement that had the greater impact. Many of the fraternisers were associated with the Anglo-German Fellowship. Essentially it was a non-political organisation with the principle purpose of promoting 'fellowship between the two peoples'. However, its annual report for 1936–7 considered that even if apolitical in intention 'its fulfilment must inevitably have important consequences on policy'. It was a role that was not without controversy.[24] Questions were asked in the House of Commons about the Fellowship's role, provoking strenuous denials of complicity by its members.[25] Mount-Temple, formerly a whip and transport minister in the 1920s, was its chairman. He had a personal audience with Hitler in 1937 and had frequent contact with leading Nazi officials.[26] Throughout 1938 and 1939 Mount-Temple regularly entertained Nevile Henderson, the British ambassador to Berlin, at his Hampshire estate, Broadlands. It was an illustration of the extent to which the Fellowship had access to the foreign policy decision-making elites. At the end of February 1938, Mount-Temple wrote to *The Times* concerning the 'rise of German nationhood'. Having read the letter, Henderson responded by expressing his agreement: 'it may not be pleasant for ourselves or others but *nothing* is going to prevent the unity of Germany during this century or the oneness of the *Deutsches Volk*'.[27] In total the Fellowship claimed a membership of nine hundred, of which twenty-two were Conservative MPs, in addition to a further eleven Conservative and eleven cross-bench peers.[28]

NEWSPAPERS

Undoubtedly, newspaper coverage had an impact, especially on the backbencher and the local activist who were not privy to civil servant briefings. Although such questions are extremely difficult to quantify, one can assume that those involved in the Conservative party were from a middle- to upper-class background, educated and therefore literate enough to read one of the broadsheet papers such as *The Times* or the *Daily Telegraph*. The popular Conservative press, the

Daily Mail and *Daily Express*, had large circulations vastly in excess of the broadsheets, and appealed to the wider Conservative rank and file and electorate.[29] In the aftermath of Munich it was the reports in the Beaverbrook press that Chamberlain had discussed colonial restitution with Hitler that revived Conservative concern about a possible colonial settlement. The press' significance lay in its role as an opinion former. As one local activist explained, 'most of them got their ideas from newspapers'.[30] It was an evaluation supported by a Mass Observation assessment in March 1940 which concluded that at the time of Munich the national press had been the most important opinion former.[31] This was not without its dangers. The leading press magnates, Beaverbrook and Rothermere, kept their empires for their own ends. Indeed Beaverbrook, whose stable included the *Daily Express*, the *Sunday Express*, and the *Evening Standard* titles, admitted to the 1937 Royal Commission on the Press that he ran his papers 'purely for the purposes of making propaganda and with no other object'. The isolationist cause was encouraged by Beaverbrook's editorial policies, which ensured that reports on the European situation were minimal and that the emphasis was upon splendid isolation from the world and defence of the Empire. As a *Daily Express* editorial explained during the 1938 May Weekend crisis, isolation 'means that Britain does not undertake to look after Abyssinia, Austria, China, or Czechoslovakia. And we are happy . . . that the first three clients are already off our books, and the fourth may be off, too, at any time now'.[32] Although none of the major papers actually condoned the dictators, there was a reluctance from editors to adopt a critical stance for fear of aggravating the international situation. The press also provided an outlet for the 'fraternisers', especially in the letter pages of *The Times* and *Daily Telegraph*, which recent visitors to Europe utilised to recount their experiences or advocate support for rapprochement, much to the exasperation of Whitehall officials.[33] For example *The Times* published a letter on 12 October 1938 from 'The Link', which praised the Munich agreement and was signed by MPs Archibald Ramsay and John Smedley-Crooke and Lords Londonderry and Mount-Temple.[34]

CULTURE

One area that must have made an impact upon Conservative perceptions of Germany and Italy was their cultural heritage. Germany was the land of Bach, Schumann, Mozart, Beethoven, Mendelssohn and Wagner. Italy was the spiritual home of opera, Verdi, Vivaldi, Paganini and Rossini. Their works were popular in Britain, and emphasised that with the exception of a few individuals like Elgar, Britain lacked its own cultural base. In the considered opinion of Neville Chamberlain, Beethoven's quartets 'knocked spots out of all the rest'. However, opera held little appeal for him. After hearing a rendition of Verdi's *Otello* he declared 'I don't much care if I never hear it again!'.[35] Since the mid-nineteenth century there had been an increased awareness of romantic German literature and authors such as Goethe, due to the influence of Coleridge, Carlyle and Arnold. German methods had been influential in the field of science, and history methodology had also benefited from the 'German school of history' during the previous century. Such links emphasised the connection of the Anglo-Saxon races of Europe and stressed the common teutonic heritage. Whilst it is difficult to define the extent to which these cultural influences encouraged Germanophile sentiments, they nevertheless must have at least suggested to Conservatives that Germany could be a civilised nation. It is perhaps significant that unlike during the First World War there was no attempt during the next war to purge the Henry Wood Promenade Concerts of their Germanic composers. The answer to this perhaps lay in the thesis expressed in 1941 by Sir Kenneth Clark, director of the National Gallery, that there was a difference between the Germany of the 1914–18 conflict and that ruled by Hitler: 'in the last war all the best elements of German culture and science were still in Germany and were supporting the German cause, whereas now they are outside Germany and supporting us'.[36]

HISTORY AND LITERATURE

The study of history appears to have been important too, and not purely because Britain had fought Germany between 1914 and 1918.[37] Undoubtedly, Chamberlain's enjoyment of historical biographies had some impact upon his thinking, although the historian R. A. C. Parker has concluded that he was 'sufficiently sensible not to stress the "lessons of history" '.[38] The one exception to this rule was to be with Harold Temperley's *The Foreign Policy of Canning* which had been published in 1925. Chamberlain read the book in September 1938, having been sent a copy by the author. The premise that 'you should never menace unless you are in a position to carry out your threat' was acceptable to Chamberlain and he used it to support his objections to giving Hitler an ultimatum during the Czech crisis.[39] Lord Maugham had also recently read the book and likewise argued most vigorously from this stance in the cabinet discussions over Czechoslovakia. Another book that appears to have been widely read amongst Conservatives was Professor Stephen

Roberts' *The House That Hitler Built* which argued that the existing Nazi party organisation would not last and that ultimately the army would become the dominant force, which made war inevitable unless Germany was able to secure her goals by threats.[40] The Prime Minister read it early in 1938 and was found to be 'much less optimistic of [the] prospects of agreement with Germany', and was even talking of trying to encircle her via an alliance with Soviet Russia. Eden had also read this anti-Nazi tract and believed it to be 'a realistic account', but one which 'said no more than the Foreign Office had been saying for months'.[41] Chamberlain overcame his initial doubts, believing that to accept the author's conclusion meant he 'should despair, but I don't and won't'.[42] Cuthbert Headlam also read Roberts' book and finished wondering whether 'the Nazi regime must lead to war if it goes to its logical development'.[43]

Duff Cooper and Winston Churchill were other examples of contemporaries who were moved by a sense of history. Duff Cooper came from a school of Conservatives which was deeply distrustful of Germany and believed that history powerfully bore out their distrust. Headlam felt that Cooper's arguments were flawed because

> if one is not prepared to fight the Germans, one has to negotiate with them. Our only policy is to treat them as civilised beings but to see to it that we are strong enough to stand up to them if they don't play the game. They recognise force and nothing else.[44]

This was despite conceding that history could reveal the German threat. For Duff Cooper, himself a former diplomat, the system created at Versailles, and a strong France with allies in eastern Europe, were the essential barriers against the resurrection of German power. Furthermore, until the spring of 1939 he was prepared to believe that Italy could be a useful ally against Germany. Cooper, as evidence of the 'German menace', drew upon the 1907 'Crowe memorandum', which had argued that Germany represented the latest in a line going back through Napoleon and Louis XIV to Philip II of challenges to the traditional British policy of maintaining the balance of power in Europe.[45] Cooper's distrust of Germany remained with him throughout the 1930s and he secured himself something of a reputation amongst the London social set for his anti-Germanic outbursts.[46]

It would appear that few Conservatives actually sought to read Hitler's *Mein Kampf*. It was first published in Britain in English in 1933, but in an edited form. In comparison to the 230,000-word German original, the English edition was a mere 80,000 words. One of those who decided to read it towards the end of 1935 was the right-wing Duchess of Atholl. Following the Rhineland reoccupation she was disquieted by the threat Germany posed and wrote to the *Manchester Guardian* warning that *Mein Kampf* clearly illustrated Hitler's hegemonic ambitions. But she found that the abridged English translation expressed little of the provocative tone of the original. As a result the Duchess, together with a group called the Friends of Europe, sought to remedy this by providing a translation of the omissions. By May 1936 she had reached the conclusion that Germany was 'the only serious danger to peace in Europe'.[47] Another Conservative who made the effort to wade through the work was Leo Amery, in May 1934. His copy was in 'the original unexpurgated German' and he

> found it very interesting and stimulating. [Hitler's] intense sincerity and clear thinking on some points, as well as really careful study of propaganda methods, attracted me very much. On the other hand he is quite insane about Jews and Socialists, and indeed entirely incapable of realising that there can be any other policy but that of the fanatical assertion of one particular race.

As a result Amery concluded that he doubted if Hitler 'will really settle down to ordinary statesmanship for long. His success all round may be a great danger'.[48] When examining the Italian regime in terms of printed text, there were more difficulties. Mussolini, although having published an autobiography in the late 1920s, had nothing comparable to *Mein Kampf*. One of the few who appears to have read the Mussolini book was Somerset de Chair in 1929, as part of his preparation for meeting the Duce.[49]

It appears that Conservatives did look back on recent history in order to support their concerns for the perceived 'nature' of the German and Italian characters. The Italians had a poor reputation. Militarily, their country's interventions in World War I had been disastrous, particularly the defeat at Caporetto. The perception that the Italian military were incompetent was reinforced by the Abyssinian campaign and the reports of it that filtered back to Britain.[50] Italy had emerged from the First World War on the side of the allies, had been a signatory of the Locarno treaty, and in 1934 mobilised its troops on the Brenner pass to prevent a Nazi coup in Austria. It would appear that until the invasion of Abyssinia there was little to suggest the threat posed by Mussolini. However, recent history was less favourable to Germany. The president of Chelmsford association shortly after Prague felt 'history was repeating itself' and roused his AGM audience with the prediction that 'if Germany made war Germany would again be defeated'.[51] This was not surprising considering that in 1938 it was only twenty years since Britain had finished fighting a major war against her, a war moreover which Germany was widely perceived as having started.[52] Certainly one does find examples of Conservatives, from both sceptic and enthusiast schools, citing comparisons and similarities between the Germany of Hitler and the Germany of Kaiser Wilhelm to justify their particular view on the contemporary situation. Birmingham association heard Austen Chamberlain in March 1935 declaring that despite Germany experiencing two revolutions since 1918, 'the old spirit is very little changed. . . . It is exactly the old German spirit which plunged Europe into war and which caused not merely her enemies but the world to fix upon her crimes the guilt of the war'.[53] Headlam, who during 1939 increasingly felt war to be inevitable, compared what he believed were the strengths and weaknesses of the Nazi state as opposed to the Wilhelmine Empire. He considered

> that Germany is not nearly so strong and united as she was in 1914, and that the Nazi domination is not so great as was that of the emperor. But of course the Nazi regime is a great tyranny – and the Nazi creed is a more powerful influence over the young in this age of mass psychology than was that of the old regime. So long as Hitler avoids war he has his country behind him – if he decides on war, it will follow him – but unless he can bring off a successful lightning war, he will be up against it, and his regime will not last.[54]

To some, nazism 'was the successor of Junkerism'.[55] In contrast, Thomas Moore, the 'fraterniser', declared in March 1937 that he did not consider Germany capable of war until Britain had finished rearming herself. The contemporary Germany had neither the power (militarily and economically), grandeur nor aggressive alliances of the 1914 regime: 'Therefore it seems to me that she has nothing except her honoured, trusted and admired leader and a spirit that is still unconquered'.[56]

Debates about colonial restitution often revealed the accepted stereotyping of the German character. During a debate amongst activists in South Oxfordshire it was argued that the mandated territories were compensation for Britain because Germany had 'held a pistol at the allies stomach for four years' during the First World War. One speaker drew on his personal experiences out in east and west German Africa before the 1914 war to validate his argument that the time was 'not ripe' for a return of mandates. Using typical liberal arguments that British colonialism was in the best interests of native populations since it both civilised, educated and protected them, he suggested that in the past Germany had treated its colonial indigenous populations with extreme brutality and posed the question: if it had been that bad then what would happen if the Nazis ruled these people?[57] At the same time it was clear with the Italian invasion of Abyssinia that in some quarters of the party the Abyssinians were viewed as little less than barbarians who required the civilising rule of the Europeans.[58]

BRUTALITY, VIOLENCE AND ANTI-SEMITISM

Conservative images of the dictatorships were most certainly tarnished by the association of brutality and violence towards their political opponents and subject minorities. This was particularly true for the Nazi regime. One of the earliest to recognise the dangers of the regime was Mavis Tate, MP for Willesden. In May 1934 she was in Berlin, at the request of several British women's organisations, lobbying for the release of a prominent German women, Frau Segar, who was being detained in a concentration camp. For Ronald Tree, who was staying in the Adlon Hotel at the same time, this was his first encounter with 'the ugly words "concentration camps" '.[59] But the majority were slow to recognise this brutality because until 1938 it rarely made an impact on areas of direct concern to them. This was in contrast to the labour movement in Britain, whose internationalist outlook and contacts with sister movements in Italy and Germany made it extremely conscious of the need for self-preservation. As Ernest Bevin, leader of the Transport and General Workers Union, told the 1936 Labour conference, 'which is the first institution victorious fascism wipes out? It is the trade union movement'.[60] Indeed, certain elements in the Conservative party were more than willing to ignore repression of the union movement and to perceive fascism as a bulwark against the left, and particularly the 'bolshevik menace'.

The Italian forces' use of poison gas in the war against the Abyssinians attracted little comment from Conservatives, judging from their private papers and diaries. However, from 1938 it was hard for Conservatives to ignore the Nazi regime's potential for oppression and inhumanity. This revealed itself following the *Anschluss*. Although the principle of German and Austrian union was not objectionable to the majority of Conservatives, the repression and brutality that the media soon began reporting touched the consciences of those from all wings of the party.[61] The diehard Henry Page-Croft felt it necessary to 'deplore the brutality of method which was employed by Germany', whilst Cuthbert Headlam thought the Nazis in Austria were treating the Jews just 'as little bullies treat the smaller boys at private school'.[62] German treatment of their Jewish populations certainly pricked the moral consciences of many Conservatives and played an important role in their decreasing receptivity to Chamberlain's efforts to appease Hitler after Munich. One joke circulating around parliament after *Kristallnacht* illustrated the changing perception of the dictators. It concerned a mother with her newly born twins meeting a friend:

FRIEND: What names are you giving your twins?
MRS THOMPSON: Hitler and Mussolini.
FRIEND: But that is surely not patriotic, Mrs Thompson.
MRS THOMPSON: Not unless you can suggest any better names for a couple of bastards! [63]

Social anti-semitism was not an uncommon taint amongst Conservatives. In 1937 for the Cheltenham by-election the local association refused to adopt as candidate the Mayor of Cheltenham, Daniel Lipson, because he was Jewish. As a result Lipson ran as an Independent Conservative against the official Conservative and narrowly won.[64] Certainly, Hore Belisha, the Minister for War, as a Jew was the butt of many anti-semitic jokes. Ultimately it cost him a place in the cabinet in January 1940, when Halifax warned Chamberlain against moving him to the Ministry of Information because having a Jew there would provide Germany with a propaganda coup.[65] 'Chips' Channon, the Member for Southend, was a well known social anti-semite. It was Channon's considered opinion when Chamberlain first flew to Germany in September 1938 that 'some Jews' and the 'more shady pressmen who hang about Geneva' would be 'furious' that war and revenge on Germany was being avoided. Following *Kristallnacht* he admitted in his diary that

> no-one ever accused me of being anti-German, but really I can no longer cope with the present regime which seems to have lost all sense and reason. Are they mad? The Jewish persecutions carried to such a fiendish degree are short-sighted, cruel and unnecessary.

Evidently Channon considered some forms of anti-semitism to be acceptable, others dangerous and unjustified. The Nazi methods of murder, assault and expulsion could not be condoned, nor could its need be understood.[66] Neville Chamberlain, although 'horrified' at *Kristallnacht*, confessed to his sister in July 1939 of the Jews: 'I don't care about them myself'.[67] Both Channon and Chamberlain, in common with many Conservatives, displayed evidence of social anti-semitism, but also an inability to rationalise Nazi anti-semitic behaviour. The ambiguity of the Conservative position to the German Jewish plight is evident from Headlam's diaries. Whilst he felt that events surrounding *Kristallnacht* were 'too appalling' to be going on in the twentieth century, he retained a wariness of Jews. It was only after he met a pair of German Jewish refugees, one of whom had formerly been a judge, that he recognised the cruelty and injustice of the Nazi system: 'the more one hears about the Nazis, the more one loathes them. They are utterly foul and their creed is the Devil's own'.[68]

Not all Conservatives took so much convincing of the plight of the Jews. Arnold Wilson, the Member for Hitchin, despite being a 'fraterniser', told parliament in 1935 that he viewed the 'recent recrudescence of persecution of Jews and particularly the latest speech of Dr Goebbels with disgust and resentment'. The following year Wilson gave his approval to German Jewish immigration, although he warned the government not to ignore the grievances of residents of the reception areas.[69] For Wilson the 'race' element in the Nazis ideology was an unfortunate but important feature that distinguished it from the Italian breed of fascism.[70] Victor Cazalet was an active campaigner for refugees and for the Zionist cause in Palestine. He wrote to *The Times* in May 1938, deploring the treatment of Austrian Jews and urging the British government to offer assistance. In the aftermath of *Kristallnacht* Cazalet found that all his time was absorbed with the refugee issue.[71] In fact Cazalet embodied a new breed of Conservative pro-Zionist who was sensitive to the Jewish plight and anxious to save them by allowing immigration to Britain and Palestine. This contrasted with the 1900s when some Conservatives, such as Arthur Balfour and William Evans Gordon, had espoused the Zionist cause as part of their desire to rid Britain of its foreign Jews and prevent any further immigration into Britain. Lord Mount-Temple resigned as president of the Anglo-German Fellowship in protest at the November pogrom, although he retained his membership.[72] One friend of Mount-Temple's wrote to suggest that since he was such 'a sincere friend of Germany' his resignation 'should bring home to the leaders of the German nation the very deep feeling aroused in this country' by the Nazis' persecution of Jews.[73]

Ultimately, the anti-Jewish activities the Nazis instigated during 1938 and especially the *Kristallnacht* pogrom convinced many Conservatives of the brutality of the German system. The issue attracted discussion in many local associations. The chairperson of Chelmsford Conservative Women after debate on the matter concluded that 'it was generally felt that this country should take a definite lead in evolving a policy to help a persecuted people'.[74] The consequences of *Kristallnacht* were effectively understated by *The Times* when it explained 'that the Prime Minister's work for European appeasement is not being made any easier – to put it mildly – by present events in Germany'.[75] All the evidence from Conservative circles suggests that opinion was so incensed by the event that had Chamberlain been tempted to continue publicly his approaches to Hitler there would then have been a universal outcry of protest, not only from the parliamentary backbenches but also from the party at large, and this helps to explain why Chamberlain eased the entry restriction for refugees into Britain.[76]

Nevertheless, the Conservative party's attitude towards Jewish refugees from Nazi Germany was complex and ambivalent. Local associations had expressed concern since 1933 at the levels of refugee immigration, especially in the areas of reception. The Member for Finchley, J. E. F. Crowder, urged stricter immigration controls in July 1937.[77] Churchill revealed his xenophobic tendency when he expressed concern in 1937 about the possibility of German and Italian aliens spying in Britain.[78] This was an argument that would be revived once war began in September 1939 by those favourable to the internment of 'enemy' aliens. Only ten days after *Kristallnacht* the National Union's labour sub-committee unanimously carried a resolution (which was subsequently endorsed by the executive) that viewed 'with grave concern the large number of aliens entering this country, and calls upon the government to exercise a closer scrutiny of their "permits" with a view to reducing the number'.[79] During December the Home Secretary Samuel Hoare received a deputation of Conservative back-benchers disquieted by the volume of Jewish refugees entering Britain. Included in the deputation were John Gretton, A. W. H. James, John Shaw, Ernest Makins, Adrian Moreing and Maurice Petherick. Makins believed the group 'put our point of view and although we did not get much change, I expect it will do good'.[80] There was a belief that alien labour was depriving British people of jobs. This economic argument was applied not purely to menial unskilled work, but also to professional careers. At the behest of the British Medical Association, during July 1938 a number of Conservative MPs received letters from local doctors who felt that the Home Office had already shown 'great latitude' and allowed alien doctors into Britain 'for no valid profes-sional reason' and every such one 'puts an Englishman out of a job'. Buchan-Hepburn, MP for Toxteth East, agreed that 'there must not be any question of great numbers of German doctors coming here and taking the bread out of the mouths of our medical practitioners' (he did, however, feel that it was beneficial that eminent refugees should be given the opportunity to work in Britain). By contrast, Vyvyan Adams, Leeds West's Member, and himself of Jewish origin, was less tolerant of anti-alienism. His information revealed that out of 50,000 prac-tising doctors in Britain in June 1938 only 187 of these were 'of

German Jewish extraction'. In no uncertain terms he informed his correspondents that he found their statements

> very disquieting. There is the extremely formidable problem of discrimination and persecution which is being carried out abroad for no reason at all except racial and religious apathy, and I should be reluctant to see our professions entirely barred to good material from abroad, which might enrich them.[81]

Once war broke out on 1939 there was renewed interest in the alien issue, particularly at the activist level, which eventually led to the internment of many refugees from Germany and Italy.[82]

It was apparent therefore that there was no straight line between Conservative attitudes to Jews and their attitudes to Germany. Some favoured an anti-semitism of exclusion, believing that Jews were not British. Others considered that the German Jews' inability to assimilate into society provoked the Nazi response.[83] British 'anti-semitic' views enabled some Conservatives favourable to Anglo-German friendship to ignore the Nazis' Jewish persecution. As Lord Londonderry wrote in March 1938,

> we must not overlook the German point of view [regarding the Jews]. We must remember that, when the National-Socialists came to power in Germany, the Jews had absorbed a very great number of positions, far in excess of the numbers which they bore to the total position.[84]

Equally, the Nazi methods of brutality were inconceivable to the British 'mind' and were considered irrational. Even those Conservatives anxious to secure German friendship found it difficult to excuse the methods. J. R. J. Macnamara, MP for Chelmsford, drew the conclusion from the German Jewish persecution that it had 'made it difficult for the friends of the Germans to argue for co-operation with their country. However, at least it should be a lesson to others not to allow themselves to be underdogs to a German'.[85] He was pointing out that the only way to deal with Germany was from a position of strength. 'Weak' enemies would only be exploited. The reports and images of Nazi brutality were important in encouraging Conservatives to question the sincerity of the German regime to secure peace. For Archibald Southby, as a keen supporter of Anglo-German rapprochement, the anti-German reaction in the aftermath of *Kristallnacht* was 'the saddest thing which has emerged from the events of the last few days'.[86]

RELIGION

Religious persuasion played a role in individuals' prejudices. Although the Conservative party has a tradition of being a bastion of the established church, it nevertheless counted amongst its members worshippers from most Christian creeds. Considering the dominance of the Church of England amongst the parliamentary party it is surprising that the 1930s cabinets were dominated to such an extent by non-Anglicans.[87] Those who drew their religious inspiration from Christian Science, as did Lord Lothian, Nancy Astor and Victor Cazalet, were conspicuous supporters of Anglo-German rapprochement. It was argued that Germany had been unduly mistreated at Versailles and felt that the judicious removal of these injustices would pacify the feared Nazi foreign policy. From within the cabinet, the nonconformist Kingsley Wood was seen to be championing this attitude, which to one junior minister appeared to suggest a 'wish to be friends with the dictators at all costs'.[88] Lord Halifax was a devout Anglo-Catholic and critics suggested his religious devotion and ability to always see the best in people allowed him to be duped by the German and Italian leaders. Even when Halifax met Goebbels, the Reich's Propaganda Minister, he found that despite himself he rather liked the man and wondered whether 'it must be some moral defect in me?'.[89] In fact, Foreign Office officials 'deplore[d] his saint-like qualities which prevent[ed] him from seeing evil in anyone'.[90] In the case of the Duchess of Atholl's squabble with her constituency association, religious divisions played a role. The Duchess's support for the republican cause in the Spanish Civil War alienated a number of influential Roman Catholic activists who favoured Franco.[91] In the case of Lord Lloyd, an Anglican, his religious persuasion encouraged his belief that the Munich settlement was morally wrong and a betrayal of Christian principles. This resulted in him attacking the pro-appeasement stance of Cosmo Lang, the Archbishop of Canterbury, during a debate on Munich in the House of Lords.[92] The role of organised religion and appeasement has in recent years received scholarly scrutiny, but there remains an opportunity for further study of the relationship of religion, appeasement and the Conservatives.[93]

HOW REAL WAS THE THREAT?

So far the possible factors influencing the perspectives of contemporaries have been assessed. With these in mind the pages below will explain how Conservatives perceived the nature and threat posed by the dictators. Not unnaturally, assessments varied over time as the international position deteriorated. Following Munich, J. P. L. Thomas, one of the foreign policy sceptics, described the Nazi regime to constituents as one which was 'fighting Christianity, which exalts paganism, and which crushes with merciless persecution in concentration camps all those who resist'.[94] Derby association heard in March 1939, shortly after Prague, how

> our beloved country is in dire peril at the hands of a man who has defined 'force' as the only instrument worth while; peace, liberty, freedom of speech, thought and conscience – even God himself – need no longer be considered; love and charity, truth and honour, are meaningless . . . that is the Nazi creed, and it is this we must fight to the death if need be.[95]

And Paul Emrys-Evans in March 1940 considered Mussolini to be 'an implacable enemy'.[96] However, the first of these descriptions of the dictator nations was presented by a Munich rebel trying to justify his stance; the second was made at a time when Hitler had destroyed all pretence of being content with his position by his seizure of Prague; and the third by an MP sceptical about the likelihood of Italy remaining neutral in the war. Typically these were minority images that few Conservatives were publicly prepared to acknowledge, in the case of Germany before March 1939 and with Italy before May 1940.

BULWARK AGAINST COMMUNISM

One foreign policy sceptic, Mark Patrick, complained that many of his colleagues were under the 'singular delusion that nazism is "Conservative" '.[97] At least until the *Anschluss*, and probably up to the time of Munich, Conservative attitudes towards fascism were ambivalent. While it was not a democratic creed they were prepared to tolerate it so long as it did not threaten British interests. Certainly many of those on the party's centre and right were able to think of fascism and nazism in favourable terms. It was a commonly held assumption that both dictators had gained power as a result of a backlash against the bolshevik threat. As Edward Ruggles-Brise, the Member for Maldon, explained to a public meeting, 'Mussolini and Hitler had both sprung into power because of communism, and both were great men for their own countries and had rescued their countries from the scourge of communism'. At a later meeting Ruggles-Brise returned to this theme of the dictators being a bulwark against communism: 'the ideology of Russia was not acceptable. Fascism and toryism were the antidotes to Soviet proposals', but he agreed that fascism, totalitarianism and communism 'were as poisons to the democracies of Britain and France'.[98] Unlike on the continent, the vast majority of the British Conservative right was never 'frustrated' enough to need its own 'extremism'. The party's leadership recognised, and the right appreciated, that policy moderation was required to secure a substantial part of the centre vote and sustain electability, especially in marginal seats.[99] The internationalist approach of bolshevism was good reason to be wary. As a member of the Kinross association executive explained, the fascists 'confine their activities to the particular country they happen to rule, while the declared policy of the communists is to undermine the ordered government of all countries'. This activist was echoing the argument articulated by Sir Patrick Ford, who had been MP for Edinburgh West until 1935, in a letter written to the *Scotsman* about the Spanish Civil War and intervention in 1936.[100] Equally, Nancy Astor told the Commons in 1937 that

> when we talk about rearming it is absurd only to talk about the menace of Germany. . . . Russia has an army far greater than Germany's, and she has an air force far greater than Germany's, and furthermore Russia has a policy of an international war. An international world war is what she wants.[101]

Ever since the 1917 Russian Revolution, British Conservatives had been fearful of the bolshevik menace. They had played upon the 'red threat' in 1924 with the forged Zinoviev letter: this was an affair believed to have been instigated by Joseph Ball on behalf of Conservative Central Office.[102] Likewise, in 1925 the Baldwin government tried along with the French to impose an oil embargo upon the USSR, whilst in 1927 diplomatic ties were severed following the Arcos raid. Consequently there was a widespread belief by the mid-1930s that many Germanophiles felt that Britain 'should let gallant little Germany glut her fill of reds in the east. . . . Otherwise we shall have not only reds in the west but bombs in London, Kelvedon and Southend'.[103] The prevalence of anti-bolshevism was enough for Rothermere to believe, in the opening months of the war, that when Germany finally turned on Russia she could 'count on the Scandinavians, the Russianised Poles, and probably Britain'.[104]

IMPRESSIONS OF THE LEADERS

If fascism was viewed positively by elements of the party because it was seen as a barrier against the spread of bolshevism, were such

favourable assessments extended to the leaderships and did perceptions change over time? Headlam, who on his 1937 visit to Germany
attended a Nuremberg rally, admitted to being 'rather terrified at their
appearance – they looked *capables de tout* and no doubt are. Hitler
himself is a bigger man than I thought, by which I mean he is of
average size: otherwise, he is exactly like his pictures'. Later on the
tour, Headlam was given a personal introduction to the Führer. Others
in the party commented upon the somewhat frosty reception they
received, but Headlam did not notice, only remembering 'that when he
shook me by the hand he fixed me with a penetrating eye and that I
gazed back at him with equal steadiness wondering why *he* had
become a national hero?'.[105] Edward Halifax on his mission to
Berchtesgaden in November 1937, when getting out of the car mistook
Hitler for a footman. Just as he was to hand Hitler his coat and hat,
Von Neurath whispered in his ear, *Der Führer! Der Führer!* Following
his meeting, Halifax recorded his impressions of Hitler, being able to
'see why he is a popular speaker. The play of emotion, sardonic
humour, scorn, something almost wistful – is very rapid. But he struck
me as very sincere'. Halifax was equally favourable of Göring, who
reminded him of an amenable aristocrat, who 'immensely
entertained'.[106] Halifax was not the only Conservative to be charmed
by the Nazi leadership. Leo Amery had met Hitler in August 1935 and
the German leader obviously made an impression. Although not
noticing the reported 'hypnotic charm', Amery 'liked his directness
and eagerness to let his hearer know all his mind'. He accepted that
Hitler had a grasp of economics and politics 'even if it is crude at
times and coloured by deep personal prejudice'. He found him to be
bigger than anticipated and wondered how the regime would evolve.
Overall, 'we got on well together I think, owing to the fundamental
similarity of many of our ideas. But I admit we didn't discuss some
controversial subjects like Austria, constitutional liberty, Jews or
colonies'.[107] This was an assessment that Amery would revise over the
next three years. Twenty years later in his memoirs, Amery presented a
very different picture of this meeting with Hitler:

> While I found him shrewder than I expected, he certainly did not
> strike me as of outstanding intellect, still less as possessing a
> peculiarly impressive or hypnotic personality. In spite of his efforts
> to be agreeable I found him unattractive and, above all, common-
> place – my first impression was that both his appearance and
> manner were those of a shopwalker.[108]

Others were equally bewitched by the regime. 'Chips' Channon, who was elevated to the Foreign Office in February 1938 as PPS to Rab Butler following Eden's departure, was to his detractors a 'little man [who] is a well-known Nazi'.[109] Channon, who was in Berlin for the 1936 Olympics, found Hitler to be

> exactly like his caricature – brown uniform, Charlie Chaplin mous-
> tache, square, stocky figure, and a determined but not grim look.
> ... I was more excited than when I met Mussolini in 1926 in
> Pergunia, and more stimulated, I am sorry to say, than when I was
> blessed by the Pope in 1920.[110]

Certainly, at least until the *Anschluss*, there was an amount of pro-German sentiment amongst Conservatives who felt that Germany had been too harshly treated by Versailles. This sympathy would only be fully dispersed when Hitler seized Prague in March 1939. Conservative descriptions of the German leadership could range from scientific phrases like irrational to paternalistic expressions that likened them to naughty schoolchildren. Prague changed all that, with the German leadership evidently becoming the 'bad guys'. It was the final proof that Hitler could no longer be trusted. He was 'nothing less than an international gangster with a vision of Napoleon and the mentality of the backstreets of Chicago'.[111] Cuthbert Headlam wondered at the oddity of a 'hysterical little ex-house painter' rising to such a position of power whereby the whole world seemed to be heeding his every beck and call. He recognised now that Hitler's ambitions to dominate left 'no room for any other empire of world dimensions remaining in existence', a position which Britain could never tolerate which would mean 'in the long run no escape from war'.[112] Even 'Chips' Channon felt betrayed by Hitler's action and felt 'his callous desertion of the PM is stupefying. I can never forgive him'.[113] What the invasion of Prague proved was that Nazi ambitions were no longer purely confined to restoring the injustices of Versailles. The Rhineland had been Germany's own backyard, Austria was historically linked with Germany, whilst the Sudeten Germans had been denied self-determi-nation; but the annexation of the Czech rump was unjustifiable. The Czechs were not ethnic Germans and the invasion could be explained as being nothing less than blatant aggression. Nevile Henderson, the British Ambassador to Berlin between 1937 and 1939, perceptively summed up the changed impressions of Hitler in a despatch to Halifax in June 1939:

From beginning to end the world has made the fatal mistake of underestimating Hitler. At first he was either a mountebank or a kind of Charlie Chaplin, an Austrian house-painter or inferior sort of corporal and now he is a madman or paranoiac. While in fact he is one of those extraordinary individuals whom the world throws up from time to time, sometimes for its ultimate good but generally for its immediate misfortune.[114]

Nevertheless, until Prague many Conservatives considered that Hitler had revived the German nation. Lord Londonderry, who was a member of the Anglo-German Fellowship, published *Ourselves and Germany* in 1938, in which he wrote that:

Herr Hitler restored the [German] sense of national pride and self-respect. He carried out his programme in the face of the tremendous difficulties which had assailed his country – of being defeated, of suffering acute privation, of passing through various stages of political revolution, of having an army of occupation within the German frontiers for a decade and finally of being disappointed and refused a fair hearing in the councils of Europe.[115]

Another of the 'fraternisers' told the BBC in 1934 following a visit to Germany that, as a result of Hitler, the German people 'rejoice to feel and believe that they are again a united nation – able to look the world in the face'.[116] It was an appeal that the sceptic, Jack Macnamara, recognised because 'the Germans, above all people, consider it impossible to be self-respecting unless one can stand up for oneself'.[117]

The perception of the Italian leadership was equally as positive at the outset as it was of the Germans. Duff Cooper was granted an audience with Mussolini during Easter 1934. He found him to be 'nicer' than expected, 'simpler, more humorous and completely lacking in pose. We talked chiefly about disarmament and were quite in agreement'.[118] For Patrick Ford, speaking later the same year to the Scoto-Italian society, 'under the guidance of Mussolini, the inspirer, rejuvenator, and patriot, a new fascist Italy confronted the world with pride and confidence'.[119] Events over Abyssinia certainly altered attitudes; suddenly Mussolini was 'a megalomaniac' who jeopardised Anglo-Italian friendship.[120] For those in the Rothermere camp there was real belief that it would lead to war, with certain defeat for a poorly prepared Britain.[121] Abyssinia did not stop the desire to reach some form of settlement with the Italians. This did not stem from any condonation of events in Africa, but from the practical realisation that a far greater threat would be posed if Italy joined forces with Germany, and no matter what an individual's personal view might be,

Italy had more recently been an ally than Germany. As the German threat increased so too did the belief that Mussolini had ceased to count. Consequently, even as Chamberlain sought to mend fences with the Anglo-Italian agreement, Conservatives who met with the Duce were warning that he was 'a real Italian peasant, and as such is extremely vindictive and I am sure that only the duress of circumstances will make him forgive us over Abyssinia'.[122] What is clear is that the relevance of Italy was increasingly questioned as the decade progressed in proportion to the emerging strength of Germany. Whereas it was accepted that Mussolini had saved Austria in 1934, and his actions over Abyssinia threatened the British positions in the Mediterranean and north Africa, increasingly by the end of 1938 the Duce was seen as little more than a puppet of Hitler. Following the seizure of Albania in April 1939, one joke circulating saw Mussolini going to Hitler and crying 'Chief, I've taken Albania', at which Hitler roared 'You bloody fool – I said "Take Rumania" '. Another joke, obviously referring to Italy's acquiescence in the *Anschluss*, had Mussolini declaring 'We have given up the Pass de Brenner for the Pas de Roma [the goose-step march]'.[123] By January 1939 Mussolini had become little more than 'an irritant'.[124]

REVISION OF VERSAILLES

The appreciation of the German leadership extended to general sympathy for their desire to revise Versailles. The Germanophile tendency of the Conservative party was highlighted by the Rhineland reoccupation in March 1936. One Liverpool Conservative observed 'everybody I meet just now seems to be pro-German or at any rate anti-French. The general view seems to be that France has been the stumbling block in the path of peace for the last fifteen years'. Another wrote suggesting that amongst his friends, businessmen and fellow constituents there was a feeling that Germany was 'largely justified' in her reoccupation and that 'this government's life would be a very short one if it in any way involved this country in hostilities against Germany on account of what has recently happened'.[125] This episode highlighted the extent to which Conservatives favoured some form of 'peaceful' revision of Versailles, and it was an attitude that persisted. Consequently, there was widespread sympathy for Hitler's wish to reunite the Germanic peoples. Sir William Brass, addressing his Clitheroe association AGM at the beginning of March 1938, declared of the Nazis' desire to unite the German-speaking peoples of Europe that 'they should be allowed to do it', arguing that it was not an affair for Great Britain 'anymore than it might be the affair of Germany to say what we should do with our dominions or any British people in other parts of the world'.[126] Brass was reflecting a commonly held belief that self-determination had been denied the Germanic peoples at Versailles due to French intransigence despite this supposedly being a guiding principle of the treaty. This sympathy for Germany was equally matched by a dislike of the French. The second Earl of Selborne, himself favourable to revision, blamed the French for the resurrection of a belligerent Germany. He believed the French had had two options available to them when Hitler began revising Versailles. First, 'to invade Germany and say "no you don't" ', but this had not been possible because France was 'now really a very pacific nation' prepared to defend her own soil but 'not willing in cold blood to invade another country'. Second, to sit around the conference table and 'make a new treaty by agreement. Every British government wanted that; but the French *would not do it*'.[127] There was also a certain attitude amongst Conservatives on the right and imperial wing of the party that eastern Europe was not part of Britain's strategical interests and they were therefore prepared to concede Germany a free hand in the east so long as this did not affect British interests in the west European and imperial spheres. As Brass continued explaining to his association, it was entirely up to the German and Italian peoples what form of government they adopted: 'it is only when that government tries to harm the British Empire that it becomes a different matter'.[128] That the 1925 Locarno agreement had not guaranteed Germany's eastern frontiers was not unintentional from the British perspective. Austen Chamberlain's comment that 'no British government ever will or even can risk the bones of a British Grenadier' for the Polish corridor still held considerable sway amongst portions of the party in 1937–8. It was the rationale behind foreign policy until it was revoked in March 1939 with the Polish guarantee. The Conservative calls for revision were made at frequent intervals throughout the Anglo-German crisis. The young Somerset de Chair spoke in parliament in July 1937 of the need to revise Versailles.[129] Inskip's PPS, Ralph Glyn, expressed sentiments favourable to revision at the height of the Czech crisis in September 1938, although he accepted that such changes could not take place under the threat of German action.[130] Even after the German seizure of Prague in March 1939, Roy Wise was publicly prepared to tell his Smethwick constituents of his 'sneaking admiration' for Germany and of the fact that he still favoured revision of Versailles – this despite the fact that to all intents and purposes Hitler had already revised the treaty.[131] Nor were the foreign policy sceptics as critical of German attempts at revision as their retrospective accounts might suggest, highlighting their inconsistency of approach. Harold Macmillan, who sat for Stockton, expressed the view to his constituents in March 1938 that the German breaches of Versailles thus far 'were not, in principle, of a kind to which real objection could be made'. Indeed, he felt 'there was a good deal of reason' behind the reoccupation of the Rhineland, German rearmament and the union with Austria. He did qualify this by adding that in Austria's case 'it was not the actual union which provoked resentment, but the brutality and persecution which would inevitably follow'.[132] But at the other end of the spectrum, sceptic MP Paul Emrys-Evans, himself a former diplomat, found it 'particularly irritating' that some junior ministers were 'liable to begin a lecture on the present position [in Austria] with a sentence such as this: "after all the Austrians you know, are Germans" '.[133]

REVISE WHICH GRIEVANCES?

Even though there was sympathy for some peaceful revision of the Versailles treaty in Germany's favour, it was another matter when it came to interpreting specifically which grievances she actually wished to be rectified. Not surprisingly in this area there was less than unanimity. Aware of the delicacy of relations between Britain and Germany, it was normal for parliamentary Conservative visitors to Germany to report their impression to the Foreign Office upon their return.[134] One theme that such visitors always noticed was the issue of colonial restitution. This was especially apparent for those who attended Nazi party rallies or meetings. Headlam visited one such rally at Nuremberg and noted 'a reference to the colonial question much applauded'.[135] A constituent of Anthony Eden's felt 'unquestionably' that the colonies aroused 'the strongest feelings' amongst German businessmen, 'the desire for the recovery of which amounts to an obsession'.[136] Such reports undoubtedly filtered back through the Foreign Office to the Prime Minister. When combined with Halifax's account of his visit to Germany in November 1937, they must have encouraged Chamberlain to believe that once more colonial returns might provide the basis for a possible general settlement. This led to the Henderson offer in March 1938. However, its rejection by Hitler, and the *Anschluss* ruled out a colonial solution in the minds of the cabinet. Nevertheless, throughout the period and especially after Munich, activists feared that the government sought such a colonial settlement.[137] The *Anschluss* firmly refocused Conservative attention on Europe. Did Hitler seek living space in the east? Would he resort to the use of force to achieve these goals? Viscount Wolmer, a foreign policy sceptic, believed Hitler now intended to 'eat up the Danubian states one by one' using 'methods of coercion and pressure rather than by war'.[138] The debate over whether to guarantee Czechoslovakia certainly suggested that Conservatives expected her to be Hitler's next target. Those who visited eastern Europe sensed the desire of the Sudeten Germans for union with Germany. One such traveller was Victor Cazalet, although he was unclear as to how far this sentiment was 'due to bad treatment [and], German propaganda'. He was, however, sure that 'general poverty and unemployment have accentuated it'.[139] In July, as a result of this visit, Cazalet felt able to assure his constituents that Germany was not prepared to absorb the Sudeten Germans for a mix of economic and ideological reasons. He believed that the Sudeten Germans were too widely scattered and therefore any annexation would include non-Germans, which was contrary to Nazi ideology. Furthermore, the union with Austria had aggravated Germany's economic problems, and absorbing any further territory would only exacerbate the situation.[140] Cazalet, during his visit to Czechoslovakia the previous April, had met the leader of the Sudeten Germans, Henlein. After a 'v[ery] interesting' one-and-a-half-hour meeting, Cazalet left the 'intelligent and delightful' man who 'makes a good impression. Honest and single. Not yet completely controlled by Berlin. He appears to be not entirely unamiable although one gather[s] it will be a hard bargain'.[141] Yet despite his optimistic public report on the unlikelihood of war, in his journal Cazalet confessed his belief that 'we have *definitely* entered the pre-war period'.[142] Certainly, a number of Conservatives feared in the immediate months after the *Anschluss* that Hitler 'may at any moment provide another shock in central Europe'.[143] Not everyone expected it necessarily to be Czechoslovakia; for a while Ralph Glyn believed Danzig (another of the Versailles grievances) to be the object of Nazi desires. Nor was the belief that Hitler intended further immediate expansion a universally held view within the party. Some felt that there was no evidence to suggest this expansionist intent. After all, Hitler had waited two years since the Rhineland seizure; what evidence was there to suggest that he would not do the same again? One such thinker was the second Earl of Selborne who confidently predicted that with the present British government following the 'right' foreign policy, it was doubtful 'if Germany will be ready for another two years', by which time Britain would be 'much stronger than we are now, both actually and relatively'. Similarly, Francis Fremantle, the Member for St Albans, believed after the Polish guarantee that this had 'collared Hitler' and it was unlikely there would be any further serious trouble.[144]

ECONOMIC FORECASTING

Although Conservatives could dispute German intentions, one factor that many felt would be crucial in determining whether Hitler embarked upon foreign adventures was the health of the German economy. It was a widely held belief amongst Conservatives that the German economic situation, due to the pressures of rearmament, was rapidly deteriorating during the late 1930s.[145] In 1937 Churchill warned the Commons that the dictators of Europe were 'welding entire nations into war-making machines at the cost of the sternest repression of all the amenities and indulgences of human existence'.[146] This belief had implications upon how best to enact foreign policy towards the dictators. One school of thought, the 'explosion' theory, argued that a grave economic position would encourage a dictator to challenge the balance of power in order to distract domestic opinion. Another line of argument believed the opposite to be true, suggesting that a dire economic situation was a restraint upon Hitler because the German economy could not cope with having to sustain a military adventure. Supporters of the 'explosion' theory suggested that 'if countries such as Germany became more prosperous, the fear of war would quickly disappear'.[147] Peter Thorneycroft, in his maiden Commons speech in November 1938, made a plea for greater coopera-tion with Germany. Although accepting that there was plenty to dislike about the German system of government, he felt 'we should co-operate with them in trade, commerce and industry; that we should try to understand them, and that we should devote our enormous resources, not to the building of armaments, but to increasing the prosperity of both peoples'.[148] It was felt that although the dictators might ignore the counsel of their expert advisors and rashly use war as a means of relieving economic instability and other domestic prob-lems, they presumably would listen to reasoned proposals for economic stability and peace. Even if the government had abandoned direct diplomatic approaches towards Germany during early 1939, more subtle efforts were being made, especially in the economic sphere.

BUT WHO'S TO BLAME?

Conservatives increasingly recognised that nazism was a brutal and undemocratic political creed; but did they automatically equate being

Nazi with being German? For those Conservatives, like Duff Cooper, who had always been anti-German, then there was no problem in distinguishing: nazism was merely further proof of all that was bad about the German character and nation. In general terms, Conservatives were able to refer to 'Germany' or 'the Germans' when using these phrases in reference to intended pursuits of the Nazi regime. For example, one Conservative peer following the *Anschluss* was fearful that 'the Germans see now they have time to devour eastern Europe'.[149] In that sentence, 'the Nazis' could quite easily have been exchanged for 'the Germans' and the meaning would not have been affected. But at other times there were deliberate efforts to distinguish between the Nazi and non-Nazi. What becomes apparent is that the more obviously 'evil' the regime became, the less Conservatives felt able to excuse the German people for not standing up to Hitler. This was especially true once hostilities commenced in September 1939.[150] Many Conservatives accepted the idea that nazism had arisen and secured its position because of grievances about Versailles, and therefore they argued that if these were removed then the Germans would not need Hitler. This view was particularly prevalent amongst government ministers, and helps to explain why during the opening months of the war they appeared unwilling to enter into direct conflict with Germany. Such views were also expressed by a number of the editors and proprietors of the Conservative press.[151] Some Conservatives believed that if a firmer stance was adopted towards Hitler it might precipitate his overthrow, since 'there are many who disapprove of present methods and that feeling is growing'.[152] Likewise during early 1939, the foreign policy sceptic Viscount Cranborne criticised the idea that Britain should offer Germany some form of economic assistance, believing that 'nothing could do more to convince the German and Italian peoples that authoritarian gov[ernmen]t based on the repudiation of obligations does not work' than a deteriorating economic situation.[153] Following *Kristallnacht* and the continued attacks upon Britain in the Nazi media, Cuthbert Headlam believed that it looked 'as if these mad creatures who are in charge in Germany really mean to have war'.[154] Headlam appears always to have been able to distinguish between 'the German people' and the Nazis. Following suggestions of a possible European conference in the summer of June 1939, he thought

> it is just possible that the effect might be to make the German people realise we were not intending 'to encircle' them . . . and . . .

have a steadying effect upon them and make them less inclined to believe that the Nazis were leading them in the right direction.

But equally, as Europe lurched closer to war, Headlam dismissed as 'nonsense' talk about the friendliness of the Germans and how little they liked the Nazi regime, recognising that 'decent people no longer count in Germany: they may dislike Hitler and his national socialism, but they dare not oppose it – and the bulk of the people do believe in Hitler and regard him as infallible'.[155]

It was apparent that Conservative perceptions of the dictators and their ambitions were constantly being re-evaluated from 1935 onwards. Although many party members visited Germany and Italy and returned with generally favourable impressions, especially of the Nazi elite, the deterioration in international relations, especially between the *Anschluss* and Prague, stimulated a gradual reappraisal of the dangers posed. Equally, as Conservative attitudes hardened to Nazi aggression and Hitler's hegemonic ambitions became more apparent, so diminished their ability to distinguish between the Nazis and ordinary Germans. As with the First World War, when Germany had been equated with Prussia and therefore militarism, in the aftermath of Prague Germany now equalled nazism which meant aggression. It was a stereotype that would be compounded by the advent of war in September 1939.

SOME BRIEF CONCLUSIONS

The various attitude groups that existed within the party, whether they were sceptics, fraternisers, isolationists or imperialists, were shaped and influenced by personal experience, prejudice and the successive international incidents of the 1930s. The impact of these influences was complex and diverse. There existed a sizeable Germanophile tendency in the party which stemmed from a mixture of guilt, sympathy and admiration. However, each international crisis steadily eroded this Conservative support for the dictators. For some, such as the foreign policy sceptics, the process was more rapid than for others, but what was apparent was that by Prague (for all bar an extreme 'enthusiast' minority) the party as a whole had come to recognise the threat that Hitler posed. As for Italy, although Abyssinia had indicated her expansionist desires, the necessity of trying to prevent her becoming a satellite of Germany persuaded many of the need to negotiate. However, by the end of 1938 a realisation was growing that Mussolini was something of an irrelevance. There is difficulty in trying to prove a 'typical' example, since the experiences, attitudes, and responses of individual Conservatives were all very different. Nevertheless, it is apparent that to consider that Conservatives of the period were either appeasers or anti-appeasers is too crude an analysis. This chapter has illustrated the complex attitudes and assumptions that existed amongst Conservative opinion, and shown that these were constantly evolving. As the following chapters will demonstrate, these attitudes were to prove crucial in shaping the party's receptivity to foreign and defence policies from 1935.

Part II

2   Abyssinia to Guernica, 1935–7
The first challenges

Within weeks of becoming Prime Minister in June 1935, Baldwin found his new administration facing an international crisis with potentially profound repercussions. A territorial dispute between Italy and Abyssinia was rapidly escalating towards war. It was quickly agreed that there was a 'desirability of showing to public opinion in this country . . . that we have made a very substantial effort to avert a catastrophe'.[1] Over the coming weeks as the cabinet considered their options, each was evaluated for its given impact upon domestic opinion. At the back of ministerial minds was the realisation that at some point in the next eighteen months the government would be obliged to submit itself to the electorate in a general election. The instrument through which the Baldwin government hoped to resolve the crisis and thereby satisfy public opinion was the League of Nations. The possibility that Britain might be obliged to take collective action against Italy under the League of Nations' covenant threatened to destroy the recently agreed Stresa Front. It had only been in March that Britain, Italy and France had agreed to guarantee the integrity of Austria with a treaty which it was hoped would deter any further German designs on the country. This chapter will move chronologically through the foreign policy crises of 1935–6. It will examine how Conservative attitudes evolved towards Italy and Germany, and evaluate the extent to which the various party factions succeeded in persuading the government of the viability of their particular approach.

THE PROBLEM OF THE LEAGUE OF NATIONS SENTIMENT

For many Conservatives the failings of the League were widely accepted. They conceded that theoretically the principles of the League were right, but in practice it had been shown to be moribund.

With many of the leading nations either absent from Geneva or never having joined, there was little point in giving it new duties which it had no hope of carrying out.[2] The constituency postbags of Conservative MPs testify nevertheless to the persistence of popular support for the League even until 1939. Privately, senior Conservative ministers concurred with the general party assessment of the League. Yet the cabinet throughout the Abyssinian crisis sought to use the League. Why? The answer lay in the perceived public support for the League. Austen Chamberlain had warned Samuel Hoare, the Foreign Secretary, that 'if we edge out of collective action . . . a great wave of opinion would sweep the government out of power'.[3] The principle reason for this assessment rested with the results from a major nation-wide referendum that was undertaken by the League of Nations Union (LNU) during the early months of 1935.[4]

The LNU was a pressure group which sought to promote the ideals of the League and to educate both public and governmental opinion. The results of the referendum were computated over a period of several months as activists went door-to-door asking residents for their answers to eight questions. Although intended as a comprehensive survey, the numbers of completed returns varied between towns and regions, being very much dependent upon the strength and activism of the local branches of the LNU. Eventually over eleven million participated in the survey, which became popularly known as the Peace Ballot.[5] Its result was taken as evidence of popular support for the League and collective security. For the National government and its supporters it presented a potential rallying standard for its foreign policy critics (and especially the Labour party) and for this reason alone was considered a threat. Yet local Conservative activists exhibited an initial unwillingness to comprehend the propaganda dangers of the ballot (as foreseen by their political superiors in Whitehall), instead embracing the populist interpretation that the ballot would be an expression of the nation's desire for peace. 'It is difficult', explained a confidant of Baldwin's, 'for the rank and file to think ill of any country's intention'.[6] This made it difficult for the government to explain properly the dangers of the international situation. Owing to the labour-intensive methods of polling for the ballot, local Conservative associations found themselves, during the winter of 1934, being approached by branches of the LNU with requests for assistance. The initial reaction of many associations was to participate, and local activists were dispatched to attend preparatory meetings.[7] The involvement of many Conservatives in the LNU and the prominence of Sir Austen Chamberlain on the Union's executive gave the organisation a sense of legitimacy in the eyes of many in the party. Furthermore, Conservatives were involved in the organising committee for the ballot, the National Declaration Committee.[8] Some felt that it was only 'right and proper' for their party to participate, not least to prevent political bias. They recognised that politically the LNU was 'a weapon of considerable menace'.[9] Others were less convinced about the advisability of participation. M. R. A. Samuel, the Conservative candidate in the November 1934 Putney by-election, urged his voters not to complete the questionnaire because of his perception that the questions were loaded.[10]

The Conservative leadership rapidly concluded that if the party participated in any capacity it would give legitimacy to the result and would consequently increase the potential for opponents to damage the government. Notice was served to the LNU by Conservative Central Office that they would not participate in the ballot on the grounds that the questions 'are not such as anyone even with full knowledge of the difficulties of the problems with which they deal could feel justified in answering just "yes" or "no" '.[11] This had not immediately been known to the grassroots, but once it became apparent local associations quickly began distancing themselves from the ballot. The excuse adopted was invariably that after consideration the association in question had decided that it was inappropriate for a political organisation to participate in a non-political event, although individual Conservatives were free to assist in the ballot.[12] In other words, Conservatives tried to camouflage the decision of non-participation underneath an expedient about wishing to preserve the integrity of the LNU by refusing to allow it to become embroiled in party politics. In Austen Chamberlain's home city of Birmingham the debate over whether to participate raged over several months. The initial decision to cooperate was called into question following a speech by Sir Austen in the House of Commons which criticised the ballot's methods. Credence was given to Sir Austen's doubts by the appearance of posters around Birmingham advocating yes answers to all the ballot's questions. The chairman of the Birmingham association was forced to conclude that 'it was evident that we were treading on very dangerous ground' and advised Conservative representatives not to attend any further meetings until clarification and direction had been sought from Sir Austen. Ultimately the association was recommended not to participate, and the chief agent wrote to the LNU expressing the decision. His letter sought to belittle the ballot's credentials by suggesting that since the issue was now being presented alongside 'other issues which were by no means simple . . . it was unlikely that any true reflection of the opinion of the country should be so obtained'.[13]

It was recognised that Conservative non-participation alone was never going to prevent the ballot occurring, so the party leadership also undertook measures to defend its record and encourage an alternative viewpoint. One such area was with regard to the overt affirmative nature of the LNU's 'green' instructions which accompanied the ballot. Central Office took to protesting. This resulted in the LNU granting the party a concession to distribute their own leaflet accompanying the ballot questionnaire. The victory was only limited – the LNU's activists and the Labour party objected to the 'blue' leaflet, and without consulting Conservative officials, Lord Cecil withdrew it from circulation. When this fact emerged two months later there were vigorous Conservative protests, but these produced only a compromise leaflet which still contained the offending passage concerning the ballot being about peace or war.[14]

Deference to the leadership ensured that any initial thoughts of participation were quickly quashed. Non-participation left the party open to the charge from political opponents that the Conservatives were not only hostile to the ballot, but to the peace movement in its entirety. In the ballot's aftermath Conservatives questioned the LNU's political impartiality, seeing it as little more than a socialist front. Some argued that they should work from within the organisation; but the debate was never satisfactorily resolved and unease continued throughout the rest of the decade.[15] Furthermore, the ballot elevated the LNU to a position of national importance. The implications of this and the Peace Ballot were not lost upon senior Conservatives. Thomas Jones pointed out that the 'country was never more pacific' which made it difficult for the government to justify anything but the smallest increases in the armaments budget.[16] Baldwin had now to balance between reconciling his party to the League of Nations by supporting rearmament and reconciling the pacifists to rearmament by supporting the covenant. When it came to drafting the election manifesto later in 1935, the government's support for collective security was top of the agenda and made a central plank of the campaign.[17] The balancing act led one backbencher to lament to the chief whip that the government 'keep looking over their shoulders at the press while the League of Nations Union seem to have a paralysing effect upon them'.[18]

THE IMPOSITION OF SANCTIONS

Whilst the ramifications of the peace ballot impacted upon the government, the Abyssinian situation continued to deteriorate. The cabinet, although concluding that an Italian conquest of Abyssinia did not jeopardise British north-east African interests, believed that public opinion obliged British support for some kind of retaliatory League action. Fearful of an electoral backlash should the League's actions fail to deter Mussolini, the cabinet agreed that it must appear that no blame lay with Britain. This was the prime motivation behind Samuel Hoare's speech as Foreign Secretary to the League of Nations in September 1935, in the course of which he pledged that Britain would stand behind collective security and the covenant. In reality the situation was that Britain would at no point act unilaterally against Mussolini. Under the circumstances this meant engineering French acquiescence for any policy action. On 2 October the British cabinet agree to support economic sanctions against Italy, but refrained from advocating military measures in light of French behaviour. Three months previously when consideration had first been given to implementing sanctions, the cabinet had been 'reminded' that they 'were almost bound to lead to hostilities'.[19] As discussions continued over the summer it is apparent that some were sceptical of the impact sanctions would make. Neville Chamberlain even went as far as to suggest that they would never be imposed because Germany and the United States of America would decline to participate. This would make them 'utterly futile' and it was a view Britain should communicate to the League.[20] Chamberlain continued the theme in cabinet, warning that any German non-participation meant Britain 'should have to be very careful if we were not to land ourselves in the war with both Germany and Italy'.[21] However, the cabinet's electoral concerns about failing to appear to support the League inexorably pushed it towards economic intervention. Nevertheless, the hesitancy continued and when the question of oil sanctions arose the cabinet declined to reach a verdict until other oil-producing nations had agreed a course of action. Throughout the crisis the cabinet sought to justify its actions in relation to the rather amorphous and unquantifiable phrase 'public opinion'. The scale of involvement in the Peace Ballot no doubt heightened the cabinet's concerns about popular protest. Yet it is clear that in the long term pressure was mounting from within the ranks of the Conservative party, and this would cause considerable problems once the general election was over.

The Abyssinian crisis, and the question of whether to introduce sanctions, produced divergent opinions amongst Conservatives from the outset. At its most simple the debate revolved around whether Britain should intervene to stop Mussolini. Those favourable to intervention argued that Britain should be supporting the League in its endeavours. For the likes of Austen Chamberlain the justification lay in the principle of fulfilling one's obligations.[22] To others, it was simply the necessity to restrain Mussolini for British self-interest.[23] Churchill combined both arguments to reason for Britain maintaining collective security.[24] These Conservatives appeared prepared to accept the constraints under which the government worked and to allow it to pursue its policy generally unhindered. From the other perspective, imperialists like Page-Croft opposed British action, fearful that sanctions inevitably meant war.[25] Similarly Lord Mansfield, a member of the Imperial Policy Group, expressed the concern that European and world commitments (outside the sphere of the Empire) only increased the risks of war and inevitably threatened universal peace.[26] It became apparent during a three-day debate on Abyssinia, immediately before parliament was dissolved in October, that the imperialist and isolationist elements of the party expected economic sanctions to be ineffective, but recognised that the government was obligated to implementing them. Nevertheless they were anxious to prevent Britain from either acting unilaterally or progressing to military sanctions.[27]

The opposition to the government's Abyssinian policy was being marshalled by Herbert Williams and Leo Amery. Both men were intent that the government should rule out any military sanctions against Italy. Having convened an initial meeting for two dozen like-minded Conservatives at the Constitutional Club ('largely young die-hards, but also some very solid moderates', Amery recorded in his diary) both men led a deputation of about one hundred to meet with Baldwin on 15 October.[28] They argued that the crisis was challenging existing interpretations about the League of Nations' role: either it was a mechanism for promoting peace and reconciliation, or it was an instrument for the forcible prevention of war. They contended that although the Locarno treaty reserved the option of military intervention, more generally the British government had assumed the League to be an agent for the promotion of reconciliation through peaceful means. These critics had little faith in the ability of economic sanctions to impact upon Italy, especially with leading nations like Germany, Japan and the United States outside the League. This left only the option of war with Italy – that was wholly unpalatable. As Lord Wargrave agreed, it would be 'madness if we are embroiled with war'. It was believed Baldwin had misjudged the mood of the people, 'all of whom hated the very idea of being dragged back into a totally unnecessary war'.[29] This was followed up by a letter sent to the Prime Minister reiterating the objections to sanctions. It was signed by forty Conservatives.[30] The 'cave' considered their deputations to have been successful when first Hoare on 22 October and then Baldwin the

following day publicly ruled out the possibility of military intervention.[31] In reality the triumph was only cosmetic – the cabinet had
already agreed on 2 October that the crisis would not be resolved militarily. On a personal level, Baldwin was inclined to agree with the
views being put forward by Amery, but he was only days away from
fighting a general election campaign with the maintenance of the
League the central policy. This required meeting the perceived desires
of popular opinion whilst placating party opinion with well chosen
parliamentary rhetoric.

THE GENERAL ELECTION CAMPAIGN TRAIL

Since assuming the premiership in June, Baldwin had been under pressure to decide when to call an election. In typical style he refused to
allow party officials to rush his decision. Certainly some MPs expected
nothing to happen until the New Year, and officials, like Robert
Gower, believed delay would be beneficial. It would enable Baldwin to
calm 'the widespread fear of war and a latent suspicion that the
Conservative party is linked up with the theory of large armaments',
which were factors threatening the Conservative vote.[32] However, other
matters were at play that made consideration of an autumn election
sensible. Labour had only recently elected a new leader, Attlee, and he
was relatively unknown. Furthermore, the Conservatives appeared
from their annual conference to be more united, having put India
behind them, than Labour, who were split on rearmament.
Additionally, economic indicators were generally favourable and a
series of defence contracts were due to be announced in the autumn.
Circumstances also moved in favour of a November election with the
Italian invasion of Abyssinia. Baldwin was aware of the need to secure
a mandate for rearmament but was equally wary of the likelihood of a
hostile backlash from the electorate. Abyssinia allowed the government to mitigate this potential resentment by justifying rearmament in
terms of helping the League. When the government policy committee,
chaired by Neville Chamberlain, reported its deliberations to the
cabinet on the manifesto, it suggested that in terms of priority,
emphasis should be first given to the position *vis-à-vis* the League and
the policy the government was pursuing, and second to explaining the
rearmament programme.[33]

The decision to fight the general election on the main plank of support
for the League of Nations meant that the scope for openly attacking the
government's sanctions policy was limited. Unfortunately, the convention of local Conservative associations to suspend activities for the

duration of an election campaign means it is impossible to source events from this avenue. However, analysis of candidates' election addresses does offer some indication of the issues at the fore of the general election. During the campaign 90 per cent of Conservative candidates spoke of the League in their election addresses; whilst 41 per cent referred to the Italo-Abyssinian conflict.[34] However, as Table 2.1 suggests, foreign and defence matters did not solely dominate the campaign. Domestic issues such as education, economic prosperity, housing and pensions were given prominence. Overall many Conservatives felt the election campaign to have been relatively tame, leaving some fearful that apathy might weaken the party's vote.[35] Ultimately, despite a reduced turnout compared with 1929 and 1931, the National government was returned with a substantial, if somewhat diminished majority. Although the government's share of seats had been reduced by 89 to 432 they nevertheless captured 53.6 per cent of the popular vote.[36] However, any expectations Baldwin held of a smooth opening session, now that he had a new mandate and the intra-party strife over the India Bill was in the past, were to be rudely shattered less than a month into the parliament.

Table 2.1 National government candidates' election addresses: issues of foreign and defence policy[37]

Issue	Ranking[a] (n. 37)	Percentage of Candidates Making Reference to Issue
Pro-League of Nations	1st	90%
Rearmament	=3rd	86%
Disarmament	14th	42%
Italo-Abyssinian War	15th	41%
Empire	16th	37%
Democracy, freedom	=27th	11%
Nearness of war	=27th	11%
Germany	=34th	2%
Peace Ballot	=34th	2%

a. Ranking is taken according to frequency with which issue was mentioned according to the 37 themes identified by Stannage.

CRISIS AND RESIGNATION: HOARE-LAVAL

News of the British Foreign Secretary's agreement with the French Foreign Minister Pierre Laval, reached over the weekend of 7–8

November, was leaked to the British press two days later. Government supporters greeted the news that Britain was willing to cede a sizeable section of Abyssinia to Italy with 'considerable bewilderment . . . upset by the suddenness of the volte-face'.[38] Within nine days Hoare was announcing his resignation to the House of Commons. The cabinet had decided that it could no longer stand by its Foreign Secretary. During the resignation debate, Baldwin portrayed the decision as being a consummate reaction to the outcry of public opinion, and similarly Hoare suggested that his position had been made untenable by the hostility of the British public.[39] In reality this was a convenient façade behind which to hide. Hoare's resignation was the result of backbench pressure, not that of public opinion. It was only a month since the Baldwin administration had been returned with a substantial majority. To suggest that a concern of electoral expediency was the foremost reason for the cabinet withdrawing its support for the Hoare-Laval Plan and the Foreign Secretary is too simplistic. Baldwin was responding to pressures from within the Conservative party and especially the parliamentary party. It was evidence that 'the whips must have been frightened or Baldwin would never have let him go', observed one recent general election casualty.[40] It illustrated Baldwin's weakness at crisis management and showed the susceptibility a government can have at the hands of its backbenchers. Furthermore it demonstrates the divisions within the party over the conduct of British foreign policy. Memories of the bitterness and factionalism engendered by the passage of the India Bill were still fresh and party managers unsurprisingly had no wish to begin a new parliamentary session in intra-party dispute.

Despite the national uproar over Hoare-Laval there is no reflection of this in the minute books of local associations. This was not because the activists did not have views on the crisis – quite the contrary – but was due rather to the timing and speed of the incident. Unless an international crisis of this proportion coincides with a scheduled meeting of a local association, events can fail to feature in the recorded minutes. Bute association was one of the few to record a response to the crisis, and this was entirely due to them holding their AGM at a rather unusual time of the year.[41] The rapidity of events makes it impossible for the associations to keep pace. To forward motions from the constituencies through the Area and National Union executive and finally onto the party leadership would have taken many weeks. In a crisis of this timescale it is the reaction in Westminster that matters. News of the plan broke on a Tuesday. As one young MP remembered, 'those of us who had campaigned at ninety meetings

against Mussolini's ruthless aggression and vowed to halt it by collective measures, were all aghast'.[42] Intra-party dissent quickly emerged
when Vyvyan Adams, supported by sixteen other progressive and
liberal-minded Conservatives, tabled an early day motion (EDM) criti-
cising the terms.[43] EDMs are motions for which no debate time has
been fixed and for which notice is given. MPs giving such notice may
hope to secure the promise of time for the motion from the Leader of
the House, but more generally they are intended merely as an expression of the MP's own views and as a means of testing opinion in the
House by inviting other members to add their names. Since 1945 the
use of EDMs has proliferated, but during the 1930s they were infrequently used (approximately sixty-five were tabled between November
1935 and September 1939 on matters relating to foreign and defence
policy) making analysis both profitable and practicable.[44] Recognising
this emerging criticism was Hoare's PPS, Mark Patrick. He wrote to
his political superior the day after Adams' EDM, warning that 'there is
great uneasiness, deeper and more widespread, for instance, than
anything we had over the India Bill at its worst moments'. Continuing,
he explained that the 'more progressively minded' objected in terms of
the League and ethics, whilst the right-wing diehards took umbrage at
the concept of ' "scuttle" before Mussolini'. Moreover, many were
complaining that they were unable to justify to their constituents
support for the plan, having just campaigned on defending the League
and collective security.[45]

However, it was the events that occurred during the next week that
most directly influenced Hoare's fate and illustrated the swelling of
opinion against the Foreign Secretary. The momentum to remove
Hoare only grew after MPs had been given the opportunity to gauge
opinions in their constituencies. This had happened over the weekend
of 13–14 November, and it was at this point that the activists had the
opportunity to make their views known. The importance of the
weekend for allowing MPs to reflect and judge the strength of grassroots feeling on matters was widely recognised, although some
exhibited scepticism as to how the decision was reached. Stanley
Baldwin reportedly declared during 1936 that he had 'always believed
in the weekend. But how they do it I don't know. I suppose they talk to
the station master'.[46] Since the 1920s politicians had increasingly relied
upon local constituency officials and agents for analysis of public or
party opinion. It is clear that the chairman, president and agent were
the principal figures an MP would consult with, although since executive committees were usually small in composition at this time, with
members who had often served for many years and so secured both

experience and respect, it was possible for them to be canvassed in the course of a weekend. At the same time, although MPs rarely, if ever, held surgeries, constituents were not adverse to writing letters to express their views on matters of issue. Many MPs were conscious that their electorate, especially the Conservative voters, was able to find little justification for the abandonment of collective security. Thomas Jones observed that whilst Walter Elliot 'had received only one letter and one postcard of protest' from his Glaswegian constituents, a Labour candidate reported receiving eighty letters from Conservatives saying that in light of events they wished they had voted Labour.[47]

When MPs returned to Westminster the following week they found that Edward Spears had tabled a new EDM critical of Hoare. Fifty-seven backbench Conservatives added their names – only ten of whom had been signatories to Adams' motion of the previous week. It was clear that a body of opinion was building against the Foreign Secretary. At the same time it is apparent that other Conservatives were sceptical of Hoare's plans for Abyssinia.[48] That same evening the backbench Foreign Affairs Committee met. The prestige of this committee rested with its then chairman, Sir Austen Chamberlain. As a former foreign secretary who had negotiated the 1925 Locarno treaty, Chamberlain was probably the most influential backbencher of the day, especially with regard to matters of foreign affairs. For him the crisis caused conflict between two ideals: the desire for Anglo-Italian accord and the belief that if the aggressor was not dealt with it would weaken the League. Although the Committee was independent of the official party structure it was given due recognition by the custom of having one of the whips in attendance at meetings. This enabled the leadership to be appraised of the Committee's deliberations. No minutes survive for the Committee; however, the presence of several backbench diarists at this particular meeting enables a reconstruction of events. Austen Chamberlain opened the meeting advocating general support for the government but regretting the Paris procedure. Harold Nicolson also spoke, but in critical terms. The tenor of the meeting, which had an attendance of about fifty, was profoundly influenced by the intercession of the Duchess of Atholl. Her typically vigorous, right-wing defence of the Hoare-Laval terms alienated many present. When it became apparent that the majority were 'so hostile' about the government's actions, Chamberlain found 'that he could not maintain the mildly critical attitude he had intended' and was obliged to sum up against the government. The Committee instructed Sir Austen to seek a meeting with Baldwin and to convey its sentiment that Hoare should resign.[49] It is important to understand with the functioning of Conservative meetings (from the National Union's annual conference to backbench committees) that the reaction and tenor of the floor to speeches is more important than any vote or motions that may be taken. From this meeting it was apparent that many of the party's leading foreign policy specialists were hostile to the Hoare-Laval proposals. For participants it was recognised the Committee served a dual purpose: it gave the 'disgruntled a chance of letting off steam in an apparently harmless atmosphere', and it enabled 'people of experience to point out difficulties which it would be impossible to mention in the Chamber itself'.[50] The party leadership would be aware of any discussions and sentiments expressed in the Committee because of the presence of a whip, whilst individual ministers, notably Eden, were kept abreast of the discussion by their PPSs who would attend on their behalf. The report that the cabinet received about the mood of backbenchers from the whips was crucial in their decision to insist on the Foreign Secretary's resignation. Indeed Margesson reported that 'Our men won't stand for it' and told Baldwin that the Foreign Secretary had to be dispensed with.[51]

However, it would be wrong to assume that Hoare was without supporters (see Table 2.2). Nor was the Duchess of Atholl alone in supporting the beleaguered minister. Her EDM secured a further twenty-six names. Moreover, Alfred Knox had tabled a counter-motion to Vyvyan Adam's EDM. This won approval from sixteen MPs.[52] In total forty-two Conservatives, principally from the right and isolationist elements of the party, were prepared to defend the Foreign Secretary. They saw that the Hoare-Laval plan offered an opportunity to resolve the Abyssinian crisis, which would safeguard British imperial interests in north-east Africa for the present whilst rearmament progressed, and would reduce the risk of Italy being driven into Germany's embrace. Numerically this level of support compared to sixty-four critics who had supported either the Adams or Spears motions. The problem was that by 17 December few were prepared to publicly side with the Foreign Secretary. One of the few was Edward Winterton. He considered the attacks to be 'the most unfair plot against him personally. There is no more occasion for him to resign, than for the whole government to do so'. It was, Winterton suspected, part of a campaign by those Tories who wished to see Eden elevated to the foreign secretaryship. It was with this motivation that Winterton proposed a compromise amendment during the censure debate on 19 December.[53] The ideological battle lines that were to later characterise the intra-foreign policy disputes of 1938–9 had been drawn. Those Conservatives with a left-centre slant were urging Hoare's resignation on the grounds that the League should be supported and the dictators

Table 2.2 Support for and against Hoare remaining as Foreign Secretary[54]

Favourable to Hoare	Undecided	Opposed to Hoare
Amery, L. 11 Dec.	Chamberlain, A. 15 Dec.	Adams EDM 11 Dec. 18 signatures
Atholl EDM 12 Dec. 27 signatures	Denman, R. 17 Dec.	Sandys, D. 11 Dec.
Carver, W.H. 12 Dec.	Nicolson, H. 17 Dec.	Hartington, 12 Dec.
Knox EDM 12 Dec. 16 signatures	Hartington, Ld. 17 Dec.	Denville, A. 16 Dec.
Somerville, A. 12 Dec.		Spears Amendment 17 Dec. 58 signatures
Denville, A. 16 Dec.		Somerville, A. 17 Dec
Winterton Amendment 17 Dec. 6 signatures		Carver, W.H. 17 Dec.
Channon, H. 17 Dec.		Foreign affairs cttee 17 Dec.
		Nicolson, H. 17 Dec.
		Whips' office 17 Dec.
		Macmillan, H. 18 Dec.
		Glyn, R.
		Cecil, Lord Hugh
		Bourne, R.C.

resisted, whilst the imperialist/isolationist centre-right was offering its support. For one observer there was the considerable irony that Baldwin was now being supported in his foreign policy by those who had been agitating for his removal since the beginning of the decade:

> It must indeed be galling for the Prime Minister to reflect on the character of the limited support which his new foreign policy is receiving. In the House of Commons many members on the government side are in open revolt; many more are anxious and distressed. The only whole-hearted supporters are to be found among the very men who for six years have been steadily engaged in fighting Mr Baldwin's main policies and undermining his leadership.[55]

It is noticeable that many of those supporting the pro-Hoare EDMs had been rebels over the passage of the 1935 India Act. Hoare's position was also being championed by the Rothermere press empire which saw the Plan as 'the possible means of saving an unprepared Britain from war'.[56] At this stage there was a possibility that Hoare may have been able to weather the storm, had not Baldwin also been faced with a revolt from within the cabinet. Walter Elliot, Oliver Stanley, Duff Cooper and Ormsby-Gore, the 'young men' of the cabinet, made their dislike of the proposals apparent. To observers it was increasingly apparent that cabinet was 'rather tepidly' supporting Hoare.[57] The crucial cabinet meeting came the day after the backbench Foreign Affairs Committee had met. J. H. Thomas, the Secretary of State for the Colonies, no doubt looking to explain backbench hostility, thought that 'Members would be going back to their constituencies to celebrate their victory [in the general election] and would find themselves faced with disintegration'. There is no doubt that some Conservative MPs were acutely embarrassed by the terms of the Plan because of the extreme close proximity to their contrary pro-League general election pledges. The situation was not lost on Baldwin, with his conclusion that it was a 'worse situation in the House of Commons than he had ever known'. The outcome of this meeting was the cabinet's decision to withdraw its support for Hoare's terms.[58] His resignation was soon received.

From Baldwin's perspective the government was not clear of danger. It was still faced with Hoare's resignation speech and a vote of censure. Baldwin acted to neutralise the situation. It was suggested to Hoare that if he went with minimum of fuss, then Baldwin would seek to return him to cabinet office at the earliest opportunity. The Prime Minister then sought to stifle the revolt from the backbenches by allowing Sir Austen Chamberlain to believe that he would be the next Foreign Secretary.[59] Dutifully Sir Austen defended the government during the resignation debate. Speaking early in the debate, his defence of the government undoubtedly carried a number of waivers, and proved equally frustrating to those disaffected Conservatives seeking a lead.

The implications of the whole episode were manifest. Baldwin felt able to confide in Thomas Jones that the

> one thundering good thing we have got out of it is the realisation of what sanctions mean. They mean that we have got to be much more self-contained. Europe had to be rearmed and to be ready, that is the conclusion which follows upon collective security.[60]

This was a conclusion to which privately many were turning. The problem was that Baldwin failed to articulate his verdict to his party. Had he chosen to do so he would have found an increasingly receptive audience. Instead his silence drew into question (once more) his own credibility as Prime Minister, both with cabinet colleagues and the parliamentary party.[61] Furthermore, as a result of promoting Eden to Foreign Secretary Baldwin had succeeded in alienating Austen Chamberlain, who became increasingly allied with Churchill, Grigg, Page-Croft and Winterton.[62] Press speculation about this quintet's 'rebellion' was rife. Over the coming weeks and months mutterings of disenchantment reverberated around the corridors of Westminster, with Neville Chamberlain increasingly being talked of as a suitable successor. For Hoare, his ambitions of securing the leadership had been scuttled by the fiasco. What is more this was the second Foreign Secretary in succession to have been offered as a sacrifice to disaffected backbenchers, which compounded an impression that the government was in the realm of foreign policy at the mercy of its supporters.

RHINELAND, 6 MARCH

With the British and French governments continuing to be distracted by events in Geneva and Abyssinia, Hitler ordered his troops to march into the demilitarised Rhineland zone. In a few hours, Germany had effectively torn up the Locarno treaty and stolen another slice of the forbidden Versailles fruit. The potential consequences were enormous 'and not unnaturally' recorded Harry Crookshank, 'the world is upside down'.[63] One MP hurried down to the German embassy to 'beg them to make concessions'.[64] For the Conservative party and the government, this event, coming at the time it did, was to have considerable repercussions. Not only did this episode oblige the party to reconsider its stance on sanctions and the League, but also it exposed their Francophobia. The crisis also put the fledgling British defence programme into perspective and forced the government to give consideration to the matter of colonial restitution. For contemporaries, a realisation grew that if punitive action was taken against Hitler it would have the effect of drawing Germany and Italy together – the very thing British foreign policy had been trying to prevent. In reverse it was clear in certain circles that to continue sanctions against Italy encouraged the exact same scenario. It was in Amery's opinion

> a most adroitly timed stroke and an interesting commentary on the folly of a policy which has broken up the Anglo-Franco-Italian

understanding. The one good thing that may come out of it is a dropping of sanctions against Italy.[65]

But would the government be persuaded of this view, and in the meantime, what was to be done about Germany?

Neville Thompson has argued that the Conservative party 'voluntarily refrained' from discussing the Rhineland crisis so as not to embarrass the government. In support of his argument Thompson cites the restraint displayed during the 9–10 March defence debate and observes that it was not until 26 March that there was a specific parliamentary debate on the Rhineland.[66] The evidence now available to the historian presents a different interpretation. Publicly, restraint was the case, but behind the scenes it was a different matter entirely. Credence is given to this thesis by contemporary newspaper reports that suggested powerful forces within the party (the Chamberlain-Winterton-Grigg-Churchill cabal) were obliging the government to respond in the manner they wished.[67] The remilitarisation of the Rhine zone jolted the party and compelled its members to begin a rapid re-evaluation of their expectations. Amery noted in both the lobbies and smoking-rooms of the House of Commons a very strong 'atmosphere of dissatisfaction with the government'. He was even approached by a backbencher, Walter Liddall, and told that 'underground dissatisfaction was rising very rapidly' and that it was hoped he would provide the disaffected with a lead.[68]

The backbench Foreign Affairs Committee provided the venue for Conservative debate. The Committee first met to discuss the matter on 12 March. The foreign affairs 'specialists' all sought to speak. Winterton, Boothby, Austen Chamberlain and Grigg all desired some form of action to force a German withdrawal. It was agreed that Hitler's action could not be condoned and that this event could mean the end of collective security. Francophile Conservatives, such as Churchill, urged that Britain should stand by her Locarno partner and called for sanctions, believing that the other nations of Europe would only be too willing to assist. However, 'opinion was by no means unanimous'.[69] Nancy Astor and Hoare believed it would be 'criminal' to fight for the Rhineland. It was pointed out that there was considerable popular support in Britain for Germany and that any notion of the nations of Europe uniting to fight Germany was at the least fanciful, they were as unprepared militarily as Britain.[70] Some like Amery were inclined to feel that the whole episode had arisen from the government's failure to sanction the Hoare-Laval plan the previous December.[71] Hoare-Laval had offered a last-ditch opportunity to restore the Stresa Front. Instead relations between Britain and France were strained and each continued to be distracted by events in Abyssinia, enabling Mussolini to strike further blows at the European order by refusing to guarantee the Italian obligations to Locarno. Other Conservatives were quite willing to concede that morally Germany had an entitlement to the Rhineland, and that recent French behaviour, by signing the Franco-Soviet pact, justified the action. Nevertheless few were publicly prepared to sanction Hitler's actions. In seeking to explain Hitler's behaviour the furthest most Conservatives were publicly prepared to lean was to suggest that 'it was [an] internal necessity' arising from the need to unify his country and consolidate his leadership.[72]

When the backbench Foreign Affairs Committee reconvened five days later the meeting was well attended, with over 200 Members crowding into the committee room. It proved an 'exciting debate mainly by younger members . . . mainly on shades rather than sheer differences of opinion as to how to treat the occupation of the Rhineland'.[73] It further demonstrated the existence of pro-German sentiment amongst Conservatives. Proceedings were opened by Victor Raikes, a right-winger, arguing that to commit too deeply to France would only result in war. It was his opinion that the country was not prepared to fight for France. This was an interpretation borne out by the constituency correspondence some backbenchers were receiving. It was apparent too that nor were the French entirely convinced that British public opinion would have tolerated a French mobilisation.[74] Raikes further argued that it would be 'intolerable' if sanctions were discontinued against Italy only to be imposed on Germany when their failings were blatantly apparent.[75] The former diplomat and recently elected Leicester East MP, Harold Nicolson, contradicted Raikes' speech with the counter-argument that Britain was 'bound morally by Locarno' and that whilst the British government should seek to 'restrain France from any rash demands we must never betray her'. It was a view seconded by Anthony Crossley. Nevertheless it is apparent that the fear that French intransigence might draw Britain into a conflict against her will held considerable sway with Conservatives. Arnold Wilson told the meeting that Britain had 'no sympathy with France'.[76] It was a concern that W. W. Astor publicly expressed when he told the House of Commons in his maiden speech that 'if we are to be responsible for defending her north-eastern frontier she must undertake not to indulge in political adventures in eastern Europe, which might provoke trouble in which we might be involved'.[77] It would appear that there was a general feeling amongst Conservatives that

Britain would never have signed the 1925 Locarno treaty if the Franco-Soviet pact had then been in existence. Certainly the Francophobia amongst the right arose from the belief that the French were hindering the inevitable Germanic expansion in eastern Europe and consequently obliging Hitler to turn his attention westward. For the imperialists a German-dominated central Europe would distract Germany from other ambitions and could be used as a means to end German demands for ex-colonies. When Leo Amery entered the fray the Committee's debate had been raging for an hour. He was again anxious that Britain should not be drawn into either military or economic sanctions, but accepted the moral obligations owed to the French. Nevertheless, it was his belief that consideration should be given to the German proposals regardless of whether the French wanted to or not. In effect, Amery was arguing again for a restoration of the Stresa Front. Amery considered that his speech had taken the middle ground between the pro-German and pro-French factions at the meeting and concurred with Winterton's assessment that 'neither . . . were so far apart'.[78]

Throughout the Committee's deliberations on the crisis, Baldwin and the cabinet were kept closely informed of the opinions being expressed via Alec Dunglass.[79] When the cabinet met to discuss its approach for the forthcoming parliamentary debate on the crisis it was 'reminded' that within the Palace of Westminster there 'was a good deal of anxiety' about British commitments to the security of France and Belgium which were not being alleviated by the public expressions of the French leader, Flandin.[80] Throughout its discussions the cabinet bore in mind the likely reaction of public opinion. At one meeting they had been warned that opinion

> was strongly opposed to any military action against the Germans in the demilitarised zone. In particular, the ex-Service men were very anti-French. Moreover, many people, perhaps most people, were saying openly that they did not see why the Germans should not re-occupy the Rhineland.[81]

Few, if any, in Britain were able to foresee the need for a French military push into the Rhineland for the sake of defending an eastern European nation; something that was clearly evident in the British criticism of the Franco-Soviet pact. As a consequence of party and public opinion the cabinet concluded that it ought to take the opportunity of the parliamentary debate to enlighten opinion, 'which was assuming that Germany was the "white sheep" and not the "black sheep" '.[82]

What the Rhineland crisis did was to harden Conservative views on the League, and what it really represented was a crisis in Anglo-French relations. When the Foreign Affairs Committee convened on 22 April there appeared to be general agreement that the time had come for a showdown. Right-wingers made the case for directing diplomatic energies to resisting Germany. This could be achieved by detaching Italy from Germany. The means to reach this end required the government to admit that sanctions had failed and in turn accept the Italian conquest of Abyssinia. This would enable the Italians to return to the negotiating table. These sentiments were conveyed to the Foreign Secretary via his PPS Roger Lumley. Furthermore, Lumley reported that the meeting had expressed support for the abolition of Article 16 of the League's covenant and that there had been a consensus for a reconfiguration of British commitments to realistic and attainable targets.[83] Less than a week later the cabinet agreed to the formation of a sub-committee to consider Britain's commitments, and at its inaugural meeting Eden referred to the views of the Foreign Affairs Committee.

THE FAILURE OF SANCTIONS

It has already been shown that, even before the British government had decided to impose economic sanctions upon Italy, there existed a sizeable element within the party which was opposed to any such measures (see also Table 2.3). The comprehensive defeat of the Abyssinian forces at the end of April and the capture of Addis Ababa led the remainder to question further the practicable benefits of maintaining sanctions. When Amery addressed a meeting of the Foreign Affairs Committee in early March he concluded that 'a great majority were wholly or largely of my way of thinking' that both sanctions and collective security had failed.[84] Unsurprisingly therefore, the suggestion of now imposing oil sanctions, which was again being mooted both in Geneva and by Eden in cabinet, gave an edge of urgency to the Conservative critics. The historian Charles Petrie, who was a member of Oxford Conservative association, felt that any suggestion of imposing oil sanctions was bluff:

> No one is going to apply oil sanctions now, and if they were applied they would be too late to be effective. The outcome of the war in Abyssinia can be no other than a dictated peace by Italy which the League will have to accept.[85]

Table 2.3 The strength and evolution of Conservative opinions on sanctions against Italy[86]

Pro-Sanctions[a]	Undecided	Anti-Sanctions[b]
Foreign affairs cttee 29/03/35	Hannon, P. 11/10/35	William, H. & 'Cave of 40' 06/10/35
O'Neill, Hugh 22/10/35	Molson, H. 22/10/35	Amery deputation 15/10/35
Wolmer, Viscount 22/10/35	Macnamara, J. 13/12/35	Nunn, W. 15/10/35
Emrys-Evans, P. 23/10/35	Foreign affairs cttee 07/05/36	Phillimore, 15/10/35
Withers, J.J. 23/10/35		Smiles, W. 15/10/35
Raikes, Victor 24/10/35		Wise, A.R. 15/10/35
Adams EDM 11/12/35 18 signatures		Winterton, E. 22/10/35
Denville, A. 11/12/35		Derby, Lord 09/12/35
Spears EDM 17/12/35 58 signatures		Knox EDM 12/12/35 16 signatures
Wiltshire North C.A. 12/04/36		Headlam, C. 16/12/35
Adams EDM 11/05/36 27 signatures		Petrie, C. 11/04/36
Adams, Vyvyan 23/06/36		Chamberlain, A. 06/05/36
Macmillan, H. 23/06/36		Churchill, W. 06/05/36
		O'Neill, H. 06/05/36
		Page-Croft, H. 06/05/36
		Knox EDM 12/05/36 28 signatures
		Denville, A. 12/05/36
		Despencer-Robertson 12/05/36
		Sandeman Allen 12/05/36
		Glasgow C.A. 25/05/36
		Horne, Robert 10/06/36
		1922 committee 15/06/36
		Petherick, M. 15/06/36
		Cazalet, V. 21/06/36
		Foreign affairs cttee 22/06/36
		Erskine-Hill, A. 22/06/36
		Russell, S. 23/06/36
		Enfield C.A. 02/07/36

a. Last known date of declared support for sanctions.
b. First known date of declared opposition to sanctions.

In common with many other Conservatives, Petrie argued that the government's attitude to the Abyssinian war had been based upon two assumptions: first, that Abyssinia was militarily capable of resistance; and second, that other nations would enforce sanctions and these would weaken Italy. Neither condition had been fulfilled and overall had 'proved to be a disastrous policy'. Lord Derby had come to a similar conclusion, feeling that any suggestion of oil sanctions was 'folly – and as it is quite useless – criminal folly'.[87]

As Table 2.3 illustrates, amongst the parliamentary party opinion was divided but increasingly swinging towards favouring the lifting of sanctions. Vyvyan Adams, anxious to stiffen the cabinet's resolve, had tabled an EDM on 11 May which approved 'the maintenance of collective sanctions against the aggressor state'. Twenty-seven other Conservative MPs concurred. But a counter motion was tabled the following day by those who felt that sanctions 'having proved power-less to restrain the aggressor state' believed 'it would be contrary to the interests of peace and world trade and employment to maintain them as a policy of revenge'. When the backbench Foreign Affairs Committee convened a few days later the division of opinion on sanc-tions was reflected: 'It is evident', wrote Harold Nicolson, 'that opinion is almost exactly divided between taking off sanctions imme-diately and maintaining them at least for the present. The right wing takes the former view, whereas the moderates incline to the latter'.[88] Another participant at this meeting was struck by the 'increasingly pronounced' swing in favour of the immediate abandonment of sanc-tions – a marked contrast to the division of opinion at the previous week's meeting between whether to act promptly or gradually.[89] Importantly, a number of those who had originally favoured sanctions, such as Austen Chamberlain, had now turned against the measure.[90] Likewise, the grassroots were increasingly opposed. In Glasgow at a local association meeting no seconder could be found for a pro-sanc-tions motion and the matter was allowed to drop.[91] It was evident that changing of opinion within the party was going to oblige the cabinet to re-evaluate its position.

The issue made the cabinet agenda on 27 May. Neville Chamberlain argued in favour of abandoning the measures, believing that it would make Mussolini more amenable. His argument 'met with a good deal of support'. But Eden remained resolute, citing his belief that by September the economic measures would be hitting Italy hard. A decision was therefore postponed.[92] The issue was returned to a few days later, with the overwhelming majority favouring their abandonment. Some speakers did express concern about the possible implications lifting would have upon public opinion and British prestige, but most agreed that the potential benefits outweighed any negative implications. Baldwin suggested, however, that a decision should be postponed until after the recess, in order for the Foreign Office to consult with the French and allow Eden further opportunity to negotiate with the Italians.[93] When the cabinet failed on 10 June to reach a decision, the policy of drift proved too much for the Chancellor. That evening at a dinner of the 1900 Club, Chamberlain burst the sanctions balloon by condemning their retention as 'the very midsummer of madness'. It was a serious breach of ministerial protocol, for which Chamberlain apologised to Eden. However, in the privacy of his diary the Chancellor admitted that he

> did it deliberately because I felt that the party and the country needed a lead, and an indication that the government was not wavering and drifting without a policy...I did not consult Anthony Eden, because he would have been bound to beg me not to say what I proposed.[94]

Some perceived this speech as a intentional attempt to undermine Baldwin's leadership and secure a possible reconstruction of the cabinet with himself as Prime Minister.[95] Whatever the reality, the whole episode did undermine Baldwin's standing and led many Conservatives again to question his suitability as leader.[96]

The immediate outcome of the Chamberlain speech was a victory for those within the party who favoured an immediate ending of sanctions. Conservative parliamentary opinion swung behind the Chancellor, with only the 'fanatics' such as Vyvyan Adams continuing to advocate collective sanctions.[97] The 1922 Committee had 'an animated discussion' on the subject after the isolationist MP Maurice Petherick had suggested that the country felt 'sanctions should be buried at once and the penal clauses eliminated from the League's covenant at an early date'. Petherick's views were unanimously accepted, although a few speakers suggested that Chamberlain had chosen 'an inopportune time' to debate the matter publicly. [98] Faced with what Amery described as 'irresistible force' from the parliamentary party, the cabinet on 17 June approved the policy of taking the initiative to propose the raising of sanctions to the League of Nations. Furthermore, it agreed that this should be first announced to the House of Commons without consulting the French or Italians.[99]

Conservative MPs were now left with the responsibility for

explaining the reversal of policy to the nation at large. The usual argument adopted was that sanctions represented an experiment that in theory looked practical but in reality was unsuccessful. It was suggested that their failure was due to Italian self-sufficiency and the failure of other nations to apply the economic measures equally. Furthermore, Abyssinia had been conquered despite the economic sanctions. Only military action would reverse this fact, but Britain was hardly in a position to achieve this. As one Scottish meeting heard, the government 'were right to try sanctions out in their honest endeavours towards international peace, but when these had proved ineffective it would be stupid and unwise to go on and endanger the whole country'. It was suggested that lessons could be learnt from the fiasco, and that these principally revolved around revising the League of Nations.[100] Paul Emrys-Evans, whose original support for sanctions had evaporated, likened the imposition of economic sanctions to 'peppering an elephant with a shotgun; it hurts but does not kill. The whole burden, the whole odium of the imposition of economic sanctions has fallen upon this country'.[101] Not all the party accepted the government's decision. In a vote of censure on 23 June Harold Macmillan and Vyvyan Adams voted against the government, with a further two or three Conservative MPs abstaining.[102] Macmillan then resigned the National government whip and remained outside the party for the next year. When called to account for his actions to his Stockton association, Macmillan articulated his belief that if the government 'had used her whole power and continued her strong leadership that we would at any rate have made Italy accept terms very different from merely the complete conquest of this province'.[103]

Surveying the international situation in the aftermath of the Rhineland affair and the lifting of sanctions, one MP in the privacy of his journal offered a gloomy assessment. He observed that

> People really getting frightened of Germans. It is hard to know how to proceed. Now sanctions have failed, I think L[eague] of N[ations] must be entirely reformed. I doubt if you can hope to restrain Germany if she wants to take over German speaking districts. Anyhow we can but reason and pray that some intervention of Providence will decide the rest.[104]

However, from the party's perspective the decision to end sanctions had the general effect of reuniting the Conservative party for the first time since the general election. The fundamental flaws that existed in the design and operation of the League had been fully exposed, especially to public opinion. The events of the past six months had clearly demonstrated the necessity for rearmament, but also illustrated the importance for some form of diplomatic initiative. From the perspective of the government it was hoped that this might be achieved through a deal on the ex-German mandated territories.

THE COLONIAL PROBLEM

One consequence of the Rhineland affair was to project the issue of colonial restitution to the top of the political agenda. After retaking the Rhine region Hitler had offered, as part of his Peace Plan, to accept a general settlement in exchange for the return of the British mandates. Whether the government would capitulate to this German demand was the express concern of a sizeable number of Conservatives, at all levels of the party. The issue of colonial appeasement was one of two themes during the period examined in this book in which the activists played an influential role. The other, as shall be shown later, was national service, in which they had a proactive function. With colonial appeasement their role was largely reactive. The topicality of colonial restitution throughout the period 1936–9 both explains and enabled the grassroots' involvement. The ideological linking of Empire with the party's core beliefs and the closeness of its association with Britain's 'greatness' also goes a considerable way to explaining the rank and files' participation in the debate. Furthermore, the theme of Empire drew together elements from all aspects of the party: diehards like Henry Page-Croft and Lord Lloyd, who saw the Empire as essential for the preservation of social order and the prestige of the nation, and who had fought the 1935 India Act; advocates of imperial preference such as Leo Amery, who saw the value of the Empire as an economic unit; and those from the left such as Vyvyan Adams, who saw imperialism as a means of educating and civilising native populations. Imperialists feared that the surrender of British mandates would signal the weakness of the Empire, threaten it strategically and hasten its demise. It is clear that Empire was intimately entwined in the lives of activists, whether by business or personal experience. The debates that took place in the constituencies were punctuated with illustrative examples from members who had experienced the imperial heritage through service in the colonial corps or military, who had relatives living abroad in far-flung corners of the globe or who merely had businesses or were employed by companies that were reliant in some way upon the imperial connection.[105] Unlike the national service debate, which was initiated by activists, with regard to the colonies the grassroots were largely observers to the

diplomatic initiatives. This did not make their contribution inconse-
quential. It was a subject the government had been considering for
some months, but recognising the hostility it generated amongst its
own ranks it decided to shelve the issue by commissioning Lord
Plymouth on 9 March 1936 to investigate the economic and political
consequences of a colonial compromise. Far from pacifying the critics
within the party, this action merely gave them added impetus to press
their case. The charge was spearheaded from within parliament by
Duncan Sandys, the MP for Norwood, and enthusiastically embraced
by many at the grassroots.[106] What is clear is that the parliamentary
opponents recognised the activists' hostility to the issue and sought to
harness this caucus.[107]

The first spat over colonial appeasement was an EDM tabled in early
February 1936 by Sandys.[108] The motion expressed opposition to transferring any mandates and secured the support of forty-seven other
government supporters. It was withdrawn on 14 February, two days
after the Colonial Secretary had taken the dispatch box to tell the
House of Commons that the government had not and would not
consider the returning of any colonial mandates.[109] During early April,
Baldwin denied in response to a parliamentary question that there had
been any change in the government's attitude.[110] The Plymouth
Committee had already been convening for a month, but to have
publicly admitted its existence would have encouraged the Germans
unnecessarily, especially in view of their recent eighteen-point Peace
Plan, and aroused the hostility of the party. Baldwin was acutely aware
of party feeling. Not only had he recently met with a deputation of
senior Conservatives from the Imperial Affairs Committee on the
matter of a colonial deal, but the National Union's general purposes
sub-committee had forwarded a motion from Bournemouth association
urging his administration 'to resist any proposals which might tend to
weaken the integrity of the Empire'.[111] In the weeks to come other
motions were forwarded by the National Union to the PM which
obliged a response. When the Central Council carried a resolution at its
June meeting, a deputation was despatched to meet with Baldwin.[112] He
'assured' the committee that the government

> had not had any consultation with any of the other mandatory
> powers upon this subject, but in his opinion the question of any
> transfer of mandated territories would rouse such grave difficulties,
> moral, political and legal, that it would appear almost impossible
> for any such transfer to take place.[113]

Baldwin was speaking with the authority of the Plymouth Report, which had concluded the impracticality and worthlessness of returning the colonies. This view was communicated to the House of Commons on 27 July in identical wording to that used for the National Union deputation.[114] If it had been hoped that this statement by the Foreign Secretary was clear and emphatic, it was evident that those Members attending the evening meeting of the 1922 Committee were less than certain. Even after discussion 'there was no unanimity of opinion as to what the Foreign Secretary really had in mind'.[115] The need for clarifying the ostensible ambiguity of the government's position encouraged opponents of restitution to ensure the issue was debated at the October annual conference in Margate. Conference echoed the mood of rejection when a large majority agreed upon a motion that considered the British mandates 'not [to be] a discussable question'. It was an evident victory for the imperialist wing of the party. As Amery told Beaverbrook:

> At the beginning of the year when Ministers gave dangerously evasive answers about the ex-German colonies, I again, not only nailed my flag to the mast, but got together a committee whom I worked up as well as educated and whose efforts resulted in the overwhelming assertion of our point of view at the Conservative conference.[116]

Certainly Amery was one of the more senior backbenchers involved in the opposition to a colonial deal. However, the young Duncan Sandys played a pivotal role at all levels of the party debate. In early 1936, having read Amery's *Forward View*, he proposed forming an Empire discussion group 'which should lead to the formulation of heads of a practical programme on which we might then enlist further supporters and workers'.[117] Sandys debated the matter of the colonies with his local association in early February. He secured the AGM's support for a resolution which urged 'an emphatic declaration' that the government had no intention of transferring mandates 'for the welfare purposes and enlightened government of whose people the British nation holds an honourable and inalienable trust'.[118] The April prime ministerial question on the colonies had been tabled by Sandys. This occurred after hearing that Stanhope, a junior minister, had addressed a meeting organised by Central Office, during which he had spoken of the surrender of Tanganyika 'as quite probable'. To give the cause further publicity he tipped off the media about the speech, securing a paragraph in the *Evening Standard*.[119] It provoked an angry response from the chief whip. He was overheard by a backbencher telling Churchill *sotto voce* to keep his son-in-law in order.[120] It must have been inevitable that rumours of the Plymouth Committee were emanating from Whitehall, which gave added impetus to opponents. When Baldwin was again pressed to declare the government's stance, Sandys and Amery decided to 'constitute a committee . . . to keep a watch on the whole situation and look out for opportunities of debate, questions etc'.[121] Amery took the chair of the Mandates Committee with Sandys as the 'energetic secretary'.[122] In accordance with the aims of the committee, Sandys instigated during July the tabling of an EDM which demanded the explicit affirmation that the transfer of any British mandate was 'not a discussable question'.[123] It secured 124 signatures, including those of many senior backbenchers like Austen Chamberlain, Churchill and Winterton. It was a clear declaration of intent from the imperialist wing of the party. The government could not have failed to notice that thirty-nine of the supporters were Conservative MPs who had opposed the India Act.[124] What is more, with the two Sandys' EDMs of 1936 opposing colonial restitution, 115 different National government supporters had expressed their disapproval – that was a quarter of the parliamentary party. With the Margate annual conference it was Sandys and Page-Croft who brought forward the resolution and carried conference despite the efforts of Hoare. Sandys felt 'the effect will be excellent. I only shudder to think what the result would have been had we *not* carried it. It would have been an unmistakable invitation to our friend Hitler to ask for more'.[125] Anxious not to alienate its supporters further and convinced of the validity of the Plymouth Report's conclusions, the government shelved the idea of a colonial deal. However, as the next chapter will illustrate, Neville Chamberlain had other ideas and the truce was short-lived.

THE SPANISH CIVIL WAR

If the problems of Abyssinia and the Rhineland were not enough to distract the attentions of the British foreign policy makers in 1936, then the events that took place in Spain over the summer months were to add a new and unwelcome dimension. From July Spain descended into civil war as the Nationalist forces challenged the Republican government for supremacy. It was a conflict that threatened to suck in the major European powers: Germany, Italy and Portugal on the side of the Nationalist forces as well as Soviet support for the Republic. For the diplomats and ministers of the British and French governments the aim was to contain the conflict within the borders of Spain, and this they sought to do through non-intervention.[126]

At its simplest the Spanish Civil War politically sharpened the divide between left and right in Britain. The Labour party, and public opinion generally, favoured the Republican forces, whilst Conservatives tended to side with the revolting army forces led by Franco.[127] More significantly it also divided the political right. Although the Conservative party was bonded by a genuine desire for peace and anti-bolshevik beliefs, there was little unanimity on how to secure that peace and how best to counter the communist spectre. The Spanish Civil War was to provoke contrasting and divisive views. On the one hand someone like Victor Cazalet felt able to conclude that Franco 'himself is the antithesis of what a military dictator is usually supposed to be' and was a man with an 'innate sense of justice'; at the same time the Duchess of Atholl's sympathies for the Republican cause brought her into direct conflict with her closest supporters and ultimately destroyed her career as a Conservative politician.[128] The motivation behind these differing views stemmed from two inextricably linked categories: the influences of the war (religion, class sympathy and the allegations of atrocities); and the implications of the conflict on the general European and world situation with its connotations of anti-communism, pro- or anti-fascism, and perceived British interests. Accepting that these factors were often mutually exclusive, the attitude of the individual depended upon their weighting of priorities. In general most Conservatives accepted the policy of non-intervention regardless of their perspective: the isolationist Maurice Petherick believed 'it was time we looked after ourselves without interfering with the affairs of foreign countries', whereas Sir Patrick Ford considered it to be 'the only possible attitude' due to British military weaknesses.[129] An exception was Arnold Wilson, MP for Hitchin, who following a visit to Spain was critical of non-intervention, which whilst 'doubtless prudent' was 'a policy of negation'. However, Wilson, who favoured the Nationalist cause, could 'in no circumstances' accept the argument that the involvement of the European powers would result in Spain becoming a satellite state for one of the dictator countries. Franco's supporters were too 'traditionalist and patriotic'.[130]

As the conflict escalated, Conservative interpretations of the war fell into three broad categories. There was the pro-Franco lobby whose anti-bolshevism led them to support non-intervention from the belief that it was operating to the advantage of the anti-Republican cause. Franco was portrayed as a leader who stood to uphold conservative ideals unconstrained by parliamentary government. This grouping was typified by Henry 'Chips' Channon. He felt that Franco 'has been so misunderstood, so misrepresented in this country' and eagerly anticipated a Nationalist victory.[131] These Conservatives saw the Republican government as either a 'red' popular front government or as a government so weak that it had abdicated authority to those of the extreme left whom it was unable to control. As Arthur Bryant recollected to Baldwin following a visit to Spain over Easter 1936, he

> saw on the walls of every village I visited the symbols of the Hammer and Sickle and in the streets the undisguised signs of bitter class hatred, fomented by unceasing agitation by Soviet agents among a poor and cruelly misled peasant and working class population.

His conclusion was that 'the foundations of civilisation are being undermined'.[132] There was a tendency to see only the excesses of the Spanish Left, in the same way that the British left saw only the excesses of the Spanish Right.[133] After the fall of San Sebastian in September 1936, 'Chips' Channon recorded that all the tales of the Reds' 'fiendish cruelties are unbelievable . . . and yet, for a race brought up on bull-fighting, a race that invented the Inquisition, nothing can be too bad'.[134] Many of these Conservatives were involved in pro-Franco organisations like the Committee of Friends of National Spain, or the United Christian Front, or the Basque Children's Repatriation Committee.[135] The second grouping was the appeasers who pursued the non-intervention policy of Eden, anxious to avoid Europe slipping into the cauldron of war should the dictatorships and democracies clash in Spain. The third group was the one that saw the threat from the Axis powers but whose actions were restricted by its anti-communism and a number of tactical considerations. Churchill fell into this category, concerned for Anglo-French relations and worried of the dangers a Francoite Spain would present to Britain. In August 1936 he declared that a Republican victory in Spain was certain to produce 'a communist Spain spreading its snaky tentacles through Portugal and France'. Certainly the political instability in France and the rise of the popular front at this time gave increased credence to these concerns. But by mid-1938 his view had reversed, as he came to consider a Francoite Spain as a threat to the British Empire.[136]

Although Spain occupied a considerable amount of parliamentary time during 1936 and 1937, the party generally considered the issue from a jaundiced perspective. Although some Conservatives took the trouble to visit Spain to see events for themselves, they generally left the matter in the hands of the government. One MP who went in the autumn of 1936 with a parliamentary delegation found himself reprimanded by his local association for breaking the spirit of non-intervention.[137] There was some debate about whether Franco should be granted belligerent rights in mid-1937, but this would appear to be the extent to which Conservative protagonists sought to influence the government's thinking on the war.[138] The party willingly gave lip-service to the claim that the Civil War had been contained by non-intervention. The involvement of German and Italian 'volunteers' did not warrant a diplomatic row if it was to jeopardise attempts to reach agreements with their governments and if their presence was helping to containing the spread of bolshevism. Occasionally Spain provided an opportunity for attacking the Opposition, for example when backbenchers tried to censure the Labour leader for visiting the Republican forces.[139] Essentially, the attitude of mainstream Conservatives was one of 'lazy indifference', unable to understand why the political left was so concerned with the war.[140]

SOME CONCLUSIONS

Although general indifference characterised the response of the majority of the party to the Spanish Civil War, a much keener interest was exhibited in events concerning Italy and Germany. The abilities of the backbencher to create a climate of such discomfort for the government as to necessitate the dismissal of a second successive foreign secretary in December 1935 was telling testimony.[141] The opening twelve months of the new Baldwin administration proved to be the heyday of the back-bench Foreign Affairs Committee. Its balance of political heavyweights and foreign policy specialists obliged the respect of ministers and whips. The committee's ability to provide a platform for criticism warranted the increased attention it was to receive from the whips' office once Chamberlain succeeded. At constituency level the activists were clearly exercised by matters of foreign policy: first with the apparent reversal in policy offered by Hoare-Laval, then with concern that the Rhineland incident might actually oblige British intervention, and finally with their hostility to a colonial arrangement with Germany. Although the role of the activist was essentially reactive in these instances, their attitudes were clearly important in setting the parameters of policy. This was clearly recognised by those parliamentarians opposed to colonial restitution who sought to harness the activists' hostility to this issue at annual conference in both 1936 and 1937.

The Hoare-Laval crisis indicated the beginnings of the dissent that would eventually congregate around Eden in 1938. At this time the key figures were Vyvyan Adams and Edward Spears. Of greater significance was the centre-right/diehard combination who opposed sanctions, supported Hoare and cautioned against reacting to the Rhineland. These individuals have tended to be overlooked. Crucial in this role was Leo Amery, who was perceived both by himself and others to be providing a lead.[142] This most probably explains the retrospective observation of Robert Bower that he followed Amery – a comment usually attributed to the Edenite period.[143] The dissatisfaction with Baldwin's leadership was clear: even Neville Chamberlain as heir apparent was feeling exasperated. In January 1936 he told Baldwin 'plainly that the time had come when he must take the lead himself'.[144] Baldwin had no intention of being manoeuvred out of the leadership, and with no formal mechanism for forcing a resignation the party had to wait until he felt it was time to stand down.

In terms of foreign policy, there was a growing feeling that action was required if Germany and Italy were to be separated. There still remained a considerable amount of sympathy for the German grievances. Rearmament, the Rhineland, and demands for colonies were considered reasonably legitimate desires for a nation state, and the regime certainly gave no indication that it would forcibly seek retribution. If any regime was considered potentially threatening during this period it was the Italian, especially given the vulnerability of the British fleet in the Mediterranean. But the desire to reach a negotiated settlement with one or other of the dictators meant that many Conservatives increasingly objected to punishing Italy too severely. The desire to re-establish Italian friendship was evident. Less than a day after the lifting of sanctions, the Italian Ambassador Grandi had already been invited to a dinner party by Victor Cazalet.[145] Although domestic matters relating to the Abdication dominated the political scene in the latter part of 1936, many Conservatives were waiting for Baldwin's retirement and hoping that a new leader would provide the necessary diplomatic breakthrough.

3   Berchtesgaden to Poland, 1937–9

The descent to war

In the two and a half years following Neville Chamberlain's succession to the premiership, the international situation (and especially relations between Britain and Germany) deteriorated very rapidly. As an issue of concern, foreign affairs was the dominant topic – to such an extent that one Conservative area chairman complained in early 1938 that it was 'the *only* thing which seems to exercise the minds of people'.[1] Historians have repeatedly scrutinised the methods and mechanisms which the British government adopted in its search to secure peace.[2] What this chapter proposes to assess is the reaction of the Conservative party to these policies, both from the perspective of the parliamentary backbenchers and those at grassroots level. What will be shown is that Chamberlain's policies were less universally acclaimed by the party than is commonly supposed. While publicly Conservatives were prepared generally to support appeasement, in private there were increasing doubts. The other theme explored is, unsurprisingly, the mounting distrust with which Conservatives regarded Germany and her territorial ambitions. Once again, one can distinguish between public and private observations of Germany. Working chronologically through the events between May 1937 and September 1939, this chapter will demonstrate how the Conservative party reversed its position of isolation and allowed Britain to become entangled in a European war for the second time in less than three decades.

A FRESH START

It was widely anticipated that Chamberlain's accession to Number Ten would mark a new departure in foreign policy. It was a field in which the 'drift' of the Baldwin years would be reversed and redirected. Anthony Eden, who retained the post of Foreign Secretary in the new cabinet, welcomed Chamberlain's succession and looked forward to working closely with his new boss. The events of February 1938 were still far away, and working relations between the two men were good. Other Conservatives too hoped for new direction in foreign affairs. The Attorney-General expected Chamberlain to be 'a great standby in foreign politics' and was confident that he would be a 'tower of strength'. Others were more specific, sensing the need for urgency: if the peace was to be saved then Chamberlain had to intervene actively.[3] This was exactly what Chamberlain intended to do. He intended the party to have only a passive role in the diplomatic process, but he required its support if he was to fulfil his ambitions. However, over the next three years its loyalty and tolerance was to be tested to the utmost.

Foreign policy, in terms of parliamentary time, during the opening year of the Chamberlain premiership was dominated by the Spanish Civil War. In terms of priorities the new administration's concerns lay elsewhere. During the first months of this new premiership the government made several approaches to Berlin and Rome, but it was not until Halifax's invitation to visit Germany in November 1937 that a tangible opening offered itself. The idea of the visit appears to have been generally welcomed by Conservatives. The broad thrust of Chamberlain's approach was acceptable to all but a few individuals. Nevertheless he took the precaution of briefing the 1922 Committee in advance of the visit. Immediately after the meeting Amery wrote to the PM, 'pointing out the weakness of the strategy'. It risked alienating the French. A more beneficial line might be to entice the Italians back into a new Stresa Front which would enable France to ditch its Russian alliance, 'and so deal with Germany'. John McEwen, secretary of the Conservative Foreign Affairs Committee, was one of a minority publicly prepared to express disquiet about the desire to seek German friendship over Italian. McEwen considered that historically, traditionally and culturally Britain had 'a great deal in common' with the Italians. To maintain that the same applied between the German and British peoples was 'a fundamental misconception of the character of that great and dangerous people'.[4] More typically Conservative public assertions echoed the official line that Halifax was going to Germany 'in order to try and find out what the Germans really wanted, and how Great Britain could help them'.[5] In private it was apparent that few Conservatives expected much to be achieved by the visit. Some were even arguing that Britain had got 'into the rut so deeply that we may find it impossible to extricate ourselves'.[6] If a consequence of the visit for Chamberlain was to highlight the similarity of views between himself and Halifax, then for the remainder of the party, particularly on the imperialist wing, it once again heightened fears that a deal on the mandated ex-German colonies might be struck. Equally, for some imperialists concerned with the rumours of further Italian expansion in Africa, it was hoped that improved Anglo-German relations might lead Hitler to 'putting the brake on' the Italian dictator.[7]

END OF THE HONEYMOON: EDEN'S RESIGNATION

Events soon overtook the party's deliberations on colonial restitution and distracted their attention. This principally involved the 'shock' resignation of Anthony Eden as Foreign Secretary in February 1938, in disgust at proposed Anglo-Italian negotiations. Eden must have been encouraged in his decision by the knowledge that only days previously the party's Foreign Affairs Committee had expressed almost unanimous opposition to any talks with the Italians, still less *de jure* recognition of the Abyssinian annexation. Churchill had wound up this meeting with 'a very warm eulogy' of the Foreign Secretary. One of Eden's closest friends considered 'this violent anti-Italian feeling is very significant and shows that opinion would back A. E.'s own instinct in this'.[8] The resignation shook the party, at least temporarily.[9] Even some of Eden's closest political allies were 'equally amazed at what had happened'.[10] The disquiet of the parliamentary party was displayed by those backbenchers who were prepared to support an amendment which deplored the circumstances which obliged Eden to resign. Although it shied away from outright condemnation of the government's conduct of foreign policy, it secured the support of seventeen MPs.[11] Despite the Speaker not accepting the amendment, most of its signatories felt obliged to abstain in the censure division, whilst one voted against the government.[12] In total thirty Conservatives abstained. These dissidents represented the younger element of the party's centre and left – about two-thirds were forty-five years of age or below at a time when the average age of a Conservative MP was fifty-one. Furthermore, many were foreign policy specialists who had previously seen service in the colonial or diplomatic corps. In terms of numbers, Chamberlain's 281 majority asserted his dominance in parliament. Nevertheless, one observer noted that those who voted for the government were generally 'obscure Members who have never spoken . . . if quantity was on Chamberlain's side, quality was in Eden's camp'.[13]

For the whips the immediate response to the crisis was to counter and discredit Eden whilst ensuring that the backbenches were fed the government line. The story was spread that Eden was ill and that as a result his judgement and mental balance were impaired, whilst also 'exerting the utmost pressure to get people to vote for the government' by suggesting Eden '*wished* Members to vote for the government!'.[14] The misinformation campaign instigated by Chamberlain through the whips' office and his 'grey cardinals' was crucial. The government succeeded in presenting an image that suggested Eden really had little reason to depart. He had gone purely over the matter of when negotiations ought to begin with Italy, and not because of any fundamental dispute about the nature of British foreign policy.[15] MPs accepted the story that Eden was ill – drained by the stresses of high office.[16] Forty years later one cabinet member still persisted with this argument.[17] The success of the government's media briefings was such that of all the daily papers only the *Manchester Guardian*, *Daily Herald* and *Yorkshire Post* expressed any sympathy with the departed minister.[18] The significance of controlling the press lay in its role as an opinion former, and in 1938 it was considered the most influential medium.

Despite concerns in some quarters, Eden's resignation was not to signal automatically a sustained revolt over foreign policy, as some contemporaries would later suggest.[19] Chamberlainite supporters were nevertheless quick to emphasise their loyalty to the Prime Minister. Many MPs hastened to their constituencies to attend specially convened meetings to explain the circumstances and to account for their personal views. In some cases it was to explain why they had failed to support the government against the Labour censure vote.[20] Recognising the need to display a united front, many associations dispatched resolutions of confidence to the PM, and if necessary sought to censure rebellious MPs. One agent was so 'anxious' to ensure 'a very strong' resolution that he approached Central Office for a draft copy of an appropriate motion.[21] Eden's popularity was a cause of concern to some, and many were openly thankful that they did not have to face an immediate election.[22] Equally, from others there was barely disguised relief at his departure, this being due to the considerable jealousy and envy aroused by Eden's relatively meteoric rise through the party.[23]

The constituency Conservative association is an important cog in the party machinery. In the event of a parliamentary rebellion the dissident MP faces not only censure from the whips' office but also their local executive committee. The executive committees possess the ultimate mode of censure, deselection, and this power of patronage provides them with a useful manipulative tool. On the other hand this patronage can work to the advantage of a rebel. If they can prevent their association from deselecting them, their own position against the challenges of the national party machine is secure. So long as they remain an official Conservative candidate then Central Office can only fight them by supporting an independent candidate. It is apparent that each side of the equation, the Member and the executive, constantly attempts to redefine the boundaries of their relationship. Some Members insist upon the right to the freedom of action on matters non-specific to the locality they represent. This approach was typified by the Duchess of Atholl and her Kinross association. However, this became increasingly blurred as she began to dissent against the National government's foreign policy, initially with Spain and then regarding Germany. When she abstained from the Eden censure vote, the Duchess was called to account for her views. Her chairman was 'very grieved' at her 'inability' to support the government and believed this was a 'universal feeling' in the association. Consequently, because this 'feeling seems to have become so strong' he felt obliged to call a full meeting of the association. This subsequently resulted in a motion of approval for the Prime Minister's policy being passed, which provoked the Duchess into announcing her decision to resign the party whip.[24] It was a lesson that Nigel Nicolson realised two decades later. His experiences in Bournemouth East and Christchurch led him to conclude that if an MP is to rebel on the party line 'he must discuss the matter with [the association] beforehand, and afterwards make the best case he can for acting as he did'. If they fail to carry a majority of the association they must accept their fate.[25] Popular mythology believes that the association executives act upon instructions from Central Office. In fact in the Atholl example the dissent against her was being actively encouraged by Colonel Blair, the secretary to James Stuart the deputy whip. However, executives are fiercely jealous of their perceived role as the guardians of grassroots Conservative opinion. Further, loyalty to the leadership is most reverent at the level of activist. These two factors combine to leave the executives requiring no second encouragement to censure a rebel. The crucial factor in preventing these rebukes becoming excessive was the relationship between the MP and chairman. For whilst in Kinross relations between the Member and chairman flamed the dissatisfaction, in West Leeds, the chairman, R. H. Blackburn, allowed the critics of Vyvyan Adams to express their dissatisfaction before intervening to encourage the withdrawal of a motion of censure. Similarly in Chelmsford, the association's president expressed the view that Jack Macnamara's abstention had been 'unwise' but prevented a resolution expressing confidence in Chamberlain being given to the local press for fear that it would further exacerbate matters between the Member and executive.[26] These examples confirm the conclusion of Epstein in his study of the 1956 Suez rebels that deselection is an option 'rarely used, and then for personal rather than ideological causes'.[27]

At the parliamentary level the forum for retribution was to be the backbench Foreign Affairs Committee. Over the coming months it was to provide a battleground between those MPs sympathetic to Eden's stance on foreign policy and Chamberlainite loyalists. The Eden censure vote had exposed the divisions amongst the officers of the Committee. The secretary, John McEwen, had supported the government; but the chairman Paul Emrys-Evans and the vice-chairman Harold Nicolson both abstained. Not surprisingly, the whips' office sought to remove the dissidents from their positions. The ability of the Committee to provide a platform for criticism of government policy from the disaffected warranted the attention the whips devoted to the Committee from February 1938. Collectively the officers placed their resignations before the Committee, but were persuaded to remain in post until April when their tenures were to expire. Both Evans and Nicolson correctly observed that many Conservative MPs had no wish for them to resign their positions so suddenly after Eden's departure for fear that it would embarrass the government even further. Emrys-Evans, having 'no desire to create a split or to cause any unnecessary embarrassment' avoided speaking in the House of Commons on foreign affairs thereafter, and 'inconspicuously' stood down at the end of his tenure in April; by contrast Nicolson continued with his belligerent stance and was prevented from succeeding as chairman when the Committee requested his resignation. Instead McEwen was elected to the chair.[28] The continued importance attached by the whips to having a loyalist as chairman of this Committee was demonstrated twelve months later when they engineered the election of John Wardlaw-Milne.[29]

Although some expressed concern that Eden's departure would provide a popular rallying call for the opposition parties, in reality these fears were to prove unfounded. The sense of crisis was soon defused as Eden removed himself to southern France for a holiday. He departed having assured Chamberlain that he would grant the premier a free run for his policy.[30] At the same time, if backbench Tories generally had concerns then they kept these doubts to themselves. Activists were no doubt aware of the uneasiness over foreign policy in the wake of the resignations, but they considered the situation best calmed by affirmations of party loyalty. Observers sensed a hardening of right-wing sentiments amongst the party and noted that Chamberlain had made 'supreme efforts' to assert his authority: 'the result is that he has the right-wing and middle of the Tory party cheering hysterically behind him'.[31]

THE *ANSCHLUSS*

The reaction of the party to the *Anschluss* a few weeks after Eden's resignation was taken as further proof by those on the party's left of a general rightward swing. The *Anschluss* had been prohibited under the terms of the Versailles treaty, but by the 1930s many Conservatives, from ministers downwards, felt this to be unnecessarily harsh and were prepared to contemplate a peaceful Austro-German union in return for a general European settlement. When the forcible annexation of Austria did occur, reaction ranged from outrage to tacit acceptance 'in principle', through to general unease and bemusement. Headlam, who had 'always regarded the Germanification of Austria as inevitable', noted that despite the 'indignation' of the press there was 'no apparent anxiety' on the part of the British population 'to rush to arms in defence of the "aggressed" nation'.[32] However, the methods by which the Nazis sought to secure the *Anschluss* rapidly eroded Conservative sympathy for their position. Even those such as Harold Macmillan, who expressed no objections 'in principle' to German revision of the Versailles treaty, felt disgust at the reports of Nazi atrocities against Austrian political opponents and Jews, and were left wondering as to Germany's next move.[33] Victor Cazalet felt Friday 10 March was 'a real black letter day' but realised 'one can't fight if the Austrians won't'. Twelve months previously Cazalet had visited Vienna. The visit left him equating Austrian independence with that of Belgium's in the previous century: 'if we do nothing we shall inevitably be drawn in and you will get the Belgium situation of August 1914 all over again'. This rationale enabled Cazalet to support wholeheartedly Chamberlain's efforts at negotiating with the dictators until at least November 1938, because by being 'willing to talk and listen . . . then by chance you may be able to influence them'.[34]

For many Conservatives the forcible Austro-German union coming so soon after Eden's resignation naturally caused them to question the viability of Chamberlain's foreign policy. It suggested that the approaches to Italy, which had cost a foreign secretary, had failed to reap any dividends when it counted most. Whereas in 1934 Mussolini had put Italian troops on the Brenner pass to check an impending German annexation of Austria, no such action had occurred in 1938. For those Conservatives who had been arguing that Italian friendship would help to guarantee Austrian independence it was a significant blow. Therefore, the *Anschluss*'s importance lay in moulding perceptions of the development of future foreign policy. Austrian independence had been lost. Since the Austrians themselves had made no efforts to resist, it was not Britain's place to intervene. It focused attention on Hitler's next widely anticipated target, Czechoslovakia. The debate was concentrated on the question of intervention, diplomatically and militarily. One association chairman noted 'the clamour' for guarantees in the weeks following the *Anschluss*.[35] During a 'stormy' emergency House of Commons debate, on 14 March, the usual foreign policy sceptics made calls for Britain to offer a guarantee to Czechoslovakia in view of the threats Hitler had made towards her in a speech to the *Reichstag* on 20 February.[36] For the next ten days Chamberlain was subjected to repeated requests from both the opposition benches and from some sceptics, like Vyvyan Adams, to guarantee the Czech republic. They argued that since Britain had been one of those responsible for the nation's rebirth at the Paris Peace settlement of 1919, it was her duty to continue to uphold Czechoslovakia's independence. Each time, however, Chamberlain refused to be drawn on the likely government response, merely reaffirming his declaration of 14 March 'that His Majesty's government emphatically disapprove, as they have always disapproved, actions such as those of which Austria has been made the scene'.[37] This delay in confirming or denying the possibilities of a guarantee 'brought about a lot of coming and going and hatching and whispering in the lobbies and smoking room' of the House of Commons.[38] Yet those favourable to a guarantee represented a minority view within the party. Certainly for many Conservatives there was considerable fear of becoming embroiled in the European quagmire by giving Czechoslovakia a guarantee. Furthermore, it was recognised that geographically Czechoslovakia was isolated, making both economic and military assistance difficult if not impossible.[39] The isolationists believed that Britain's vital interests lay in the consolidation and protection of British assets, which in practice was the motherland and the Empire. To their minds eastern Europe was not a British sphere of influence and most certainly not worth sacrificing British lives for.

Alan Lennox-Boyd, MP for Mid-Bedfordshire and Under-Secretary to the Ministry of Labour, appears to have been echoing these fears when in a speech to constituents on 18 March he declared that Britain ought only to go to the assistance of other European nations if her security was directly threatened, and as far as he was concerned Germany 'could absorb Czechoslovakia and Britain would remain secure'.[40] Had Boyd not been a member of the government (and admittedly he was only a junior minister with no position in the cabinet) this speech would probably have gone largely unnoticed by the national press. Instead it caused a sensation and an outcry from

Francophiles, sceptics and opposition MPs, who claimed Boyd's words were being used for propaganda purposes in the Sudetenland.[41] It was Boyd's tactless choice of words and frank assessment of British self-interest, rather than the sentiments he expressed, which embarrassed the government. Chamberlain was forced to defend the government in a debate upon the subject and deny that the speech had been intended as a Trojan horse for the government. Boyd apologised for his conduct and claimed that he had been speaking as an individual MP and not as a member of the government.[42] In fact, at the time Boyd made his speech the cabinet had still not confirmed its response to the alleged threat. The cabinet Foreign Affairs Committee which had met on the afternoon of Boyd's speech heard Halifax, the Foreign Secretary, suggest that a refusal to commit Britain to action would have the effect of keeping France and Germany 'guessing'. The uncertainty would restrain them both. It was a view that Chamberlain echoed. However, it was not until 22 March that the government's policy of 'bluff' received cabinet approval. At this cabinet meeting Chamberlain offered a concession to public opinion by redrafting his prepared statement to be given to the House of Commons in order to make it friendlier to France.[43] This at least conciliated the francophile First Lord of the Admiralty, Duff Cooper, who had risen from his sickbed to attend the cabinet meeting and defend the French perspective.[44] Mark Patrick, an Edenite sympathiser, probably reacting to the rumours emanating from Downing Street and the Foreign Office on 22 March, felt that 'the emphasis has been shifted towards what they call "realism", which in practice means towards isolation'.[45]

When Chamberlain addressed the House of Commons on 24 March 1938, the statement he gave appears to have been universally welcomed by Conservatives both publicly and privately. The ambiguity of the declaration meant that Chamberlain succeeded in more than just keeping the European powers guessing: he also managed to satisfy almost all shades of Conservative opinion. It was a speech demonstrative of Chamberlain's political acumen. Maurice Petherick, an isolationist, hailed the speech as 'a very wise one and a courageous one'.[46] Victor Cazalet, only recently returned from central Europe and 'rather anxious for a clear statement as to our intentions if C[zecho]s[lovakia] was invaded', believed it to be 'a really great and important speech' which 'satisfied' his view.[47] Leo Amery, who privately felt that the speech 'was all right as far as it went', observed that the Prime Minister 'had the party solidly behind him and even Winston [Churchill] could not criticise it beyond suggesting that he might have been a little more definite over Czechoslovakia'.[48] Likewise

Mark Patrick, who only days previously had been critical of the government's apparent move towards isolation, admitted that the speech

> was far better than I had hoped. I have no doubt at all that it has averted any serious division of opinion, on our side, for some time to come. Some of the isolationists feel that we are committed too far, but on the whole it has been a very successful compromise.[49]

Leonard Ropner, one of those who abstained on the Eden censure motion, explained the following week to his Barkston Ash association that at the time of Eden's resignation 'there were not a few' government supporters who felt themselves to be more in accord with Eden's views than the policy announced by the PM.

> Last week Mr Neville Chamberlain made a speech which in our view, went far to meet those we had expressed, and although some differences of approach to the urgent questions arising out of foreign policy may still remain, it is in complete confidence that I can now confirm that had a vote been taken after the Prime Minister's speech last week, no supporter of the National government would have voted against the government.[50]

Indeed, when Labour forced a vote of confidence a few days later on the government's foreign policy, Ropner was amongst those in the government lobby alongside fellow sceptics Macmillan, Macnamara, Emrys-Evans, Spears, Bracken and Keyes.[51] Party activists also received Chamberlain's speech warmly, as Table 3.1 illustrates. Several MPs who had returned to their constituencies felt it necessary to write to the Prime Minister recounting the grassroots' 'whole-hearted support' for his stance.[52] Without doubt the 24 March declaration did much to restore Chamberlain's reputation following the setbacks of the Eden resignation and the *Anschluss*.

The situation in terms of by-elections was nevertheless presenting problems. It rested essentially with the presentation of policy. Eden's resignation and the *Anschluss* meant that the government was 'handicapped' because it 'dare not press too violently' its foreign policy. Hacking was advising his leader 'that if we seemed even negatively to attack Eden the British instinct of not liking to see a man kicked when he is down would send votes against us'.[53] Furthermore, domestic issues always loom large in elections, something clearly borne out by Mass-Observation polling in West Fulham, the venue for a by-election in early April. One survey found that 54 per cent of the sample thought home affairs more important than foreign affairs,

Table 3.1 Responses to Chamberlain's 24 March speech

Favourable	Critical
Amery, Leo	Adams, Vyvyan
Bosworth CA	Atholl, Duchess of
Bracken, Brendan	Boothby, Robert
Cazalet, Victor	Chorlton, A.C.
Emrys-Evans, Paul	Churchill, Winston
Finchley CA	Herbert, Sidney
Keyes, Roger	Perkins, Robert
Kingston-upon-Thames CA	Sandys, Duncan
Kinross CA	Thomas, J.P.L.
Leicester East CA	Withers, J.J.
Macmillan, Harold	
Macnamara, Jack	
Patrick, Mark	
Pembroke CA	
Petherick, Maurice	
Rickards, G.W.	
South Edinburgh CA	
South Midlothian CA	
Spears, Edward	
Sueter, Murray	
Tynemouth CA	
Wolmer, Viscount	

with only 21 per cent believing the reverse. It made little difference whether the voter was a Conservative or Labour supporter.[54] Fulham was lost by the Conservatives by a swing of 7.3 per cent. Observers believed that the floating vote went against the Conservatives whilst their own voters abstained.[55] The constituency had been highlighted by the CRD as a 'key' seat, which if lost in a general election would 'be dangerous for the government'.[56] This result compounded the Ipswich defeat of February when Richard Stokes secured the seat for Labour with a 10.3 per cent swing against the Conservatives. He succeeded in overturning a majority in excess of 7,000. Although suggesting that the Labour candidate lacked socialist credentials, enabling him to secure crucial Liberal support, Douglas Hacking still believed that 'when we are able to be more emphatic we can expect to do better'.[57] Although during June the Conservatives retained three seats in Aylesbury, Stafford and West Derbyshire, the results were not as resounding as the candidates were apt to claim.[58] Consequently, the CRD warned that these results, especially West Derbyshire, illustrated the vulnerability of the government's candidates should the Liberal contender withdraw at the general election (see Table 3.2).[59]

Table 3.2　Pre-Munich by-election results[60]

By-election	Date	Percentage Share of Vote				Swing
		Con.	Lab.	Lib.	Others	
Ipswich	16/02/38	47.0	53.0			−10.3
West Fulham	06/04/38	47.8	52.2			−7.3
Lichfield	05/05/38		50.9		49.1	
Aylesbury	19/05/38	54.1	19.1	26.8		−5.8
West Derbyshire	02/06/38	48.6	32.5	18.9		*
Stafford	09/06/38	57.6	42.4			+1.2
Barnsley	16/06/38		64.4		35.6	
Willesden	28/07/38	56.6	43.4			−4.8

* No percentage swing can be calculated since in 1935 the Conservative candidate had been returned unopposed.

A FAR AWAY COUNTRY? THE CZECH CRISIS

During the summer of 1938 Czechoslovakia became the focus of foreign policy attention. Against this increasingly volatile international situation, Conservatives began privately to express concerns and doubts about the wisdom of conciliating Hitler. However, as this crisis evolved parliament was in summer recess, and most constituency associations followed their MPs and did not meet for the duration of the summer. Consequently, as the crisis deepened most Conservatives could be little more than passive observers as their political masters sought to deflect it. Despite its best intentions the British government found itself being drawn deeper into the crisis. This involvement was effectively signalled with the dispatching of Lord Runciman to the region in August. Some Conservatives had reservations about Runciman's mission, but typically these were kept private.[61] Equally, it was recognised that the region was a potential flashpoint, in view of Czechoslovakia's mutual assistance pacts with France and the Soviet

Union which would be sanctioned by a German assault on the Sudetenland. As the agent for Leeds West association explained to one correspondent critical of intervention in European affairs: Czechoslovakia was 'the powder barrel of Europe' and any explosion would involve Britain:

> it cannot be said that it is interference if efforts are being made by this country to bring that controversy to a peaceful issue. . . . it will have been interference well worth while if the results achieved prevent our country from going to war.[62]

Czechoslovakia was crucial, for whilst there was 'uncertainty about the future' wrote one MP, 'there is little chance of easing the tension that exists everywhere today'. However, to then assert that Germany, for a mixture of economic and ideological reasons, was not ready yet to absorb the Sudeten Germans displayed an element of naivety.[63] By September such denials were impossible in light of the blatant German propaganda. Yet the government still persisted with its approach 'to keep Hitler guessing, while we pressed Benés to get on with negotiations'.[64] Certainly critics, such as Cranborne and Emrys-Evans, looked on with a degree of glee at the government's predicament. Although the Czech situation was 'all very revolting', they thought it would 'be interesting to see how the policy of appeasement deals with a mobilised army of a million men'.[65]

Hitler was due to make a keynote address to a Nuremberg rally on 12 September and the British waited tensely.[66] Ralph Glyn listened to the speech on the radio, and found 'it gave one an extraordinary feeling of a kind of mad revivalist meeting'. This MP felt 'the time has come for a "show down" and we should all say to Hitler that this uncertainty and methods of intimidation are impossible and he must declare if he does not recognise the sovereignty of C[zecho]S[lovakia]'.[67] Edward Winterton decided that although 'the speech did not make things any worse [it] certainly made them no better'. It had been a 'clever abusive speech'.[68] With the Nazi leadership 'beating the big drum', many feared that it was intent upon war.[69] Of course with hindsight the historian is only too aware that Hitler planned to annex Czechoslovakia on 1 October.[70] Hitler had not, however, calculated for the personal determination of Chamberlain to avoid war. The diplomatic coup the British Prime Minister secured with his proposal personally to fly to Germany to meet with the Führer thwarted any German ideas of a forcible annexation of the Sudetenland for the present.

When 'Plan Z' was made public it caused a sensation, and left 'the world completely astounded'.[71] In the more recent era of 'shuttle diplomacy' it is all too easy not to be able to appreciate the uniqueness of Chamberlain's action in September 1938. It was seen by contemporaries to be all the greater because Chamberlain at the age of sixty-nine was flying for the very first time. The contrast could not have been more marked: Neville, with his winged collars, Edwardian dress sense and umbrella, flying as an ambassador of peace to Nazi Germany to be confronted with a man twenty years his junior, dictator of the most powerful continental nation.

While in public Conservatives continued to express satisfaction with Chamberlain's actions as he shuttled between Britain and Germany, in private doubts were apparent – and from more than just the usual sceptics. Even the party chairman was 'dubious' about what he saw as Chamberlain's policy of surrender. Others considered it 'very odd' that Chamberlain had only taken Horace Wilson and William Strang with him as advisors.[72] Cuthbert Headlam's daily diary entries for September reveal something of the tension, fear and bewilderment contemporaries experienced during the crisis. Confident of a successful and peaceful outcome one day, by the next Headlam's optimism may have evaporated. In common with many other Conservatives, Headlam became increasingly concerned at the apparent betrayal of the Czechs, although equally conscious of the practical realities of the situation. Following Berchtesgaden he saw trouble in reconciling the Czechs to a plebiscite, or in expecting them to give up their frontier with its strategic and economic implications. He felt that

> it all comes from making impossible little states. They were created by woolly headed idealists and extreme nationalists who never seem to have contemplated a revival of Germany, or that the League of Nations must inevitably be a wash-out.

A week later, with little apparent improvement, Headlam was of the opinion that 'this time we shall be lucky if we get out of the mess without a war'. However, he believed Britain, even though not pledged to assist the Czechs, ought to intervene since she was 'a party to the calling into existence of their unhappy country and [we] are supposed to stand up for the smaller nations'.[73] But Headlam was well versed in military matters, having seen service in the First World War, and through a historical/practical interest as editor of *Army Quarterly*. As a consequence he reached the conclusion, in common with the Chiefs of Staff, that Britain 'cannot prevent the Czechs being annihilated even if we do go to war on their behalf'.[74]

Certainly by 28 September many Conservatives expected war to occur within a matter of days.[75] Chamberlain felt it necessary to broadcast to the nation. During the course of his talk he referred to the Sudeten crisis as being 'in a faraway country between people of whom we know nothing'. The broadcast left one group of foreign policy sceptics with the impression 'of a broken man', which was something they felt would only encourage Hitler.[76] For the agent of Sedgefield Conservatives it meant 'that peace is hanging on a hair and that we may be faced with a world war almost immediately'.[77] It was under this sense of crisis and foreboding that the following day parliament was recalled to debate the situation. Chamberlain had expected to announce the failure of his mission, except that part-way through his speech an invitation was received to return to Germany for a four-power conference to be held in Munich. Relief more than anything explains the eruption from Members as the announcement was made to the House.

DIVISION AND RETRIBUTION: THE IMPACT OF THE MUNICH AGREEMENT

In due course Chamberlain returned from Munich claiming peace in our time and proudly waving the scrap of paper which, on the spur of the moment, Hitler and he had both signed, agreeing friendly relations between Britain and Germany. But the initial euphoria about avoiding war quickly subsided. Although in public most Conservatives expressed satisfaction with the Munich agreement, many privately revealed reservations. The Duke of Atholl, president of Kinross association, was 'very nervous' about 'Europe being handed over to Hitler', nor did he 'like the confession that our armaments are insufficient, and only being told so at the last minute'.[78] It was especially this latter point that caused Conservatives the most concern. It would be rearmament rather than foreign policy that proved the more divisive issue for the party in the latter part of 1938. Those Conservatives who went public in their criticisms of Munich were subjected to pressure from the whips and local associations. It was an issue that outwardly gave the impression of being capable of splitting the party. However, it was a schism that was to the greatest extent kept private, and one that was far less serious than at first supposed. In part this was a tribute to the whips and party managers, but even more it was because the party prided itself on loyalty. To some observers the Conservative conception of loyalty was, and still remains, the party's greatest asset: 'people outside, and foreigners in particular, are apt to underestimate the silent and almost undying support that the normal Conservative MP will give to his elected leader and his chief whip'.[79] Veneration and loyalty to the leader were extremely powerful forces in the party, and dislike of factionalism could subjugate any desire for a change of policy or leader. Such beliefs help to explain why the overwhelming majority of Conservative MPs backed the government during the four-day Munich debate despite many having private doubts. Harry Crookshank, who had tried to resign as Minister for Mines, decided after a personal interview with the Prime Minister that his 'reservations would remain mental not vocal'. In fact Crookshank believed he had won a moral victory over the PM, for the private threat of resignation had enabled him to present an 'ultimatum' which Chamberlain had agreed to: to take back the words 'peace with honour'; to press on with rearmament; aim at collective arrangements for diplomacy; and not to dissolve parliament.[80] The pressing of claims in private to ministers and whips was widely accepted to be a more lucrative exercise than public criticism which only provoked hostility and invariably retribution. The subject of loyalty helps one understand to an even greater extent why the activists reacted, almost violently at times, against rebels in the constituencies.[81] The emphasis upon loyalty was always strongest and most extreme at the grassroots. Munich was very much Chamberlain's policy and therefore an attack on the Agreement was perceived as an attack on the Prime Minister. The exception taken by members of the Winchester association to a suggestion by one of their executive in March 1939 that Munich had caused 'national humiliation' illustrates the cult of the leader.[82] Dissident MPs claimed that Central Office had been encouraging local associations to censure their actions. However, in the case of Duff Cooper and St George's, the chief organisational officer at Central Office said they had actually intervened to prevent the retribution getting out of control.[83] Local association executives needed no second encouragement to reprimand dissidents. This was also demonstrated in the constituency of Aldershot, home to Neville Chamberlain's spinster sisters Hilda and Ida. They had thought about 'ginger[ing] up' the local women's association against Wolmer, but were very pleased to discover that the 'local association far from needing a lead was bristling with indignation'.[84]

How then did supporters of the Munich agreement justify their acquiescence? Since May 1940 Munich has become synonymous with betrayal and humiliation, and many who supported it in October 1938 sought to distance themselves from the agreement. The fact that Chamberlain secured an overwhelming majority in the parliamentary debate was testimony to the contemporary Conservative support

Munich received. Yet historians have failed adequately to explain why, and it has been too easy merely to label these backbenchers as 'yes-men'. A critique of these men has been that few had much understanding of the conduct of foreign policy, but it seems hard to believe that in 1938 when foreign policy dominated the news these MPs had not formed their own opinions of the situation. Certainly some voted with the government purely from loyalty and because of pressure from the whips' office. Yet many did accept that Munich was a victory for peace. One such Member who believed this admitted retrospectively he may have been 'over-optimistic' when Chamberlain returned, but 'we regarded him rather like an Old Testament patriarch who had returned with God's blessing to preserve peace in our time'.[85] The contemporary public defence that supporters of Munich mounted is all the more interesting in view of the growing private unease about the agreement. How therefore did Conservatives justify the transfer of the Sudetenland to Germany? Roger Lumley, formerly an MP and at the time governor of Bombay, had 'not the slightest doubt' that were he still in parliament he would have cheered himself 'hoarse' about Munich. For this reason he believed he would 'find it hard to be patient with those who, now that the danger is over for the present, are no doubt beginning to criticise the Munich agreement'. He agreed that the principle issue was nazism versus decency:

> but if a struggle on that fundamental issue has got to come I would prefer (a) to have it over a pretext which is better and less likely to cause doubts than the Czecho[slovakian] issue, and (b) to have it when we are ready.[86]

Arthur Heneage had a series of correspondents who criticised Munich. There were three lines to his argument. First, that 'we should not go to war because we dislike other countries having dictators . . . that is their own business'. Although dictators have an inherent inability to be peaceful, this has been proved wrong in Germany's case 'and the contact established between this country, France and Germany in admitting injustices should go far to make possible further peaceful negotiation'. Second, Heneage felt it was

> a bad case to have three million Germans in a country where they do not want to stay, and certainly a bad case on which to go to war. You cannot have self-determination for some nations and refuse it for the Germans.

Third, it was argued that one could not go to war for a country that was indefensible and it was 'evident that Czechoslovakia would have been overwhelmed and wiped out'.[87] Peter Thorneycroft explained to his association that Munich was only one part or incident in Chamberlain's foreign policy. Such a foreign policy had been working when Chamberlain and Mussolini established friendly relations in February 1938, and this had borne fruit when during the autumn Czech crisis Mussolini had been prepared to intervene to secure peace rather than war.[88] However, there must be a distinction made between public and private statements, which reveal the party's general unease about the whole situation. During the Munich debate a quip went round the backbenches which likened the crisis to St George, who having failed to rescue the maiden remarked that she would not have been worth it anyway.[89] The unease was further illustrated by the behaviour of Captain C. G. Lancaster, who stood as the Conservative candidate in the November 1938 Fylde by-election. In his election addresses Lancaster stood by the Munich agreement and argued that it had created 'a new spirit' that had to be fostered so as to make the likelihood of war impossible.[90] However, upon his election to parliament, Lancaster aligned himself with the foreign policy sceptics. This action came as no surprise to the Fylde agent, who felt that at the selection interviews Lancaster

had not been very satisfactory in his statement about his political views and had given you to understand that he was not prepared to give whole-hearted support to the present government whom he thought behaved all right at the [Munich] crisis but were to a certain extent responsible for all the trouble and unpreparedness now.[91]

Party officials appear to have been alert to the unease. Central Office produced a propaganda leaflet *Chamberlain the Peacemaker*, which they encouraged associations to purchase and distribute.[92] As the secretary of the Scottish Conservative association, Colonel Blair, explained, this leaflet distribution was of 'the highest importance' because 'of widespread misrepresentation and misapprehension regarding Mr Chamberlain's policy'.[93]

The foreign policy sceptics had tried to coordinate their voting during the Munich debate. They had met regularly throughout the crisis, and had considered Duff Cooper's resignation a boost. Churchill had favoured voting against the government, but was persuaded to join an *en bloc* abstention.[94] His damning of Munich in the parliamentary debate as a total and unmitigated defeat would ensure that he came to be seen as the central figure in British opposition to nazism and Hitler. In fact Eden and Amery came very close to supporting the government, after Chamberlain's closing speech appeared to suggest to them a new line of realism. Nevertheless, a sense of loyalty to his followers made Eden stick to the pre-arranged plan, but both he and Amery took the precaution of ensuring that the Prime Minister was aware of the situation.[95] Usually historians suggest that around twenty-five Tories followed Eden's example and abstained. However, analysis of the voting behaviour of Conservative MPs on foreign policy votes during 1938 suggests that this number was greater, possibly as many as forty. This is certainly a figure that fits more closely with the retrospective claims of Churchill and Eden. Amongst those who abstained were a number of unfamiliar names: John Gretton, Ernest Makins, J. J. Stourton and Victor Raikes. This quartet of right-wingers voted against the Labour amendment but were absent from the vote supporting the government. Boothby acted similarly. Duff Cooper's PPS Hamilton Kerr followed his former political master and abstained.[96] But not all supposed sceptics were consistent in their criticisms of foreign policy, and a number actually supported the government during the Munich votes. Interestingly, J. R. J. Macnamara, as well as Mark Patrick (who had resigned as a PPS in February in sympathy with Eden) and Ronald Tree walked into the government lobbies. Tree explained to Eden that he felt the government motion had been phrased to refer only to the immediate crisis. Therefore he had felt able to support it, although he would have considered abstention if he had believed it would have been of definite assistance to Eden. This action was later overlooked by Tree, who declared in his memoirs that he 'had consistently abstained from voting with the government on matters of foreign policy'.[97] However, in early November Tree did resign his PPS position in objection to foreign policy.

It is worth considering the motives behind the dissidents' abstentions. They were at pains, especially to their local associations, to emphasise their personal admiration for Chamberlain's selfless action of flying to Germany. Such declarations were always appended to their objections. These criticisms were both specific to the Munich agreement and to the government's policy in general. Though many of them accepted that there was a need to revise the 1919 Versailles treaty, they argued that the government's pursuit of a misguided foreign policy had contributed directly to the Czech crisis and made the 'humiliation' of Munich necessary. Many pointed to the weakness of Britain's defences and argued that unless Britain had a strong enough military capability she would continue to be at the dictators' mercy. Munich was 'a victory for brute force' and merely 'a stepping stone' to further outrages. To have supported the government in the votes would have implied general support for both past and future foreign policy, the consequences of which could be profound. Wolmer felt that the issue at stake was 'whether Europe shall be dominated by equity or force. That is an issue for which England has repeatedly gone to war, because we have known that if we do not resist such force we shall be crushed by it'. Specifically, many questioned the terms of the Munich agreement, particularly the guarantee of Czechoslovakia's new borders. As Emrys-Evans told his association chairman, when the Czechs had their army and border defences there had been a degree of British interest in preserving her integrity,

> When, however, Czechoslovakia is indefensible, when every British interest has disappeared, the government has guaranteed a state whose frontiers do not yet exist. They cannot fulfil this obligation without placing immense new burdens on this country and without recasting the whole scheme of our defences.[98]

Ernest Makins, MP for Knutsford, was one of those Conservatives who clearly felt dissatisfaction with Chamberlain's policy during 1938, but who made no attempt to ally himself with either the Churchill or Edenite camps. He had a reputation as a right-wing diehard, who had originally tried to enter parliament after the First World War as a member of Page-Croft's National party. In fact his sympathies rested with the Eden camp, perhaps in part because his son Roger served in the Foreign Office and frequently briefed his father on the international situation. When Eden resigned, Makins' 'sympathies' were with the former Foreign Secretary although he still voted for the government. In June 1938 he considered the government to be 'rather feeble' in the realm of foreign affairs, and these private doubts finally surfaced when he abstained from the government's Munich motion. Although after Munich he returned to supporting the government in parliamentary divisions, he did so 'reluctantly' and wondered as to 'how long I can go on doing so and keep my self respect?'[99]

It is impossible to gauge the impact Munich had upon Conservative membership, since detailed membership numbers do not exist. Despite some thirty to forty Conservatives abstaining from the Munich divisions (this was only one-tenth of the parliamentary party) only one MP, the Duchess of Atholl, felt obliged to resign her seat and fight a by-election on the issue.[100] The cabinet suffered only one resignation, that of Duff Cooper, while the usual ministerial malcontents – Winterton, Elliot, Crookshank and Oliver Stanley – overcame their objections in the euphoria of peace.[101] Indeed Winterton considered the agreement was better than the Godesberg terms and believed

'Neville was right to sign it in the circumstances especially as it was accompanied by a mutual affirmation of goodwill' between Britain and Germany.[102] It is even more difficult to ascertain the impact looking down towards the rank-and-file membership. It would appear that while the overwhelming majority of local associations sent messages of congratulations to Chamberlain, there was some unease. Indeed many of these communications from the activists carried appendages. This was demonstrated by the mass meeting organised by Stone association, which carried a motion congratulating Chamberlain on securing peace but which also called for 'a ministerial statement to say what was the government's future plan of appeasement'.[103] This demand reflected a widely held fear amongst activists that Chamberlain proposed further concessions to Germany, especially in the colonial sphere. The apparent weaknesses of defence, as revealed by the crisis, became the major point of disquiet. There were divisions of opinion over Munich that not all the minute books could conceal and there were certainly Conservatives who resigned their positions (especially in constituencies represented by dissident MPs).

One member of the Newbury executive committee resigned in protest, whilst in Newcastle the local agent noted the sense of guilt felt amongst supporters over the betrayal of the Czechs.[104] In Derbyshire, Hugh Molson, the prospective candidate for the High Peak constituency, actively considered withdrawing his candidature. Molson saw the whole business of the Czech negotiations as 'a complete and abject surrender to Hitler'. At the height of the crisis he had urged Eden to attend the Newcastle National Union conference (which was ultimately cancelled) and 'either oppose any motion of approval or move a vote of censure on the gov[ernmen]t'.[105] Ultimately Molson did remain because he was elected at the 1939 by-election, caused by the death of Alfred Law. His views about the government's foreign policy did not change and he associated himself with the sceptics and ultimately voted against the government over Norway in May 1940. Equally, in another of Derbyshire's constituencies the dispute between MP and chairman reached a climax, the latter resigning in protest at the MP's continued opposition to Chamberlain's foreign policy. Relations between Emrys-Evans and his chairman had been rather volatile since he had abstained from the Eden censure motion. Through a series of misunderstandings and failed compromises the situation continued to deteriorate during the summer of 1938. Evans' Munich abstention was the final straw. Until this point both parties, as far as was possible, had wished to keep the divisions over foreign policy out of the public domain. After Eden's resignation, Evans had refrained from speaking in the House of Commons on foreign policy and sought to counter the press speculation concerning his proffered resignation from the Conservative Foreign Affairs Committee. As he assured Doncaster, 'you may rely upon me to be as discreet as possible. If, however, I was convinced that the public interest demanded it, I would feel bound to speak out again'.[106] Munich provided that opportunity, and when Evans notified Doncaster of his intention to publish a letter in the local newspaper explaining his actions, the chairman objected:

> If you desire to send to the press a considered statement of your attitude then that is a matter for your personal discretion but until South Derbyshire association has had an opportunity of considering and deciding upon the action to take such a course would be manifestly unfair to those who have worked for you.[107]

Doncaster decided to resign following a series of further misunderstandings and doubts about whether Evans was going to be able personally to present his views to the association. Doncaster considered it 'invidious' to remain chairman of an association which declared itself

> to be in complete accord with the Prime Minister *and his policy* yet in effect it pledged itself to support a Member who not only openly expressed his hostility to that policy but quite honestly stated that he would continue to act in that spirit.[108]

This time around it was Doncaster's turn to prevent the dispute being publicly aired by only giving his reasons to the association executive at a private meeting.[109] In Yorkshire the sceptical attitude of the *Yorkshire Post* aroused activists' hostility. York association passed a motion which 'deplore[d]' the paper's Edenite stance, believing that it was 'doing a signal disservice to the country in general and to the Conservative party in particular'. This was forwarded to Arthur Mann, the paper's editor, and other constituency associations were canvassed to act likewise. West Leeds concurred with the York resolution but had no desire to exacerbate the situation, 'generally agreeing that no useful purpose would be served in sending this or any similar resolution to the press'.[110] The dispute continued into 1939, with the paper's editor continually fighting to retain editorial freedom. This example and that of South Derbyshire demonstrate the party's natural instinct for maintaining a façade of unity at all times.

These instances of MPs being called to account for their behaviour

Table 3.3   Conservative MPs censured by local associations for criticism of foreign policy, 1935–40

Date	MP	Association	Occasion
02/06/37	Atholl	Kinross	Pro-Spanish republican attitude. Vote of censure defeated
28/02/38	Adams	West Leeds	Voted against gov't re: Eden
03/03/38	Macnamara	Chelmsford	Eden abstention
22/04/38	Atholl	Kinross	Criticism of gov't foreign policy
13/05/38	Atholl	Kinross	Special general meeting to confirm vote of censure of previous month
27/05/38	Atholl	Kinross	De-select MP over attitude
Oct. 1938	Thomas	Hereford	Opposition to Munich (no resolution)
Oct. 1938	Cranborne	Dorset South	Opposition to Munich (no resolution)
Oct. 1938	Law	Hull South West	Opposition to Munich
22/10/38	Wolmer	Aldershot	Opposition to Munich
04/11/38	Churchill	Epping	Opposition to Munich (defeated)
11/11/38	Duff Cooper	St George's	Opposition to Munich - threat of de-selection
13/11/38	Sandys	Norwood	Association's 'regret' at Munich abstention. Chair resigns in protest at criticism of Sandys
23/11/38	Sanderson	Ealing	Regarding views on Germany
13/12/38	"	"	"
17/04/39	Churchill	Epping	De-selection challenge over attitude to foreign policy. Defeated
Aug. 1939	Cartland	King's Norton	Attacked PM in parliament. Severely reprimanded.
15/12/39	Culverwell	Bristol West	Reprimanded for defeatist attitude.
06/05/40	"	"	Told that unlikely he would be re-selected.

illustrate a number of features about rebellion in the Conservative party. They concern the role of local associations, their intolerance of disloyalty, the part played by constituency chairmen, their financial solvency and the degree of independence an MP was allowed. For example, the Duchess of Atholl was not alone in being censured for her attitude on foreign policy. Other dissidents experienced similar responses, as Table 3.3 illustrates.[111]

The crucial factor in preventing these instances of censure going further was the degree of support from the association chairman for the MP. This is particularly illustrated by comparing the experiences of Wolmer and the Duchess of Atholl. Both were subject to deselection moves from disaffected activists. As was the case with the Duchess, moves were made by some elements of Wolmer's association to deselect him. James Paton, the Duchess' chairman, initially seemed unsure of his position and was then unwilling to use his personal prestige to prevent the splitting of the Conservatives in the Kinross constituency. In contrast, Colonel Charrington warned the Aldershot executive that if Wolmer was deselected he would resign his own position.[112] In both of the cases of Churchill and Boothby, only the intervention of their chairmen prevented their local executives passing resolutions condemning their criticisms. In Leamington Spa, Eden was to find the support of Sir Spenser Flowers absolutely crucial in safeguarding his position.[113]

Invariably in any of these clashes between MP and association, the issue at stake was the extent to which the MP felt able to assert the right for independence of action. The Duchess of Atholl felt that her opposition to foreign policy was justified under the terms agreed with her association at the 1935 election, allowing her the freedom of action on issues that did not directly affect the constituency.[114] In other associations the parameters were defined by those who on the one side expected their MP to represent their views, and on the other by those activists who felt that they had no qualifications to pass judgements on matters before parliament.[115] The middle ground was occupied by the chairman who told his MP that

> whilst not accepting your point of view, [I] admit your right to exercise your independence in so far as you have already done so, but I wish to be very frank and to say that we do not expect you to harass the government.[116]

Another element taken into consideration by associations when allowing their MPs freedom of action was the solvency of the association and the degree to which it relied upon the support of the Member. Not untypically many associations during this period experienced some degree of financial difficulty and relied upon the generosity of their MP and wealthier members to maintain activities. In short, the greater the reliance upon the MP then the more likely the association was to tolerate the independent actions of that Member. The extreme case was that of Harold Macmillan and his Stockton association. In 1936 Macmillan had resigned the National whip in opposition to the government's Abyssinian sanctions policy. Despite returning to the whip in 1937 Macmillan's criticism continued; he abstained from most of the foreign policy votes during 1938, including Eden's resignation and the Munich agreement. At no point did his association censure his action, but during 1938 Macmillan was paying the salary of the agent and women's organiser because the association carried a £700 over-draft. The following spring he waived £400 rent on the association's premises. As the chairman told his executive 'if it were not for the generosity of Mr Macmillan, it would be impossible for the organisa-tion to carry on'. Further, Macmillan seems to have been careful when speaking to his association on matters of foreign policy to adopt a conciliatory tone.[117] This can be neatly contrasted with the position of the Duchess of Atholl. Her husband had been forced to sell the family seat of Blair Atholl Castle in the early 1930s. In 1938 the Duchess' subscription to the Kinross association was £5. It was at this point that the chairman warned her to start following the party line on Spain or else a number of wealthy members would withdraw their subscriptions from the association.[118] Certainly the financial relationships between MPs and their associations was a major point of disquiet to both parties during this period. Ultimately the 1949 Maxwell-Fyfe report attempted to resolve such anomalies, but what is often forgotten is that such questions of democratising the party were already under investi-gation by 1939, only to be interrupted by the war.[119]

AN EARLY GENERAL ELECTION?

One concern amongst Conservative dissidents in the months after Munich was that Chamberlain would call an early general election. Sidney Herbert, during the Munich debate, had intervened to warn Chamberlain:

> We can be led but we cannot be bullied. I am not talking so much about what appears in the press, but if it is a case of going into the lobbies and if we are told that only those who vote straight are to get the coupon, then I say, quite honestly, that there will be a great many people in the Conservative party who will not vote straight.[120]

Herbert's cautionary words carried all the more weight because he was a highly respected backbencher who was rarely moved to intervene in debates. Some considered the possibility of fighting such an election as independents or even possibly forming a new political party.[121] For Members such as Churchill and Wolmer, the deselection threats from their local associations made this issue one of pressing concern. If they could prevent their association from deselecting them, their own position against the challenges of the national party machine was secure. So long as they remained official Conservative candidates then Central Office could only fight them by supporting independent candidates. It was a prospect that exasperated Douglas Hacking because he correctly observed that an independent fighting against 'men like Winston, Duff Cooper and Harold Nicolson' could only hope 'at best' to fight with no realistic chance of victory.[122] From the perspective of the local association executives, the possibility of an early election may also have explained the hostility with which they treated dissident MPs – an association's duty was to uphold Conservative values in its constituency and ensure the election of its candidate. To have a Member standing for re-election who dissented publicly from the Prime Minister's foreign policy, the issue most likely to dominate the campaign, would not augur well.[123] Some Conservative supporters sought to foster these sentiments. Lord Rothermere tried unsuccessfully to persuade St George's association to adopt his nephew in preference to Duff Cooper, whilst encouraging loyalists to stand against Eden in Warwick.[124] When the Newbury association executive heard that their current MP, Clifton-Brown, would be standing down at the next election, they agreed that the new candidate must be loyal to the government's foreign policy.[125]

There were certainly elements within the party who favoured the electoral option so that the party might gain political capital from Chamberlain's personal prestige. But powerful forces within the party organisation were urging caution. The party chairman thought a snap election would be 'fatal'. He believed that the administration needed to retain the goodwill of the trade unions for the purposes of rearmament, and that it was possible, if a decision was taken to widen the government, that 'the bitterness engendered by an election would prevent that'. His preferred option was to have an election in the next few months 'before people have forgotten the gas masks'.[126] Sections of the party machine had for some time been preparing for an election. The Conservative Research Department (CRD), acting upon Chamberlain's instructions, had already prepared a short list of 'danger' seats. Its regular analysis of by-election results was always measured in relation to possible general election performances. During mid-November D. F. Clarke of the CRD confidently reported that analysis of by-election results since 1935 left the impression that a general election now would make 'very little difference' to the government's current majority. But two weeks later the analysis was more worrying. In an urgent memorandum to Joseph Ball, the CRD's director, Clarke concluded that the political situation had deteriorated with the outlook being 'far less promising'. The large number of seats held by only small majorities meant that 'only a small turnover of votes would defeat the government'. The assessment carried a further 'important' warning that, 'while a general election would be fought largely on foreign policy, home issues would not be put entirely in the background'.[127] This report coincided with a *News Chronicle* commissioned poll which indicated a 2 per cent fall in 'satisfaction' levels with Chamberlain and recorded a 40 per cent level of dissatisfaction.[128] Chamberlain continued to keep an open mind about the possibility of an early election, not least because it offered an opportunity to force the reunification of the party. But the deteriorating electoral situation cannot have escaped his attention when he suggested to his sisters in December that he had abandoned plans for an election because of the 'behaviour of the dictators'.[129]

JEWS, COLONIES AND BY-ELECTIONS

While the vast majority of Conservatives were prepared to tolerate the Munich agreement, it was apparent that many were unprepared to accept further concessions to Germany. The Nazi pogroms against the German Jews in November 1938 underscored this sentiment. The news of *Kristallnacht* was received with obvious disgust.[130] Although social anti-semitism was not an uncommon trait amongst Conservatives, the intensity and violence of Nazi anti-semitism was abhorrent to most. Such behaviour pricked the moral sensibilities of Conservatives and suggested something of the true nature of nazism. It must also have been recognised that public opinion was incensed by the atrocities. To have talked of further concessions to a regime capable of such brutality would have brought a wave of public condemnation.[131]

This Nazi savagery occurred at a time when the party was expressing concern about the possibility of Britain returning her former colonial territories to Germany. The need for Nazi anti-semitism to resort to murder and brutality was an unacceptable development, and it led Conservatives to question the advisability of continuing negotiations with the Nazi regime. As was shown in the previous chapter, for activists during the latter half of the 1930s the return of former German colonies was a question that aroused considerable opposition (see Tables 3.4 and 3.5). Both the 1936 and 1937 National Union annual conferences had adopted motions opposing any colonial restitution, and such similar sentiments were very visible during 1938. Rumours, particularly in the Beaverbrook press, that Chamberlain had talked to Hitler about colonial returns observably stiffened hostility and brought a wave of protests from local associations.[132]

Table 3.4   Examples of Conservative associations' resolutions passed on colonial appeasement, 1936–39

Against		For	
Date	*Association*	*Date*	*Association*
07/02/36	Norwood	No examples found from sample CAs	
24/04/36	Bournemouth		
	Battersea North		
16/05/36	Wessex Area		
10/06/36	Scottish Eastern (Withdrawn)		
19/06/36	Norwood		
24/06/36	National Union Central Council		
18/12/36	Birmingham		
27/02/37	Northern Counties Area		
01/05/37	Wessex Area		
18/06/38	South Oxfordshire (Withdrawn)		
20/10/38	Inverness		
04/11/38	Chelmsford		
09/11/38	South Oxfordshire		
19/11/38	Harborough		
25/11/38	Greenwich		
14/12/38	National Union Executive		
21/02/39	Maidstone		

An example of the colonial debate during 1938 at the local level, and the stiffening of attitudes, was provided by South Oxfordshire. At its AGM in June a resolution that the time was 'not ripe' for returning Germany's former colonies had been debated. Supporters of the resolution argued that the last war had been at Germany's instigation and that the colonies were compensation for that conflict. Equally it was felt that Germany was demanding these colonies as a right and not as a settlement. The opposition of the dominions was considered important, especially since they held some of these mandated territories. The strategic significance of some of the colonies, like Tanganyika, was also pointed out. Perhaps unsurprisingly, the German character was called into question with a portrayal of the Germans as bad colonialists who maltreated native populations. The current German regime was revealing its intolerance towards subject and ethnic minorities, and therefore any native population surrendered to the Nazis was likely to be ill treated. Opponents countered by questioning the loyalty of the proposers and moving an amendment which felt that acceptance of such a resolution 'would make it appear that they had lost faith in the government'. Disloyalty was a loaded term in Conservative circles and such a charge was enough to encourage the withdrawal of the original resolution. The question of colonies was forced back upon the South Oxfordshire executive in November when their Peppard branch sent a resolution expressing 'alarm' at press speculation about colonial restitution. Gifford Fox, their MP, had also been in correspondence with a constituent about the same question in which he too expressed objections. The executive concluded that they were only prepared to consider colonial returns if they meant 'an absolute guarantee of peace', but this could not be done until Germany disarmed both numerically and morally.[133] Similar views were not uncommon amongst Conservatives and in colonial circles. A further argument, which may have stemmed from an imperial arrogance and a prejudicial view of the German character, was that no colony should be returned without the consent of the native populations.[134] This view must certainly have seemed credible in light of the Nazi mistreatment of their Jewish populations and political opponents.[135] Certainly *Kristallnacht* was a catalyst. 'Even some of the staunchest supporters of the government are puzzled and disconcerted' observed *The Times* on 15 November. The paper's political correspondent

> understood that this feeling was reflected in speeches at last night's meeting of the 1922 Conservative Private Member's Committee, when the subject of ex-German colonies was raised. These speeches,

and the way in which they were received, appear to show a stiffening of the attitude of a number of government backbenchers.

That same day an EDM was tabled in the House of Commons which urged 'that no agreement should be made under which any British colonies or mandated territory should be transferred to Germany without the consent of the people of Great Britain'. It soon had thirty-seven signatures including those of Adams, Amery, Ruggles-Brise, Crawford Browne and Cary.[136] The signatories were a mix of loyalists and foreign policy sceptics. For those with an imperialist tradition, the fear existed that surrendering the mandates would weaken the Empire, threatening it strategically and hastening its demise. The opposition of the disaffected sceptics came from the desire to avoid any further concessions to the Nazi regime. Sections of the media speculated that Chamberlain had given Hitler some verbal assurances at Munich about the return of colonies. These rumours particularly aroused the suspicion of the dissident Conservative foreign policy critics.[137] Eden was being urged by supporters to 'come out very strongly' against colonial restitution and request a ministerial statement. They felt that a very large part of the party were 'disturbed and anxious' and that an appeal 'put with vigour would have a disturbing effect on the back-benches and would rally many doubtful supporters in the country'. Eden 'would speak as a Tory for Tories'.[138]

Of course, not all were opposed to returning former German colonies (as shown in Table 3.5). Oswald Lewis, the Member for Colchester, 'doubted' in December 1938 if there could ever be 'any settlement with Germany until something was done to meet her half way in the matter of the colonial question'.[139] Nevertheless, most accepted that in the last months of 1938 such advances were not prac-tical given the current political outlook, and this view applied equally to the cabinet, parliamentary party and constituencies. As the National Union executive agreed in mid-December, such returns 'would not be conducive to the maintenance of peace'.[140] Certainly Chamberlain felt frustrated at the attitudes of the dictators in the months following Munich. Even the prospect of an early general elec-tion to capitalise upon the euphoria of peace had to be ruled out because the dictators appeared incapable of behaving themselves.

Unable to make any immediate approaches to Hitler, Chamberlain sought to maintain the initiative by improving Anglo-Italian relations. At Mussolini's request, Chamberlain set out to reward him for involve-ment in the Munich conference, by a hasty ratification of the Anglo-Italian agreement. When it was presented to the House at the

Table 3.5 Conservative MPs' and Peers' attitudes to colonial restitution

Opposed	*Favourable*
Leo Amery*	Thomas Moore (Oct. 1933)
Duncan Sandys*	Lord Redesdale (March 1936)
Harold Nicolson*	Arnold Wilson (December 1938)
Charles Ponsonby*	Oswald Lewis (December 1938)
Earl of Selborne*	
Viscount Stonehaven*	
Lord Lugard*	
48 signatories to Sandys' EDM 10/02/36	
124 signatories to Sandys' EDM 22/07/36	
105 signatories to Sandys' EDM 15/02/37	
37 signatories to Adams' EDM 14/11/38	
5 signatories to Ponsonby's amendment 05/12/38	
15 signatories to Amery's amendment 05/12/38	

* All members of the Colonial League, an organisation opposed to returning the former German colonies.

beginning of November there were only a few abstentions, with a number of leading foreign policy critics supporting the government. The ratification process illustrated the distinction many Conservatives drew between appeasing Italy and appeasing Germany. John Withers and Joseph McConnell were implacably opposed to giving concessions to Mussolini and were consistently absent from votes concerning Anglo-Italian relations. In contrast, Sidney Herbert and Leo Amery supported the government's implementation of the 1938 Anglo-Italian treaty, but found themselves sceptical about the government's German policy from the time of Munich. For others it was all about political manoeuvring. Eden, who was one of the abstentions, explained that he 'could not vote against the government without voting with Labour. Moreover it would be impossible to vote against the government on a major issue such as this without refusing the government whip and ceasing in effect to be a government supporter'. It would have meant a by-election.[141]

With many of the Munich rebels still experiencing trouble from their local associations, such considerations of expediency were not surprising. In Kinross the Munich agreement forced the issue. Having already been deselected for the next election and finding the terms of Munich unacceptable, the Duchess of Atholl resigned her seat and fought a by-election against the official Conservative candidate. She was defeated – none of her fellow rebels had been prepared to speak on her behalf. Only Churchill gave a degree of public support by sending the Duchess an open letter of endorsement. Bob Boothby considered intervening but was warned off by the whips' office.[142] As it was, the government had to fight eight by-elections between Munich and Christmas 1938 – losing at Bridgwater and Dartford (see Table 3.6). CRD analysis concluded that the degree of public interest in the by-elections was due to the 'emotional and abnormal atmosphere produced by the uncertainties of the international situation and of national defence, and aggravated by the strong feeling aroused by the Jewish persecutions'.[143] These results, and the international situation, were enough to persuade the party chairman that the government should 'hold off an election as long as possible'.[144]

Table 3.6 By-election results October 1938–December 1938

Date	Constituency	Result	% Swing For/Against Conservatives
27/10/38	Oxford City	Conservative hold	3.9% against
07/11/38	Dartford	Labour gain	2.9% against
16/11/38	Walsall	Conservative hold	0.4% against
17/11/38	Doncaster	Conservative hold	2.6% against
17/11/38	Bridgwater	Independent gain	7.6% against
24/11/38	West Lewisham	Conservative hold	7.6% against
30/11/38	Fylde	Conservative hold	2.4% against
21/12/38	Kinross	Conservative hold	*

* It should be noted that the Duchess of Atholl who had stood in the 1935 general election as the Conservative candidate fought the by-election as an independent and lost to the official Conservative candidate.

THE IDES OF MARCH AND THE COUNTDOWN TO WAR

Certainly a number of Conservatives were by February 1939 becoming increasingly concerned about Hitler's next move. During January conflicting rumours emerged from Berlin which suggested that London might at any moment be subject to a 'mad-dog' air raid or that Hitler's attentions were turned to the Low Countries. Ralph Glyn admitted that it would be a 'critical fortnight' but he still believed that 'peace and reason' would be preserved.[145] The foreign policy sceptics were less confident about Hitler's intentions and were fearful that Chamberlain proposed to launch a fresh diplomatic initiative.[146] Their gloomy assessment was being echoed by some sections of the press, causing Scottish Conservatives to complain that 'the persistent pessimism of widely read organs, from which government support might ordinarily be expected was doing great harm by creating an atmosphere of undue anxiety among people of all classes, besides giving a false impression abroad'.[147] It was perhaps to counter these defeatist press reports that Chamberlain told lobby correspondents in early March that the international situation was so hopeful that disarmament talks might begin before the year's end. This was despite the government being aware of rumours that Germany was now intending to absorb the remainder of Czechoslovakia, and of the German forces being massed on the Czechoslovak border.[148] When news reached London that advanced mobile German units had entered Prague, blatantly flouting Munich, it signalled the failure of Chamberlain's appeasement policy. This was certainly the prevalent view amongst the party: Prague should mean the end of all dealings with Hitler, who henceforth should 'be treated as outside the pale'.[149] Although Chamberlain stoutly defended his position to a hostile House of Commons, its reaction meant that a few days later, during a speech to Birmingham Conservatives, he effectively signalled the end of appeasement. Pressure had been brought to bear by Halifax, who recognised the very real danger of the government falling from power if they persisted in their current vein. The House of Commons debate had revealed the concern amongst Conservative ranks. Wolmer seized on Chamberlain's declaration that he would persevere to keep the peace of Europe. In a speech laced with sarcasm, Wolmer asked 'what sort of peace are we enjoying today? Is it proper, legitimate, right and sensible to describe the state of Europe today as one of peace? I do not think it is'.[150] Richard Law was equally damning:

> It is no time to apportion blame. But at the same time we must admit that that policy [of appeasement] has not worked out as we

were told it would work out. We must admit that the predictions which were being made by critics of that policy have been fulfilled in a most alarming degree, and that every published calculation of the supporters of that policy has been falsified by the event.[151]

A few backbenchers did try to defend Chamberlain but declarations like Archibald Southby's 'that the policy of appeasement is still right . . . [and] . . . is the only policy which we can expect to gain a peace that will last' did not really sound convincing.[152] The parliamentary debate had been, as one Chamberlainite loyalist admitted, a 'great day' for the disaffected.[153] The situation had not been alleviated by the impression that Chamberlain had not performed 'very convincing[ly]'.[154] If publicly some Conservatives felt obliged to support the Prime Minister, the majority remained silent. In private however, the leadership was left in no doubt about their criticisms, the hostility of the parliamentary party being expressed at a meeting of their Foreign Affairs Committee.[155]

Chamberlain's Birmingham speech, which was extensively reported in the press and relayed live to some local associations, averted a party revolt and the tributes from the activists were soon dispatched to London. The prospective candidate for Barnard Castle proposed for the Northern Counties association one such resolution of 'confidence' which promised 'unqualified support' for the Prime Minister.[156] A similar resolution was approved by Derby association, an action repeated by many other associations around the country.[157]

The government after consideration responded further on 31 March by guaranteeing Poland's territorial integrity, as well as that of a number of other European nations. Measures were announced that doubled the size of the Territorial Army, and finally conscription was introduced in April. Once again, activists were quick to assure Chamberlain of their support for the new foreign policy emphasis on 'guarantees'.[158] The parliamentary party, including the sceptics, publicly received the new measures positively. Even Churchill 'did not harangue the government, but actually praised it'.[159] Christopher York felt the guarantee meant 'that the blame for any war now rests solely on Hitler and the PM has manoeuvred him into the position that he will have the whole world against him including probably America'.[160] Although one area chairman thought it ironic that 'now possibly the next European war may arise in defence of the Polish corridor! How odd that would be'.[161] Amery later wrote that with Poland 'the Germans often had better grounds for complaint than in the case of Czechs and Sudetens the year before. Polish crowds were far less restrained in venting their anti-German sentiments, while some Polish newspapers . . . were openly provocative'.[162] Despite this, Conservatives still continued to refer to the dictators in conciliatory terms; members of the cabinet were asked to refrain from making personal attacks upon Hitler, while the suggestion that Britain was trying to encircle Germany was denied.[163] Instead, Conservatives insisted that Chamberlain was merely creating a peace bloc whose role was defensive not aggressive. The City of London association heard how Hitler had 'betrayed' Chamberlain and that now the Prime Minister had 'adopted the only other method available – a peace front with other European countries. . . . the great prestige enjoyed by the country was [being] shown by the readiness with which other countries had accepted our guarantees against aggression'.[164] One Yorkshire MP assured his local association that since Prague

> we have re-oriented our foreign policy and we have been building up a peace front which will be able to confront Germany and Italy if they start on any further acts of aggression with force equal to or superior to their own. This peace front has no hostile or aggressive intentions but it was determined to preserve its integrity.[165]

To many observers, Soviet Russia was the key to any successful 'peace bloc' Chamberlain may have been wishing to create after the Prague spring. Certain elements within the Conservative party had been suggesting since early 1938 that the British government should try to incorporate Russia into some sort of anti-fascist pact. This was being most vocally expressed by Churchill and his suggestion of a 'grand alliance'.[166] This envisaged a network of nations assembled around Britain and France in a mutual defence pact based upon the covenant of the League of Nations and 'sustained by a moral sense of the world'.[167] Critics of the Munich agreement were by 1939 arguing that Britain and France would have had the help of Russia, Poland and Czechoslovakia if Chamberlain had stood firm against Hitler in September 1938.[168] Following the fall of Prague and the threat being placed upon Danzig and Poland, these advocates of the 'grand alliance' suggested it was all the more essential to secure an agreement with Soviet Russia. But to the vast majority of Conservatives any thoughts of an alliance with the communists was anathema. Many, especially those to the right of the party, were of the opinion that many of the world's troubles could be attributed to communism, and they argued that Hitler and Mussolini had come to power because of it. Some were even prepared to argue that Hitler 'stood as a bulwark' against Soviet Russia.[169] Not even all the foreign policy sceptics were agreed that it was necessary to approach Russia. Amery was always very cynical of the value of Soviet help. During the Czech crisis he had argued vigorously with the other foreign policy sceptics against involving Russia, and was again during 1939 less than enthusiastic for an alliance.[170]

Prague did force Chamberlain into an approach to Moscow, but there was an apparent lack of enthusiasm on the British part. One motive behind the negotiations was to prevent Stalin making a pact with Hitler. Headlam saw this as the 'only reason' for an agreement with Russia.[171] Whilst the thought that fascism and communism, two supposedly irreconcilable ideologies, could reach terms was inconceivable to some contemporaries, others were aware that both Germany and Soviet Russia had their sights on Poland. The replacement of Litvinov as Soviet Foreign Minister by Molotov meant that a sympathetic Germanophile was in place. Indeed there were rumours emanating from Moscow that suggested negotiations were taking place. Dissident Conservatives were inclined to believe that Chamberlain was not doing enough to entice Russia. Amery considered the trouble to be that Chamberlain was being 'pushed all the time into a policy which he does not like, and [he] hates abandoning the last bridges which might still enable him to renew his former policy'. Even the loyalist 'Chips' Channon was inclined to admit that he felt Chamberlain's heart was not in the Russian talks.[172] Particular criticism was made of the failure to establish direct personal contact with Stalin in the opening stages.[173] William Strang, from the Foreign Office's central department, was despatched to Moscow in July to conduct the negotiations. Many observers, and not least the Russians, felt that if Chamberlain had been prepared to fly to meet Hitler, then at least he or another senior cabinet minister ought to have tried to negotiate with Stalin – at the very least it would have revealed the genuineness of the British approaches.[174] Halifax had suggested the possibility of dispatching Eden, while Churchill had offered his services to David Margesson, the chief whip. Chamberlain believed that if either man was sent to Moscow it would only legitimise their claims to be recalled to cabinet office.[175]

In the summer months of 1939 Conservatives were imbued with a fatalistic consciousness of the impending doom. Ralph Glyn wrote to his mother explaining that 'the only way in which to keep sane is to farm and do things that Hitler and Co. cannot control'.[176] As the crisis moved towards Danzig and the Polish corridor the situation was such that one MP felt that 'the present impasse can only be ended in two ways. 1. by peaceful agreement. 2. by war'. This Member was confident that the government would tolerate no further aggression, arguing that the dictators had been given their chance.[177] Other Conservatives were rather more doubtful about the government's resolve. Chamberlain's decision to allow parliament to adjourn for the summer recess brought a tirade of abuse from some backbenchers who were fearful that the Prime Minister might try and negotiate another Munich in parliament's absence. In an outspoken attack, fellow Birmingham Member Ronald Cartland rounded on Chamberlain, suggesting it was more important 'to get the whole country behind you than make jeering pettifogging party speeches which divide the nation'.[178] Certainly throughout August the signs emanating from Germany were unpromising. Cranborne noted the media talk of 'a war of nerves' and observed that

> If they mean by this phrase that the Germans still hope to bully us into another Munich without war, no doubt that is Hitler's game. But if they mean, further, that he is bluffing, I'm not so sure. He may, equally, be confident or desperate – I see today that the German press seem to have orders to say that Germany's honour is involved. This is a bad sign, as it is taking up a position from which it is very difficult for them to retreat.[179]

By August it does appear that many were reconciling themselves to the inevitability of war. The Polish corridor was the sole remaining vestige of Versailles and there was little to suggest that Hitler would be deterred. The only difference this time was that the Poles were unprepared to stand back and Britain was obligated to assist her. Moreover, the British public was unprepared to tolerate a second Munich. Headlam admitted 'the issue now depends on the Poles – if they really mean business, we shall really have no alternative but to go in with them'. Soon he was musing about 'how many English people will be called upon to die' for Poland.[180] News of the Nazi-Soviet pact confirmed many peoples' worst fears. Channon 'realised that the Russians have double-crossed us, as I always believed they would. They have been coquetting secretly with Germany, even as our negotiations proceeded. They are the foulest people on earth. Now it looks like war, and the immediate partition of Poland'.[181] Walter Elliot was relieved to find at cabinet 'that we intended to stand by Poland whatever the result of the German Russian talks'. He admitted that,

> the business looks rather bad – not so much because of the pact itself, which may mean anything or nothing, but because of the psychological reactions. I should think it could be interpreted by

Hitler as a free hand in the east. In that case, so far as I see, there will be war. On the other hand Hitler may start guessing as to what the Russians really mean and that may delay things a little.[182]

Unbeknown to the British, although not totally unexpected, the Nazi-Soviet pact contained a secret clause which agreed the annexation and division of Poland between the two signatory nations. *Fall Weiss*, the German directive to invade Poland, was now in countdown. On 1 September 1939 at 6 a.m. German troops crossed the Polish border.

SOME CONCLUSIONS

With Chamberlain in charge from May 1937 it was clear that it was not just foreign policy, but also party leadership that was to be pursued with vigour. The Prime Minister was determined not to blight his administration with Baldwinesqe drift. The backbenches and activists were to be relegated to a passive role, meekly sanctioning the government's policies. The power of the backbench Foreign Affairs Committee was curtailed, with the whips ensuring that 'sound' MPs acted as its officials. Chamberlain had no intention of allowing them to dictate terms, as had often been the case under Baldwin.

It was apparent that the majority of Conservatives were publicly prepared to back the Prime Minister's policy of conciliation and negotiation until the seizure of Prague. Therefore, to this extent Chamberlain's actions were justified. In private, however, doubts were certainly more apparent. These first emerged during August and September 1938 and became very noticeable in the few months after Munich. These private doubters were obliged to express their disquiet behind the scenes. The retribution delivered upon the foreign policy sceptics following Munich was probably enough to deter others from going public and thus attract the unwelcome attention of either the whips or local grassroots zealots. The party's uneasiness with Chamberlain's foreign policy, especially between September and November 1938, was more considerable than has been previously supposed. Nevertheless, Chamberlain was able to weather the storm. This was due to three factors. First, the inability of his opponents to present a viable and cogent substitute foreign policy. Second, the reality was that to many Conservatives, both MPs and rank and file alike, there was no credible alternative to the Prime Minister. And finally, there did not exist at that time any formal mechanism whereby the party could oust their leader. By the summer of 1939 Eden had failed to capitalise upon his popularity and present himself as a worthy alternative; whereas Churchill, although he had done much to improve his stature, was still viewed with considerable suspicion. Moreover, it is apparent that to consider the foreign policy sceptics as one 'anti-appeaser' bloc is an overly simplistic analysis. Sweeping generalisations have been made that categorise these MPs as consistent critics, yet it is apparent that many were inconsistent in their approach, attitude and response to foreign policy during this period. Their numbers were limited, being less than a tenth of the parliamentary party, while as a political force they were scattered and disorganised. A number of the disaffected, such as Churchill, Amery, Horne, Eden and Duff Cooper, had seen government office at one time or another. Naturally, being ex-ministers, these individuals commanded a greater degree of influence in the lobbies and corridors of Westminster than the remainder of their junior backbench associates, but the extent to which they were able to influence policy was negligible. Under Chamberlain the nature of foreign policy critic altered. Whereas Baldwin had found himself being attacked from both left and right, Chamberlain moved the party rightwards. The diehards and centre-right Conservatives who had played a central role in the opposition to Indian reform were divided in their attitude and response to Chamberlain and how to respond to the dictators: some followed the Churchillian calls for rearmament, the remainder gave their support to Chamberlain's methods.

4   The rearmament debate, 1935–8

In March 1935 the government announced a white paper which planned to increase the all-round spending upon rearmament for the first time since the end of the First World War. From that moment onwards debate was to be waged in media, military and political circles over the priorities for rearmament: was the air force, army or navy of greatest importance? Should the Royal Air Force prioritise bombers or fighters? And was a continental expeditionary army necessary or not? By 1935 few Conservatives denied the necessity for rearmament. There had been growing momentum from the grassroots upwards since early 1934 for some increased defence expenditure.[1] Nevertheless, there were concerns that the British population would not tolerate such expansion. This domestic concern had to be balanced against the deteriorating international situation as the European dictators attempted to consolidate and then expand their spheres of influence. This was the backdrop to the British rearmament programme. It also provides the starting point for this chapter's examination of the Conservative party's attitudes and expectations of the National government's rearmament programme from 1935 to the end of 1938. It will highlight the link between the deepening international abyss and Conservative concerns that British rearmament was failing to deliver. After considering the formative years of the programme, the means by which rearmament was funded will be examined. An assessment will then be made of the party's reception of the Inskip defence review and the subsequent impact this had upon defence requirements. Rearmament was perceived in terms that required the prioritisation of the best deterrent capabilities, but what did Conservatives judge to be the greatest deterrents? The Munich crisis was to shatter any illusions held about the improved defence position. What will become apparent was that as 1938 drew to a close, it was defence policy and not foreign policy that proved the most controversial and divisive of topics.

THE BEGINNINGS OF REARMAMENT

The party welcomed the 1935 defence white paper.[2] The years of financial austerity had impacted hard on the defence services. It meant that disarmament had taken the country to the 'verge of risk'.[3] Hitler's reaction in announcing the reintroduction of German conscription and then declaring that the *Luftwaffe* had parity with the RAF highlighted the need for an expansion of the defence programme. The private response of some Conservative grandees was not so positive. Events abroad were 'critical', and although the government was moving in the right direction the reverses were inadequate. The problem was that if these weaknesses, were exposed by public debate, then potential harm would be done to British prestige, both at home and abroad. Furthermore, the perceived pacifist nature of public opinion posed problems.[4] The response of the government was to alert opinion gradually to British weaknesses, thereby averting hysteria. This process had begun as early as November 1933 when Baldwin, addressing the Lord Mayor's banquet, warned that 'there is a point when the possession of arms of offence by other nations forces the hands of pacific nations and they feel compelled to accumulate material for defence'.[5] From the beginning, rearmament was couched in League phraseology – emphasis being placed upon acceptance of the League's principles because of Britain's preference for negotiation and discussion as opposed to war. The 1935 white paper stressed that no country had tried harder than Britain to secure peace through arms limitation, through collective security and by the promotion of international understanding. The argument was made that these measures offered the best guarantee for peace.

In order to continue the electorates' education, Central Office published a leaflet, *The True Facts*, which elaborated upon the decision to expand the defence programme.[6] It was evident that local activists undertook to vindicate the programme's existence to the electorate. In common with the Westminster line, stress was laid on the benefits for peace, the deterrence factor and the ability the measures gave Britain to fulfil her obligations to the League of Nations.[7] When Baldwin addressed the Bournemouth party conference in September, his first since becoming PM in June, he told delegates that collective security backed by rearmament offered 'greater security than can be obtained by any other policy which we have yet seen advocated'.[8] In a matter of weeks Baldwin had dissolved Parliament and gone to the country, resolved to having rearmament and its contribution to collective security as the major theme. The Abyssinian crisis provided the government with the best possible justification for its plans to rearm. Throughout the campaign it is apparent that candidates took the opportunity to explain their support for the defence programme: 84 per cent of Conservative candidates declared their approval for the programme.[9] Candidates did embellish their declarations to suit both their own beliefs and those of their constituents. In North Salford, John Morris laid stress upon the benefits to collective security of strong British defence forces; whilst in Caernarvon, with its nonconformist tradition, the candidate went to lengths to explain the necessity of British rearmament in order to persuade others to adopt disarmament.[10] The success of the election for the Conservatives may have finally provided their leaders with an electoral mandate to rearm, but this was only the first victory in what would be a protracted war. The skirmishes over priorities were only just beginning and the need to justify both the programme and its expenditure to the wider party and electorate remained ever present.

HOW WOULD THE NEXT WAR BE FOUGHT?

At this point it is important to outline contemporary perceptions of what form another war would assume and what implications this held for the rearmament debate. Few expected the next war to be one of attrition, as the First World War had been. For example Chamberlain, having read the theories of Liddell-Hart, wrote in 1936:

> I cannot believe that the next war, if it ever comes, will be like the last one, and I believe our resources will be more profitably employed in the air, and on the sea, than in building up great armies.[11]

The advancement of technology, particularly in terms of aviation, encouraged this belief. Many feared that on the declaration of war Britain would be subjected to a massive air attack aimed at forcing a quick surrender, primarily through the collapse of civilian morale.[12] Declarations made by public figures, such as Stanley Baldwin suggesting that 'the bomber will always get through', and the pictures of the bombed Spanish town of Guernica in 1937, added greatly to the popular fear of a knockout blow.[13] Consequently, British rearmament was preoccupied with the needs of the RAF and ensuring parity with the *Luftwaffe*. By contrast, the demands of the British army were deemed of lowest priority.[14] At the same time, during the late 1930s there was growing concern about the inadequate nature of Britain's air defences. These defences had initially been designed to provide protection for London and south-east England against attacks from France. The rise of Germany as a belligerent power meant that the Midlands and north were now exposed to the possibility of enemy aerial assaults. This made the provision of air defences a matter of considerable urgency.

THE NEED FOR RE-EVALUATION

The Abyssinian conflict presented a test case for British defence policy. Hitherto defence planning had been based on the assumption of conflict with Germany and for the need to deter Japanese expansion against imperial targets in the Far East. Now the Mediterranean was a potential hostile zone with the strategical threat to the Suez canal.[15] It is evident that the consequences of this for rearmament were seen in quite differing perspectives by the party and the military planners. Whilst the military were concerned with tailoring the defence schedules to meet these challenges, debate within the party centred around whether the government was taking on too many foreign commitments without regard to military capability and the primacy of home defence. Amongst the party the defence debate was both diversifying and specialising. The causes of supply, air defence, recruitment and imperial defence were all being taken up.[16] This was reflected in the topics that guest speakers lectured the 1922 Committee on. In 1935 three guests had spoken on defence-related matters. In 1936 four guest speakers delivered talks on defence organisation, imperial defence, supply and air defence.[17] Furthermore, 1936 saw the politicisation of the defence debate. Conservatives openly addressed the subject and were prepared to highlight what they perceived to be the deficiencies. This was particularly the case with air defence. Lord Rothermere, through his press empire and the Air League, was proactive in the air debate. When Ward Price, foreign correspondent for the *Daily Mail*, reported to him a remark by Göring that the Germans were building a new plane every half-hour, a note was immediately sent to the cabinet on the matter.[18] Churchill also began championing the cause. In November 1936 during a defence debate in which Baldwin admitted to the weaknesses in the defence programme and claimed that he could not have begun rearmament any earlier because he lacked a mandate, Churchill rounded on the government's rearmament record. For his supporters it was 'one of the best speeches of his life' and helped to draw a crowd of one hundred and fifty to the next 1922 Committee meeting (this was over twice the normal audience) the following month when he spoke on defence.[19] However, the extent to which Churchill's concerns were gaining currency amongst the party more widely, at this time, is questionable.[20]

FINANCIAL PRUDENCE VERSUS REARMAMENT

The years of neglect experienced by the three armed services since the cessation of the First World War meant that the task facing the British authorities was a phenomenal one. To make matters worse the British economy was depressed and the balance of payments fragile. It was a situation not alleviated by the financial pressures of the defence programme. For example, the level of rearmament between 1937 and 1938 diverted attention away from exports towards imports and conse-quently produced an adverse balance of payments of about fifty-five million pounds. Further, the funding of rearmament through domestic loans weakened confidence in financial institutions.[21] Consequently, there was a battle not only over priorities, but also over funding, with the Treasury attempting to tailor the demands of the service chiefs with the practical realities of what Britain could afford. During the 1930s Neville Chamberlain occupied a pivotal position in the debate, firstly as Chancellor of the Exchequer from 1931–7 and then as Baldwin's successor to the premiership. Ultimately, the Treasury's view that rearmament should be constrained within the boundaries of what could be afforded prevailed. Not surprisingly, when Chamberlain became Prime Minister in May 1937 there was no change in emphasis.[22] Under the influence of Chamberlain, rearmament was increasingly based upon the concept of limited liability. This was the idea that Britain should limit her defence responsibilities and classify those that she did accept in terms that provided the greatest deterrent capabilities combined with value for money. This defence concept, which some historians have suggested was little different to Britain's former policy of splendid isolation, reached maturity with its applica-tion in the Inskip defence review of 1937.

Since 1935 the cost of rearmament had risen at so rapid a pace that by early 1937 the projection was for £1,500 million over the next five-year period. Such expansion meant that the Treasury was forced to look for alternative or new sources of income – in practical terms this meant either greater borrowing or greater taxation. The former held the risk of fuelling inflation and weakening still further confidence in Britain's financial institutions, whilst the latter was a potential electoral liability. Indeed, from as early as 1933 Conservative back-benchers had been warning that armaments expenditure should not be allowed to interfere with tax reductions.[23] During the 1936 budget debates the differing schools of thought within the party came to the fore. Those such as Russell and Salmon argued that the Chancellor's line should be approved provided that strict economy was exercised over armaments.[24] Michael Beaumont took a rather more diehard view, arguing that economies were required in the social services budget to cover the costs of defence.[25] Conservatives favourable to imperial preference approached the matter from a differing perspective. They argued that protectionist tariffs could be levied, believing that these would enable the Chancellor to circumvent income tax increases.[26] Churchill's intervention in the proceedings was to argue that whilst he welcomed the increase in arms expenditure he felt that the limited nature of the expansion failed to warrant the corresponding rise in direct taxation.[27] It was view that his lieutenant Boothby echoed. He offered the Chancellor a practical suggestion: capital defence projects, such as aerodromes, could be financed via loans, taking advantage of cheap money; and recurrent expenditure could be met from annual revenue.[28] Unfortunately from the Treasury's perspective the cost of rearmament continued to rise during 1936, obliging the Chancellor to explore new avenues of revenue generation.

THE NATIONAL DEFENCE CONTRIBUTION CONTROVERSY

In his final months as Chancellor, Chamberlain decided upon the income option with a new temporary tax, the National Defence Contribution (NDC).[29] As a result, instead of the smooth transition to the premiership he had hoped for, Chamberlain found that the turbulence caused by the question of funding rearmament 'risked' the premiership.[30] The NDC proposal was introduced to the House of Commons in his last budget during April 1937 when Chamberlain warned that 'the national finances have, and must continue to be dominated and governed by the vast expenditure on defence'.[31] The Chancellor explained that his motive behind the NDC was to avoid imposing 'a succession of new taxes hitting first in one direction then in another', whilst also ensuring that the general expansion of trade was not hindered further. He proposed a graduated tax on the growth of business and industrial profits in excess of £2,000 during the period of the rearmament programme.[32] Chamberlain anticipated that this would immediately yield over two million pounds, a figure which would increase to somewhere between twenty and twenty-five million pounds within a full year. The NDC tax was designed not only to raise revenue for rearmament, but also to forestall severe labour unrest in the event of serious price rises and prevent the possibility of excessive profiteering by defence contractors.[33]

B. E. V. Sabine, the fiscal historian, has suggested that the parliamentary Conservative reaction to the proposals 'showed an interesting division of opinion, not of course amounting to anything like a real split in the ranks'. As evidence, Sabine cites the cautious welcome for the NDC from backbenchers Loftus and Somerville and compares the criticisms of Wardlaw-Milne and Boothby.[34] This analysis needs revision principally because Sabine sourced his assessment from the parliamentary debates. Invariably, parliamentary etiquette and rhetoric as well as party loyalty prevented Conservatives from directly and publicly expressing their objections. Equally, when this measure was first announced there was considerable uncertainty over the precise nature of the proposal. This was because Chamberlain's budget speech had only given the briefest of outlines about the new tax. He admitted that he 'could hardly expect Hon[ourable] Members to grasp at the first hearing all the implications of the system', and it is apparent from the first two days of debate that many MPs were clearly unsure what the proposal entailed. Indeed this confusion extended to the Chief Secretary to the Treasury, John Colville, when concluding the debate for the government.[35] Only after time had allowed for greater analysis of the precise nature of the plans did Conservative criticisms crescendo to an almost intolerable level.[36] In private even the initial reaction of Conservatives was critical. Winterton saw it as 'one big surprise'.[37] Amery noted the 'hostile buzz' in the lobbies as soon as the proposal was announced, and his diary entries over the next few months reveal the continued furore against the tax.[38] Many Conservatives, at both national and grassroots level, felt that the measure was the sort one would have expected a socialist government to introduce. Victor Cazalet, although finding morally and ethically 'much to recommend the idea', nevertheless considered the NDC to be in practice the 'most unfair tax ever been put forward'.[39] The Conservative Finance Committee with a 150 members present passed a 'strong' resolution demanding its withdrawal.[40] The growth of opposition at all levels is apparent from the constituency correspondence files of backbench MPs, which testify to the hostile response of businessmen, and to that of the big industries and the City, who lobbied vigorously against the measures while clandestinely aided by a Central Office insider.[41]

Winchester association executive discussed the tax in May, just days before Chamberlain succeeded as Prime Minister. The debate exposed not only the executive's attitude to the NDC but revealed confusion about the extent to which an association could expect its Member to reflect its concerns in parliament. Critics desired the tax to be 'less onerous and more equitable'. One speaker felt the proposals would penalise those companies who had made no profits between 1933 and 1936. Similarly, another argued that 'the businessman would be penalised and the professional man would escape'. Others cautioned against hasty decisions, believing that the Chancellor was still considering compromise and suggested that the issue was one for parliament and not themselves to decide. Some on the executive felt the proposed motion tied the hands of their Member and would push the MP against the government. This provoked one activist to explain that the association's 'one duty' was to keep their MP informed: 'all opinions should be weighed and he should know about it'. Continuing, he indicated he 'was against people keeping their mouths shut when they disapproved of anything and from what he had heard he thought the tax should be modified'. This interjection carried the day and persuaded the chairman to modify the motion so as not to stifle the meeting's disapproval. Their MP was urged 'to use his influence' to have the tax 'made as fair in its application as possible under the circumstances'. Other Conservatives at the grassroots were equally critical. One Lincolnshire man felt 'it will crack the foundations of the Conservative party which will ultimately crumble'. The chairman of Kinross association met one businessman who was 'foaming at Mr Chamberlain's new tax. Says it is the most "socialistic" measure ever introduced by Unionists – he refuses to subscribe to our association in future'.[42] The threats of financial sanction could not be taken lightly. The situation was such that one party worker warned his MP that he found among the 'thinking people' a 'distinct dislike to the present government gradually growing through allowing such taxation'. The prominence of local businessmen and the professional elites on local association platforms meant that the party leadership could not afford to overlook their views.[43] As a consequence this hostile reaction, not only from natural supporters of the Conservatives but also from backbench MPs, publicly (during the report stages of the budget) and in private (to whips and ministers), forced a humiliating climb-down by the government. Chamberlain's successor at the Exchequer, Sir John Simon, was obliged in June to introduce a general flat 5 per cent rate of taxation on profits.[44]

The negative reaction of Conservatives to the NDC tax demonstrates something of the contradiction being experienced over rearmament. They were prepared to declare that 'we have to rearm, [and] the cost must be met, that is of course a certainty and is generally recognised', but in the same breath they would shy away from any measure that might have been electorally unfavourable, or that was in conflict with their own self-interest.[45] A likely explanation for this inconsistency was the inability of many Conservatives to conceive the sense of 'crisis', and because few really believed that rearmament needed to be made a 'national' rather than purely 'party' issue. Some of this may have stemmed from a delusion about the 'greatness' of Britain and also from a failure to comprehend fully the danger that Germany posed to post-Versailles Europe – these assessments would be radically reversed over the following eighteen months. In the meantime the problem of financing rearmament remained. It is unclear exactly where these critics of the NDC tax expected the additional finance to be found. Certainly in comparison to German business, which was subject to a 40 per cent tax on profits, British business escaped relatively lightly.[46] Some, such as Charles Williams, argued that borrowing was the answer since they believed direct taxation imposed a 'heavy burden on trade and industry'. Others confessed to concerns about further borrowing but believed that under the current circumstances it was the lesser evil. In contrast, backbenchers such as Wardlaw-Milne and Boothby felt that the necessary money could be secured by income tax and surtax increases.[47] However, Chamberlain believed that the threepence in the pound income tax increase he announced with his budget was the most that could be squeezed from that source.[48] The level at which income tax was already pegged was considered high enough by most contemporaries. During the 1931 financial crisis, income tax had been one of the principal means of trying to bridge the deficit (it being levied at five shillings in the pound). Thereafter, income tax rates were seen as an indicator of the healthiness of the economy. If Chamberlain had gone any higher than the 5s. 6d. rate he now introduced it would have created the impression of financial crisis.[49]

The costs of rearmament explain why the topic featured heavily in the addresses MPs made to their associations between 1935 and 1938 justifying its necessity. 'Nothing', explained one Yorkshire MP, 'was more calculated to ensure the peace of the world, to inspire the small nations with confidence and certain powerful nations with prudence', than the defence programme. It meant 'the English taxpayer was saving civilisation'.[50] The need to justify rearmament in 1937 was particularly necessary because internationally it was a relatively crisis-free year, with the events that were to occur in 1938–9 by no means appearing predictable. Consequently, rearmament was explained in terms that emphasised Britain's role as a leading world power, and that underscored the deterrent capabilities of a strong Britain.[51] Deterrence was to be the rationale of the British rearmament programme from its inception in 1935 to the outbreak of war in September 1939.

THE PROBLEMS OF JUSTIFYING REARMAMENT

If the inter-war period was the era of the League of Nations, by the late 1930s it was apparent to many Conservatives that the League had failed. From the very beginning the absence of the United States of America seriously debilitated it, whilst the 1931 Manchurian crisis first publicly highlighted the League's failings, merely confirming what many Conservatives thought privately. The disarmament conferences of the early 1930s achieved very little and were effectively scuppered by Hitler's announcement that Germany would be leaving the League in 1933. However, by-elections, such as East Fulham in 1933, which John Wilmott won for Labour, suggested to the Conservative leadership that pacifism still persisted and that there still remained popular support for the League.

From the beginning, rearmament was being justified in terms of the League of Nations' ethics. This was clearly necessary in 1935 given the League's popular support, but in light of its failure over Abyssinia and the increasing awkwardness of the dictators it is perhaps surprising that this approach was still in evidence in 1937. The difference was that by 1937 a subtle change of emphasis had occurred in the line of argument. It was pointed out that Britain had led the way in disarming but that it was now only too apparent that other nations had little or no intention of following suit and were ultimately threatening the European balance of power by their own rearmament programmes. If Britain was to make collective security a working reality, she had to deter aggressors, and this could only be done 'if we were strong enough'. As one MP explained, rearmament 'was meant to restore that respect for the word of Britain' which had been absent during the Abyssinian crisis because of British military weakness.[52] An activist in Kinross believed that the government's foreign policy

> must be largely governed by the strength of our defence forces, and it is perfectly evident these forces are not up to [the] standard aimed at, especially our air force, and in the event of war with a weak air force our towns would suffer badly.[53]

The assumption was that military might also give diplomatic strength. This was now being explicitly argued and was to become the standard argument justifying rearmament during 1938 as Hitler began further to challenge the European order.

Rearmament was considered necessary for more than purely defensive purposes. A sizeable number accepted that there were also economic benefits. Indeed it had been Chamberlain's argument during the 1935 general election that if rearmament had been made *the* leading issue it would have secured their party crucial votes in Labour heartlands such as Tyne and Wear with their shipyards.[54] In fact the decision to fight the general election in November was taken in the knowledge that a number of lucrative defence contracts were to be announced during the campaign. On 31 October the Admiralty announced its 1935 construction programme. Nine ships were to be built and in a reversal of government policy the tenders were given to shipyards in areas of high unemployment (including Clydeside, Tynemouth and Birkenhead) rather than to those that had submitted the lowest quotations.[55] When the 1922 Committee in 1937 debated the siting of an aircraft factory near Waltham, a number of speakers felt it should have been sited in one of the official Distressed Areas so as to help alleviate unemployment. Fifty-four Conservative MPs then followed the lead of the 1922 Committee's chairman and signed an EDM declaring the Waltham site 'unsuitable'.[56] Nor did every Conservative accept war to be the inevitable outcome of rearmament. But there were concerns expressed about the over-reliance of the British economy on rearmament. A number, including Chamberlain, felt able to talk during late 1936 and 1937 of a possible scaling-down of the programme. Consequently, it was felt necessary to consider the implications for the British economy of a reduced defence scheme.[57] The suggestions of reducing armaments production were not inconceivable. Despite the Spanish Civil War there was little on the international scene that suggested the imminence of Armageddon. The Spanish situation had been sidelined by Anglo-French non-intervention, making it little more than a bloody and noisy regional conflict. Equally, some Conservatives were confident that the defence gaps would have been plugged by 1937, enabling a reduction in the defence budget.

PARTY SCRUTINY AND THE ISSUE OF SUPPLY

Because rearmament was a domestic issue it was subject to the scrutiny of local associations. These associations, while not denying the necessity for a rearmament programme, were not always prepared to accept the optimistic rhetoric of their MPs. They had concerns of both general and specific natures. These concerns were communicated to the leadership via resolutions that progressed up through the party structure from local association to regional level to the National Union executive. The National Union executive decided then whether to forward these resolutions to specific ministers, or if it warranted, to the party leader. To this extent the National Union was a barometer of activist opinion. Some activists felt that defence had to be placed within a broader framework that allowed for more than purely armaments. This meant the adoption of a strategy that made allowances for all aspects of supply, including foodstuffs and raw materials, that would be crucial in wartime. When the National Union took up the matter of food supplies with Baldwin in July 1936 he assured them that the matter was receiving the government's 'urgent attention' and that 'action would certainly be taken when it was considered necessary'.[58] In fact, despite the activist and media support during late 1935 and early 1936 for the supply issue, the government did not deem action necessary until 1939, when it reluctantly decided to establish a ministry of supply. In the interim the issue never entirely disappeared from Conservative thought. For example, the Northern Counties Area Union at its 1937 AGM considered a resolution on air defence which called for greater emphasis to be placed upon the production of aerodrome ground equipment and the organisation and conservation of food supplies.[59] In due course, the National Union forwarded this resolution to the Air Ministry.[60] At the back of many of these Conservative minds was the realisation that any future conflict would be of similar proportions to the 1914–18 war – the first 'total war' – and that Britain could no longer rely upon her island status to shelter her population from involvement in war. The cult of the bomber made this all too apparent. However, the supply issue, in 1938 following the *Anschluss*, mutated into a question concerning the supply of manpower. It was an issue that many grassroots members believed would have a more profound and obvious impact upon the ordinary elector than a ministry of supply.

The concern about supply was reflected amongst the parliamentary party in their criticisms about the coordination of the rearmament programme.[61] Traditional service rivalries encouraged the fear that technical developments which cut inter-service boundaries were being overlooked. Argument over who controlled the Fleet Air Arm typified this concern. In response, and after considerable deliberation, in May 1936 Baldwin appointed Thomas Inskip as Minister for the Coordination of Defence. With a remit 'to oil the wheels' Inskip quickly admitted to the difficulties of coordinating industry. It was a situation hampered by the lack of executive power and resources. Furthermore, his civilian background did little to alleviate the 'near impossible task' he faced.[62] Churchill had been widely tipped to secure the appointment, and his continued criticism of the post owed much to sour grapes. Even so, Inskip's remit found itself under continual attack from other backbenchers with an interest in military affairs. Winterton considered Inskip's appointment 'calamitous' and was surprised that neither Churchill nor Hoare, who were 'by far the most competent men for the job' had got it.[63] In July 1937 Wing Commander James offered an interpretation that deplored the lack of strategical planning. Like other Members, he believed that the departmental battles 'continue[d] unabated' and considered there to be 'grave disappointment' amongst the services at the lack of results.[64] In the same debate, Leo Amery questioned Inskip's role and expressed his 'profound dissatisfaction' with the job description. At the same time he felt Inskip had failed to answer the case

> for an organisation such as Germany possesses, which could provide a minister who would be the minister primarily responsible to the cabinet and parliament for the general defence, and for its proper co-ordination, with a staff of his own to help him work that out.[65]

THE INSKIP DEFENCE REVIEW

In response to these criticisms and in light of the continued financial strains imposed by rearmament, Inskip was commissioned in October 1937 to assess Britain's rearmament and strategical priorities.[66] A number of strategical factors also suggested the need for a reappraisal. The development of radar and a new generation of monoplane fighters, like the Hurricane, meant there now existed the possibility of providing a viable form of air defence. The Chiefs of Staff were warning that Britain could not hope to fight Germany, Italy and Japan simultaneously. Furthermore, the estimates of German air capacity underlined the failure of parity as a deterrent. Despite this the core of the air staff continued to press for long-range heavy bombers.

It was with this backdrop that the cabinet accepted the recommendations of Inskip's interim report in December. It recognised that economic stability was the 'fourth arm of defence', and consequently agreed that defence expenditure should be kept within the Treasury's £1,500 million limitation. It also identified the defence priorities: the direct defence of Britain was deemed of primary importance, followed by the preservation of her trade routes, and then the defence of the Empire. The field force was given lowest priority, making the army's primary role one of home and imperial defence. The report also dismissed the long-held view of the air counter-offensive by seeing the RAF's primary role as to prevent a knockout blow. It was fighters and not bombers that were needed. Priority-wise the Inskip review was little different to the 1891 Stanhope memorandum, which had placed home and imperial defence foremost and argued that involvement in a major European conflict was unlikely. However, the major significance of the review was to switch defence spending from the limited, short-term diplomatic reinforcement of the last three years to a basis for war preparation – the implications of which were readily noticed by Halifax when he warned that preserving economic stability placed 'a heavy burden on diplomacy'.[67]

LIMITED LIABILITY VERSUS CONTINENTAL COMMITMENT: THE CASE FOR THE ARMY

The limited liability concept embodied in the Inskip report was generally welcomed by Conservatives. For most, the idea of a continental expeditionary force was abhorrent. The backbench delegation which met Baldwin in July 1936 made this abundantly clear, with Edward Grigg arguing that such a 'fear' was the greatest single deterrent to recruiting.[68] In early 1937 the Minister for War, Duff Cooper, had tried in a private briefing to the 1922 Committee to present the case for the army. Looking back, he observed that Napoleon had survived after Trafalgar a further ten years, and that in more recent times Britain's naval blockade of Germany had failed to secure a swift conclusion to the 1914–18 war. As for air power, this 'had not by itself enabled Italy to conquer Abyssinia nor had air bombing brought the war in Spain to a rapid conclusion'. To the chagrin of some present he felt it was 'impossible to give an undertaking that the army would never be used abroad in the event of a European war'.[69] Consequently, during the 1937 army estimates, backbenchers once more publicly voiced their opposition to a continental commitment. In fact, recruiting and the failings of the 'Cardwell system' – whereby the army needed to keep as many battalions at home as abroad so as to ensure a regular flow of relief and replacements – were the dominant sources of debate. Winterton thought it 'obvious' that the system was 'breaking down before our eyes' but admitted difficulty suggesting an alternative. Likewise, Amery and Knox criticised the system. They feared that as long as the army was considered a second-class citizen it would fail to attract enough recruits, which would have the cumulative effect of threatening not only the defence of the Empire but also of Britain. In short, the army was suffering from imperial overstretch. It made recruiting a pressing concern, and Members were anxious that the army 'should not be considered the last resort'. Equally, the fact that the army was under its establishment was 'undoubtedly making a serious, [and] a very unfortunate impression' upon the dictators. If these Conservatives were opposed to a field force, then what role did they envisage for the army? What they foresaw was the regular army providing the nucleus of home defence as well as imperial defence, whilst the Territorials assisted with home defence. By home defence Conservatives meant 'defence against air attack', which envisaged anti-aircraft batteries and other fixed air defences, as well as passive defences for the civilian populations, such as ARP.[70] Concern over the recruiting position continued throughout 1937, with the 1922 Committee deeming it necessary to send a delegation to Leslie Hore-Belisha, the new War Minister, 'on this most important matter'.[71]

Twelve months later, the interest in the army estimates was more acute.[72] These were the first estimates presented by Hore-Belisha and were the first of the 1938 estimates to be announced that took account of the new Inskip defence priorities. Chamberlain had acquainted parliament with these priorities three days previously on 7 March. Then, he had disclosed that rearmament now took into consideration the resources of manpower, of productive capacity and of finance, because 'wars are not only won with arms and men; they are won with reserves of resources and credit'.[73] Interest was further aroused because of the deteriorating situation in Austria. Hore-Belisha's proposals generally appear to have been well received both publicly and privately by the army's parliamentary supporters; only Alfred Knox expressed concern that the army was being restricted in size. He suggested that if it was acceptable on the continent then 'there must be something in that idea of these big armies still'.[74] During his speech Hore-Belisha confirmed that the army would be responsible for home coastal and anti-aircraft defence, whilst overseas its responsibility was imperial defence. Regarding a continental field force, Hore-Belisha felt that assistance to allies could be best made in other areas – on the sea and in the air.[75] Precaution was taken to brief beforehand those Members most likely to be critical.[76] Although it was evident from the 7 March debate that the army was still considered the least important of the services, it was also apparent that for those Members who took an interest in the army the emphasis was now on value for money and ensuring that the army was not only adequately supplied but also properly trained in its required role, 'the defence of this country against air attack'. As a consequence, the issue of national service arose. This was a subject that increasingly attracted the attention of Conservatives at all levels over the next year.

THE ANSCHLUSS: A TURNING POINT

The *Anschluss* marks a turning point in Conservative attitudes towards rearmament. It reminded them that Hitler still posed a threat to European stability. Hoare and Amery concluded that to 'hurry on even more determinedly with our military preparations' was the 'only practical conclusion' that could be drawn.[77] As another backbencher decided, 'Germany respects force and force only, and the moral is that we must do everything in our power to increase our forces and everything to increase the speed of our rearmament programme'.[78] The *Anschluss* emphasised the continued necessity for rearmament if merely 'for self-protection'.[79] In public, Conservatives expressed their continued satisfaction with the state of Britain's defences: MPs reassured both constituents and activists that it had been 'carried out just in time', that it was an 'insurance premium' and no premium was too great for peace; whilst associations continued to pass resolutions welcoming the defence programme.[80] Privately, however, concern was being expressed. Ralph Assheton spoke codedly to his Rushcliffe association about defence being the country's 'greatest need', whilst to political colleagues he was swearing that rearmament was 'going badly wrong, or rather unavoidably slowly because (1) there is not enough drive at the top (2) there is no *real* business direction'.[81] Others feared that by the time Britain had sufficiently rearmed everything worth saving in Europe would be gone.[82] Lord Tyrrell, a Tory peer and former British ambassador to Paris, was so concerned about the state of affairs that during April 1938 he was in contact with TUC leaders, attempting to enlist their assistance. The necessity was urgent because he believed rearmament to be the 'one language' that Germany understood.[83] Tyrrell advised that in any conversations with the government concerning the dilution of skilled labour and rearmament, the TUC 'insist' on being shown the 'rearmament figures before they consent to any agreement'. These he believed 'would be so damaging that they would then be able to insist on [Chamberlain] widening the government by taking in A[nthony] E[den] again as Foreign Secretary and Winston [Churchill] as defence minister and two TUC leaders'.[84]

These doubts were also being expressed in parliament, although disguised behind parliamentary rhetoric. Even with the role of the army, which had almost universal approval less than two weeks previously, there was now increased scepticism. Jack Macnamara, formerly an officer in the Indian army, expressed doubts about the reliability of the Maginot Line and questioned 'our strategy at home [which] relies, in the first place, on somebody else's line abroad, and secondly, on a very small army of very young men'.[85] Likewise Edward Grigg, an advocate of national service, criticised the 'extremely questionable doctrine that man power counts less than machine power in modern war'. The fact that the army was still 20,000 under establishment when 'facing difficulties and contingencies such as we are facing at the present time' was dangerous. He believed that the army's role

> must be carried out by great mobility, great versatility and by training in that offensive spirit that it has always possessed. I believed that doctrine holds true wherever you may have to apply it – whether in the east, the Middle East or the west.[86]

Anstruther-Gray believed the recruiting situation was bedevilled by complacency and warned that 'we are in the position where one other emergency would strain the army to breaking point'.[87] One backbencher, Roy Wise, even went as far as explicitly expressing his doubts about the doctrine of limited liability. As he explained, the theory behind a limited liability war meant a British contribution would be small but also superlatively good:

> In other words it must be composed of adequate numbers, full establishments and men of high quality. I doubt whether that is, in fact, the case today. . . . I do not believe that on mobilisation a British expeditionary force would be the equal in the field, in training and in practice, to a corresponding number of men in a continental conscript army who had just finished two years' service.[88]

Wise was a little ahead of his fellow Conservatives with this declaration. Yet twelve months later such pronouncements became the norm.

REVISED PLANS

The *Anschluss* forced the government not only to make a ministerial statement concerning the diplomatic situation but also to announce alterations to the recent defence estimates. Chamberlain explained to the House that

> acceleration of existing plans has become essential and, moreover, that there must be an increase in some parts of the programme, especially in that of the Royal Air Force and anti-aircraft defences.

In order to bring about the progress which we feel to be necessary, men and materials will be required, and rearmament work must have first priority in the nation's efforts.[89]

The revision was welcomed by the party, but there nevertheless remained a certain amount of concern.[90] Wolmer accepted 'that there should be one last effort at appeasement' but warned that if the dictators 'shut the door altogether to a general agreement, they will make a war in the near future inevitable'. The democracies, he argued, must make sacrifices and go to the same lengths in military preparations as the dictators because it was 'no use hoping that democracy can be defended unless it puts its entire heart into the task of defence'.[91] Victor Cazalet noticed 'most think we shall have to fight Germany – not a pleasant prospect', but he drew comfort from the fact that 'rearmament goes a-pace' and was to be accelerated. Two weeks later he dined with Churchill and found him 'v[ery] anti-gov[ernmen]t for not having got on with rearmament. We are, apparently, lamentably behind, but of course it's all a matter of degree'.[92]

THE CASE FOR THE RAF

Apprehension about the rearmament position erupted in Westminster during May 1938 in a debate on air defence during which Edward Winterton, recently appointed Chancellor of the Duchy of Lancaster and House of Commons spokesman for Air, gave a singularly inept performance.[93] For the Chancellor, it was a speech for which 'the first hour of it was better than the second!'[94] Senior cabinet members feared political repercussions. Hoare felt 'very worried'.[95] He was acutely aware of the party's attitude to air defence because of the generally critical reaction he had received the previous week when addressing the 1922 Committee on ARP preparations.[96] Churchill reacted by tabling an EDM, supported by twenty-four other Conservatives, demanding an enquiry into Britain's air defences, a call that the opposition parties took up when they moved a formal motion on 25 May.[97] Other reactions to the Winterton speech were far from complimentary. Eden felt this debate 'made a very poor showing' for the government. Like many Conservatives he seemed perplexed by the decision to abandon parity. 'It does not seem to me exactly "realistic"', he told the editor of the *Yorkshire Post*, 'to surrender the determination to maintain our parity with Germany, and excuse it by saying it would be impolitic to mention that country's name'. Eden's solution to the problems of rearmament was a government of 'national unity and national inspiration' which he believed would enable Britain to parallel the efforts of the dictators.[98] Part of the problem was due to the Air Minister, Lord Swinton, sitting in the House of Lords. It was an arrangement that many backbenchers found unsatisfactory.[99] As a consequence, Winterton (who had only been in the new position a matter of weeks) endured the full fury of the House of Commons for mistakes or alleged errors made by his predecessors. Chamberlain nevertheless turned the affair to his own political advantage, taking the opportunity to eliminate his critics in cabinet. It was a move that confounded his detractors who were urging a widening of the government. Swinton was removed and Ormsby-Gore, the Colonial Secretary, dismissed. For Ormsby-Gore his elevation to the House of Lords as Lord Harlech was the justification – it being argued that the Lords–Commoners ratio in the cabinet could not support another peer as minister. Ultimately, Winterton's poor performance was merely a pretext for Swinton's dismissal. In reality, Swinton was a longstanding critic who had annoyed Chamberlain by his fight for extra resources and for advocating the need for the state to take compulsory powers to overcome skill shortages in the rearmament industries.[100] Winterton, for his part in the fiasco, escaped relatively lightly and kept his post in the cabinet, although he was relieved of parliamentary responsibility for the Air Ministry.[101]

Since the 1935 defence white paper, parity between the *Luftwaffe* and the RAF had been the desired aim. Chamberlain, as Chancellor, had played a significant role in ensuring the RAF's primacy. He had argued that a large army was superfluous, accepting Liddell-Hart's view that the army of the future would be a small, professional, mechanised affair and that the 'British way in warfare' demanded spending on an air force and navy. Public opinion was a crucial catalyst in prioritising the RAF.[102] Memories of the Somme and Passchendaele, propaganda organisations like the 'Air League of the British Empire' and popular writing on air power, such as P. R. C. Groves' *Behind the Smoke Screen*, encouraged the belief that a strong RAF was the best defence as a deterrent.[103] It was a view that held sway with many Conservatives. In 1933 Churchill described the RAF as 'almost a complete protection for the civilian population . . . against destruction'.[104] During the wrangling over a possible continental commitment in the course of 1936, Chamberlain had objected to a field force on the grounds that mobilisation would be too slow, and argued that 'a strong offensive air force' had greater deterrence value. Ultimately the CID sub-committee on defence policy and requirements agreed that the RAF programme should have latitude 'so as to improve its offensive power and constitute the most effective deterrent against Germany'.[105] These views were acceptable to the majority of Conservative MPs, who had no liking for an expeditionary field force. For them the necessity was parity and it became their watchword over the coming years. Problems arose from defining parity. The poor quality of long-range intelligence predictions, personalities at the Air Ministry and rivalry between the Foreign Office and Air Ministry (which led to a lack of coordination between military and economic intelligence and a failure to appreciate the German air force strategy properly) all hindered accurate predictions of the threat posed.[106] The overriding fear of a knockout blow blinkered official and public minds.[107] The 1937 air estimate debates revealed backbench concern that the British programme was failing to make parity. Criticism was levied at the Air Ministry for its 'overbearing' attitude towards manufacturers and its failure to show due regard for continued research. Concern was also expressed at the lack of shadow factories. When Admiral Sueter suggested that under the circumstances industry was coping, Churchill responded with a broadside that claimed the current first-line air strengths to only be 44 per cent of their projection. Likewise Oliver Simmonds believed that during 1937 Britain's air 'inferiority will be ever increasing. We may only hope that the European skies will clear during this year, but it does behove the government and the Air Ministry to apply themselves with ever increasing vigour'. Churchill's claims did not go unchallenged.[108] Nevertheless, the Inskip defence review of the same year accepted that parity had failed as a deterrent. It had decided that the priority should be fighters and air defence as opposed to the long-range bomber force favoured by the Air Ministry and many Conservative backbenchers. Indeed, during the 1938 air estimates debates the Conservative backbench air protagonists were deeply critical of the decision to abandon parity and of the skilled labour shortages in the air construction industry. As Wing-Commander Wright explained, government supporters like himself had 'been so staunch that we have been prepared to accept everything that we have been told with regard to rearmament [now] certain things had happened which made us feel anxiety ourselves'.[109]

THE WEAKNESSES OF DEFENCE EXPOSED

Conservative anxieties about defence were to be displayed again in the aftermath of the Czech crisis. The ramifications of the Munich agreement were not purely confined to the political map of Europe and the unity of the Conservative party. The emergency revealed serious inadequacies in Britain's defence programme. As Victor Cazalet told his constituents, rearmament was shown 'to be sadly behind what is necessary and essential if this country is to play its proper role in Europe'.[110] At the height of the incident trenches had been dug, air-raid shelters hastily erected, gas masks distributed, anti-aircraft batteries mobilised and the Royal Navy placed on alert. The private fears many Conservatives had been sustaining since the *Anschluss* now appeared to have been realised. The chief whip admitted he had 'never looked forward less to the opening of a session – everyone with a complaint about guns or sheep or Czechs or something'.[111] Emrys-Evans expressed 'profound disquiet' at the position of Britain's defences, and cited it as one of the reasons why he abstained from the Munich votes:

> It is impossible to have a foreign policy at all unless there is adequate force to support it. The recent mobilisation displayed to all the world the alarming inadequacy of our preparations. Three years after the mandate had been given to rearm and after hundreds of millions had been voted we found ourselves in a position of the utmost peril because we were not ready. I cannot help feeling that the government have been half-hearted in rearming, and they have given assurances to the House of Commons which have simply not been carried out.[112]

One confidential memorandum drafted by a group of Territorial Army officers, and circulated amongst Conservative MPs by Edward Spears, considered that the crisis had revealed the whole organisation of anti-aircraft defence in London to be 'grossly incompetent'. The report considered this situation to be 'principally due to the fact that the War Office is only interested in the organisation of expeditionary forces, and attaches virtually no importance to anti-aircraft defence'. The authors concluded that there would be no change unless the War Office was stripped of control for AA defence.[113] Sources suggested this was a deliberate move to engineer the War Minister's downfall.[114] In a debate on ARP during the opening week of the autumn session, Hore-Belisha, who 'had got wind' of the document, tried to defuse the situation by 'boldly' announcing the AA deficiencies himself during his speech: 'For this he got a good deal laughed at', one backbencher observed, but considered that it 'undoubtedly weakened the effect which would have been produced by subsequent disclosure'.[115] At the time of the crisis RAF fighter command only had twenty-nine squadrons of fighters, and the ninety-three Hurricanes in the command were useless above 15,000 feet because their guns jammed from cold. A group of foreign policy sceptics was horrified to hear how air headquarters in London had no means of getting through to their bombers in Suffolk except by sending two military police down by motor car.[116] The implications of such weakness in Britain's defences were only too painfully apparent not least because they 'grievously injured our power to reason with dictators'. The situation left many feeling 'disgusted and appalled at the position'. Sidney Herbert effectively summarised the party's opinion and fear when he declared

> that this lack of rearmament is known. Of course it is known to Herr Hitler. It is known to the children in my village. . . . I am deeply dissatisfied with what the government have been doing for many months beforehand.[117]

But who was to blame? Here Conservative opinion divided. Some argued that the electorate was really responsible since they had supported pacifist ideals for so long, and professed through such things as the Peace Ballot to favour disarmament, which had prevented the government from implementing an adequate defence programme soon enough. Indeed, this theme was expounded by Oswald Lewis during a public meeting in Essex in December. He warned his audience that 'it was at present a very dangerous situation, and up to the present it had been very difficult to interest public opinion in the matter'.[118] Others though felt that only the government was responsible. Wolmer suggested that it was the failure of the government to make rearmament a national issue rather than one purely of party politics, believing that if MPs in past years 'had not sometimes allowed their personal loyalty to their leaders to outweigh their judgement, we should not now be in our present arrears in regard to national defence'.[119] Some Conservatives supporting this argument tried to suggest that Chamberlain was free from responsibility since he had only been in charge eighteen months – the fact that he had been Chancellor and absolutely crucial in shaping the 1935 and 1936 defence white papers was conveniently overlooked. For Churchill and other Munich rebels, the inadequacies of the defence programme validated some of their warnings and consequently helped to dilute the anger felt by loyalists towards them. Wolmer stressed this point during correspondence with his local chairman following his Munich abstention. He assured Fell that, in view of Chamberlain's emphasis on the need for greatly accelerated rearmament, 'that is a policy I have advocated for four years and I shall do everything in my power to support it'.[120] Similarly Churchill's supporters in Epping used such arguments.

Consequently, instead of immediately facing a resolution critical of his disloyalty to the leadership, Churchill found himself being urged 'to continue his work for national unity and national defence'.[121]

It has been argued retrospectively that Munich bought additional time for Britain's rearmament programme.[122] Conservative apologists and historians have suggested that the months between October 1938 and September 1939 were crucial because vital improvements were made in Britain's anti-aircraft defences, radar and the development of fighter aircraft. It has, however, been assumed that this was a retrospective argument devised by contemporaries in their memoirs to justify their past and divert some of the criticisms of their Munich prosecutors. This was the purpose of the short polemical tract *The Left Was Never Right*, written in 1945 by Quintin Hogg.[123] Somerset de Chair maintains to this day his firm belief that Munich had bought Britain a breathing space.[124] Whilst it can not be denied that the additional eleven months of peace proved invaluable to Britain, equally it gave Germany additional time to prepare for conflict. It would seem, however, that historians have failed to appreciate the extent to which contemporary Conservatives actually saw Munich as a delaying tactic. At the height of the Czech crisis one Central Office official wrote to Rab Butler to explain that as a consequence of Chamberlain's negotiations with Hitler 'every day may make the preparations on the other side greater *but it is also quite invaluable to us*'.[125] During the Munich debate a number of Conservatives argued similarly. Wardlaw-Milne suggested 'there can be very little doubt that we shall be considerably better off a year or two hence than we are today. Germany's rearmament has gone very far; ours still has a long way to go' (although he did warn that the crisis had illustrated the need to push on with rearmament, especially in the sphere of civil defence, and to this end a national register was 'essential').[126] Southby took the argument to the government's prosecutors, asking them 'to consider whether we ourselves are entirely ready for a world war at the present time and whether we should not be in a better position in two years' time?'[127] In fact one such critic, Wolmer, who had been a protagonist for rearmament since the mid-1930s, was prepared to concede in October 1939 that the additional year had been invaluable when comparing the relative military positions between September 1938 and 1939. A similar attitude was adopted by Lord Chatfield who, speaking to the 1936 Club in June 1939 as Minister for the Coordination of Defence, declared that 'every day that war is postponed . . . is of the greatest value to us'.[128]

REMEDYING THE DEFICIENCIES?

Following Munich, Chamberlain quickly sought to remedy some of the deficiencies in the rearmament programme.[129] Once more the revisions were justified in terms that emphasised the necessity of a strong defensive force in order to maintain Britain's diplomatic prowess.[130] Although generally welcomed by the party, there were suggestions that more was required.[131] Accelerated rearmament at a time when Chamberlain was supposedly claiming to have secured peace invariably left the Prime Minister open to jibes from critics. It was apparent from the public declarations of Conservatives that there were deliberate efforts afoot to contradict these criticisms and place the expanded rearmament programme into a viable context. C. G. Lancaster declared during the Fylde by-election in November that Chamberlain was

> bent on building up this country's defences because he realises that weakness in armed strength means weakness in diplomacy and negotiation, and that it is only by being armed ourselves that we can ever hope to persuade other countries to agree to an all-round reduction of armaments.[132]

This was Lancaster's public stance. In private he was inclined to blame the government for the predicament in which it found itself.[133] Once again rearmament was being justified from the ethos of deterrence. It was 'simply taking reasonable precaution against the emergency'.[134] At the same time attempts were being made to try and alleviate the concerns about Britain's defences that public opinion and activists were experiencing. The situation was, as Heneage told a constituent, such that 'if it comes to a contest between dictator ruled and democratic countries, we shall be in a better position, both morally and materially [than Britain was before Munich]'.[135] A similar vein was adopted by Charles MacAndrew when addressing his Bute association AGM. He defended the government's programme, reminding his audience that with a five-year programme 'obviously' the first year or two had to be employed 'arranging the workshop and so forth'. He sought to reassure his listeners by explaining that he possessed private information which 'convinced him that there was in fact an immense output of aeroplanes, and that this country was in a position of which we need not be ashamed'.[136]

Privately, Conservatives continued to feel concerned at the rearmament position. This was especially true of the foreign policy sceptics who were not so readily assured of the situation. Emrys-Evans believed the government and dissidents were drifting further apart not only on foreign policy but on defence. I have had two conversations with Jock McEwen, who is now frankly, much more defeatist than anyone I have talked to, and some importance must be attached to his view point as he is close to the PM. . . . He says that he doesn't really think it worth while making a really big effort to rearm.

Eden found himself 'inclined to agree' with Evans' analysis of the government's attitude towards rearmament and felt McEwen to be 'probably fairly representative' of Conservative backbench opinion.[137] The air situation still gave grounds for disquiet, with Eden unsure whether the emphasis upon fighters only was 'wise'. He believed that they were not as great a deterrent as bombers. At the same time, Eden appears to have questioned the strategy of limited liability, unable to believe 'that we can be secure in our tight little island and ignore the rest of the world'.[138] Boothby's declaration in the House of Commons during November that 'a great number' of Conservatives 'feel that no real effort is to be made by the government, even now, in this question of rearmament' was simply giving public expression to backbench private sentiment.[139] Inskip addressed the 1922 Committee at the beginning of December and made what many considered to be a 'lamentably feeble statement'. As a consequence, the committee agreed to bring forward their planned defence debate. Amery opened this talk with a broad survey of the military position if Britain and France had to fight the axis powers. 'I had hardly realised myself, till I attempted the survey', confessed Amery in his diary, 'how serious the situation is and I think my talk profoundly affected the 60 to 80 Members who were there'.[140] At a constituency level there was equal concern at the defence situation which compounded the calls for national service. Discontent was not merely confined to the backbenches and grassroots. A number of junior ministers were actively considering resigning over the situation. Their criticisms would have remained within the confines of Whitehall had not Randolph Churchill leaked the news of this 'under-secretaries revolt' to the *Evening Standard*. Oliver Harvey, a civil servant in the Foreign Office, noted that 'they wish to resign because of their dissatisfaction with rearmament, failure of the Munich policy and agricultural policy'.[141] In meetings with Chamberlain the malcontents let him 'know that they think [Hore-] Belisha, Inskip, Runciman and Winterton all incompetent and that defence is in a hopeless condition'.[142] It was observed that the ministerial plotters were 'hesitant because of the risk that the PM will spring an election on them'.[143] They were afraid that an election in the wake of their resignations would expose them to the risk of being dropped as official Conservative candidates. The premier emphasised this during personal interviews with the ministers before persuading them to withdraw their resignations.[144] Many observers suggested that Chamberlain would remove these malcontents in the new year once media interest had died down. This was believed to be especially likely for Strathcona, who it was felt had made his position with Hore-Belisha impossible by his betrayal.[145] Indeed, Chamberlain reflected that 'the recent appointment of younger men have saddled me with a number of colleagues whose judgement I cannot trust and who are always a source of trouble in difficult times'. However, he was loath to make any reshuffle because he could foresee it making no change in the situation.[146]

SOME CONCLUSIONS

It is evident that there was an inexorable growth in concern about the defence position from 1936 that climaxed in September 1938. There was a discernible change in 1936 as the debate became politicised. Conservatives began to give public expression to their doubts by championing particular causes, whether it was Churchill calling for a ministry of supply or Lord Rothermere championing air rearmament through the National Airmen's League. Those favouring greater, or more rapid, rearmament sought to utilise all the channels available, parliamentary, party and extra-parliamentary. Activists ensured that their doubts were being expressed via the National Union; whilst parliamentarians optimised the use of the floor of the House of Commons, committee rooms and ministerial deputations. Ministers were not being left in any doubt of the party's concerns. The semi-mobilisation necessitated by the Munich crisis highlighted the gaps in British defence plans, especially in the anti-aircraft sphere. British fears of an aerial knockout blow meant that air defence was the primary priority for many Conservatives. As the next chapter will reveal, the growth of support for national service would be encouraged by the desire to rectify these deficiencies in air defence. Although rearmament was accepted as a 'twin pillar' with foreign policy, it was increasingly perceived during 1938 as the issue of greater concern. A strong defence programme would enable a government to negotiate with the dictators from a position of strength, whilst if that negotiation failed, an adequately prepared defence scheme would repel the initial aerial assault and ultimately ensure victory.

5 The call for national service, 1937–9[1]

The growing awareness of the challenge presented to Britain by the dictators had, as has been shown, a direct bearing upon the party's support for defence and foreign policy. As will become apparent in this chapter, this was especially true for the national service debate. For some like Leo Amery and Roger Keyes, it was a cause long advocated.[2] From the government's perspective it was something they had no wish to introduce.[3] However, during 1938 the question of the marshalling of manpower and resources became the central theme of the defence debate for many Conservative activists and parliamentarians. As 1938 drew to a close it was *the* issue for the party. Just as in the Edwardian period, activist support for compulsion was always more advanced than the leadership either wished to believe or acknowledge.[4]

THE CHRONOLOGY OF DEBATE

Four phases emerge in the debate between 1935 and the introduction of conscription in April 1939. The initial phase ends with the German annexation of Austria in March 1938. As was shown in the previous chapter, the matter of national service was of limited importance, being restricted to a few long-term advocates. There was some debate about supply. More generally the preoccupation was with the pace and nature of the rearmament programme. This concern about rearmament does not diminish after the *Anschluss* – quite the contrary. Rather, national service was increasingly recognised as the missing component of the rearmament programme, and rapidly assumed considerable prominence. The period between March and September delineates the second phase. Support for some form of national service, and in particular a national register, was reaching a crescendo. In parallel was a widening distrust of Germany. Although the Munich settlement temporarily suspended the expansion in support for

national service, as many Conservatives tried to reconcile the contradiction of adopting greater measures of rearmament at a time when a
supposedly new era of international cooperation had been inaugurated, the realisation dawned of the reality of the Nazi threat. Events
such as *Kristallnacht* reinforced this trend. During the third phase it
was apparent that the principle of national service had been accepted;
the question was whether it should be voluntary or compulsory. It was
during this period that the government opted, in December 1938, to
introduce a voluntary register and proposed a scheme of voluntary
national service. The final phase runs from the introduction of this
scheme in January 1939 through to the introduction of conscription
on 26 April. The period was one in which the party recognised the
failure of voluntarism and clamoured for compulsion, to show both
Germany and Britain's allies that it meant business.

TERMS OF REFERENCE

It is necessary to define the terms of reference used in the debate.
'National service' during the Edwardian era had meant anything from
conscription by ballot to compulsory military service for all males to
compulsory training.[5] Now in the late 1930s degrees of confusion were
exhibited over the meaning of the measures advocated: national registration, national service and conscription. Essentially national
registration meant compiling details of the special qualifications citizens possessed. This would enable the advance assignment of wartime
roles whilst allowing essential industries to shelter their skilled labour
from call-up. Problems arose over whether such a register should be
compulsory. Ought the government or another body be responsible for
its compilation? And what were the limitations of registration: should
it be purely restricted to vocational skills or should it also be a registration of wealth?[6]

To advocates of national service, registration was the essential
precursor to any scheme of service. It was in defining 'service' that the
confusion occured. Some conceived it as being synonymous with
conscription. In fact there were two forms of service countenanced by
contemporaries. One was a scheme of annual or periodic training for
individuals in civil defence. The argument was made that should
mobilisation occur the transition would be smoother and more efficient if individuals had already been familarised and primed in their
roles. The second form to be discussed was military national service –
most probably taking the form of duty in the reserve services.[7] If
backed by compulsion it would be reminiscent of military conscription

as experienced during the First World War, with all the connotations of slaughter. This to an extent provides some excuse for the confusion and distrust of national service. Naturally, the controversy centred around whether either scheme should be adopted at all, and if one was, whether it ought to be compulsory or voluntary.

In the event of war, there was a consensus that the conscription of manpower for military purposes would be introduced. It was considered to be the fairest means of evenly distributing the burden of hostilities. Whether peacetime conscription could be justified was another matter and provoked considerable contention. But by the 1930s conscription meant more than just compulsory military service. The twentieth century was the era of 'total war', and it was agreed that a nation's staying power during hostilities was just as important as the forces it could send into battle. Important war industries, such as munitions, would require both skilled labour and special powers to ensure priority in the supply of materials and orders. The administrative and organisational confusion of the 1914–18 war had amply shown the necessity of such measures.[8] Supporters of compulsion suggested that the creation of a ministry of supply would prevent any repetition of the chaos witnessed in the last conflict. Additionally there was a third form of conscription, namely of wealth. This could be applied by methods such as a tax on excess profits during wartime to prevent any one profiteering from the emergency. As was shown in the previous chapter, the controversy over the NDC tax bears testimony to the Conservatives' distrust of such measures. The conscription of wealth was a socialistic measure. Throughout the national service debate, Conservatives thought solely in terms of the conscription of manpower, but not in terms that envisaged a million strong field force, as had been the case in the Edwardian situation. Rather, this manpower was required to resolve the recruitment shortages in realm of anti-aircraft defence.

To this extent, the national service debate was linked with the fate of the army since this was the most manpower-intensive of the three services. However, the debate was not to be conducted along the lines of the Edwardian discussion. The assumption that support for national service automatically meant support for a continental commitment will be disputed.[9] What will be shown is that the emphasis on national service did not contradict the idea of a small professional army concerned primarily with home defence and imperial duties. Rather, it dovetailed with the doctrine of limited liability and deterrence. It was envisaged primarily as a measure of home defence which would help cushion the nation from the feared aerial knockout blow. It became an issue for Conservatives from the time of the *Anschluss* as German aggression led to questions about whether Britain's air defences, not just in London and the south-east of England, but also in the Midlands and North could resist a German aerial assault. As Grigg explained to the 1922 Committee in May 1938:

> Speeding up rearmament was not enough, organisation of the nation was essential. 'Key-men' had been recruited into the anti-aircraft units and would not be available when required. Three things were necessary for efficiency: (1) compulsory national registration: (2) concentration on the organisation for defence of vital spots: (3) setting up of air defence authorities for important areas. The moral effect of such action on Germany would be tremendous.[10]

Although conscription was introduced after the abandonment of limited liability and following the re-acceptance of a continental commitment, the emphasis remained on home defence. The first batch of conscripts was expected to spend six months training in AA defence before serving a further three-and-a-half years as members of the Territorial Army, which had been responsible for AA ground defence since 1923. But it experienced difficulty attracting enough recruits before September 1938.[11] Such measures were unacceptable before March 1939 to government ministers obsessed with the 'fourth arm of defence' and the belief that war mobilisation during peacetime would disrupt the economy, whose strength was also vital in the event of war.[12]

THE GENESIS OF THE DEBATE

The *Anschluss* signalled the opening of the second phase in the debate. In part this was because it occurred during the AGM season for constituency associations, making it possible to chart the reaction of the party's activists. Although Austria was never deemed an area of direct strategical importance to Britain, it was Hitler's first foreign adventure outside the boundaries of the Reich. Furthermore, it high-lighted the level of compliance between Italy and Germany, something British foreign policy had been trying to avoid. Contemporaries wondered whether Hitler would be content with Austria alone or whether this expansion was the beginning of something infinitely greater and more menacing. Even though many Conservatives had expressed sympathy for Hitler's desire to unite the Germanic peoples, as the brutality employed to enforce the Austro-German union became apparent, so the doubts emerged.

In the week before the *Anschluss,* debates on defence occured during which various Conservative MPs made calls for the adoption of compulsion. Churchill repeated his demand for a ministry of supply,

Table 5.1 Examples of Conservative associations discussing national service, January 1937–July 1938

Association	Date	Summary of Outcome
Edinburgh North	27/01/37	Junior Imperial League pass motion urging conscription's immediate introduction.
Somerset Area	29/01/37	Carry motion pledging support for the voluntary system.
Midland Area	30/04/37	Carry motion recognising importance of national service.
Kinross	17/03/38	Chairman reports level of support for limited conscription amongst activists.
Winchester	26/03/38	Conscription motion carried by 90 per cent. Forwarded to National Union.
Altrincham	11/04/38	Women's branch 'strongly' urge universal registration.
North Wiltshire	21/04/38	Universal service motion discussed but rejected 24-15.
Kennington	29/04/38	MP declares support for 18 months compulsory military service.
Chelmsford	06/05/38	MP raises subject of service, but discussion postponed.
West Stirling	11/05/38	Prospective candidate declares his support for training.
Chelmsford	27/05/38	Motion calling for military and labour national service discussed. Hope to send to annual conference. Amended to call for voluntary scheme of fitness and training.
Norwood	24/06/38	National registration motion carried, 17-8. Forwarded to National Union.
National Union central council	30/06/38	Debate and carry Norwood motion.
South East Area	20/07/38	Carry motion urging national registration. Forwarded to National Union resolutions sub-committee.

whilst Grigg advocated a register in order to allocate individuals to home defence and safeguard those in key industries from call-up. This was followed by a plea from Beamish for compulsion, to assist in recruiting for the Territorials.[13] Occurring at the time when parliament annually debated the defence estimates meant the *Anschluss* altered Conservative opinion to its ramifications for British rearmament, particularly regarding the increased likelihood of British vulnerability to German air assault. This was reflected by the parliamentary calls for national service and the similar demands being echoed by associations around the country (as illustrated in Table 5.1). The chairman of Kinross association reported that several members had expressed support for the suggestion 'that a mild form of compulsory service would be good and have a wonderful effect on the continent'.[14] Similarly in Winchester the association's AGM backed a call for conscription, believing 'the inability of the League of Nations to deal with major world issues and the unfortunate but obvious advent of an age of power politics' necessitated its introduction.[15] The emerging support for conscription was not universal. North Wiltshire association rejected, after debate, such a motion. The proposer, Colonel Fitzgerald, complained that he had been outvoted 'by an opposition which immediately raised the cry of "conscription"'. Fitzgerald had visited Germany in May 1937 and like so many Conservatives who stayed in the Nazi state had been 'impressed' with the 'vigour and efficiency of that country'. Nevertheless the experience had left him in 'little doubt that the dictators treat our policy almost with contempt because they know that we have neither the power nor the will to carry out a strong line'.[16]

The debates that occured amongst Chelmsford activists, as noted in Table 5.1, demonstrate the dilemma of accepting the ideal of national service. It was an ongoing debate that was not finally resolved until early 1939. The local MP Jack Macnamara played a proactive role, with the close assistance of the association's president General Wigan. Both men were clearly anxious to have a universal scheme of basic military training, and whilst there was support from other activists there was evident concern about the implications of advocating compulsion. It was feared that this 'virtually meant conscription and that as such did not consider the country would accept it'. Ultimately the executive could only agree, in the interim, on a motion advocating a voluntary scheme of fitness and vocational training.[17]

The debates in Chelmsford and North Wiltshire illustrated the danger that the term national service could be interpreted as conscription. It reflected a fear that conscription was unacceptable in peacetime and an electoral liability. As with before 1914 when leading Unionists had feared that the adoption of compulsion as a party policy would wreck their electoral chances, so now the worry existed that with a general election due in 1939 or early 1940, any popular suspicion that the party was advocating conscription would destroy their chances of re-election.[18] This was certainly the official belief in Leeds.[19] In addition to these thoughts of electoral expediency, there existed the philosophical argument that compulsion was not the 'British way'. One of those who had argued in this manner before 1914, the fourth Marquess of Salisbury, was by 1938–9 putting his signature as a member of the Army League to motions calling for compulsory national service.[20]

From the perspective of ministers there existed an additional practical argument which generated considerable concern. This was the fear that any measure of compulsion, whether it be in the field of defence or industry, would incur the wrath of the trade unions, the opposition of which would ensure the disruption of industry as a whole, with disastrous consequences for the rearmament programme. Limited approaches had been made to TUC leaders to enlist their support for the rearmament programme, but fears were expressed by ministers of the possible implications of such negotiations.[21] As it was, little was established by the talks. Individual Conservatives were, as previously shown, independently 'sounding' the Labour party and unions on various matters of defence.[22] These approaches reflected a belief that the issue of national defence should be above party politics. Further, the very deliberate attempts by advocates of national service to emphasise that they were not championing conscription were in the hope of making their proposals more palatable to the unions.

Confident that parliamentary support for a national register was growing, Amery and Grigg actively promoted the issue during 1938. At Whitsun, the 1922 Committee had given its backing to the cause.[23] A backbench deputation, which included O'Neill, Grigg and Makins, met Chamberlain to argue their case at the end of May. Unfortunately, they found the PM's attitude disappointing and left viewing the situation with 'increasing anxiety'.[24] Further evidence of the swelling support emerged when 174 backbenchers pledged, in July, to support a motion on national service. It was a reflection of the belief that voluntary recruitment would only be stimulated by registration.[25] Efforts were also undertaken during the summer vacation by senior figures to lobby the government over, including a national register in the King's address for the new session.[26] Advocates kept up the debate in extra-parliamentary circles by writing to the press. In one such letter Roger

Keyes told the *Daily Telegraph* that he had 'no doubt if sufficient people would show their desire for registration now, the government would only be too glad to carry it out'. It would serve as a warning to the dictators; whilst if there was a delay in setting up it would 'lose half its value, as under modern conditions of war, the whole population may well be involved from the start'.[27] The cabinet were unable to accept the necessity for such a proposal. A fear existed that the introduction of registration would be considered the first move towards conscription. Alternatively, to delay adopting such a scheme until war appeared more imminent might be interpreted as tantamount to mobilisation. After reflection the prefered option was to do nothing for the present.[28]

THE IMPACT OF MUNICH

The Munich crisis emphasised the debate over national service and heralded a new phase. The serious deficiencies in Britain's defences, particularly with anti-aircraft defence, exposed by the emergency provoked a number of MPs during the Munich debate to urge the introduction of at least a national register.[29] For them the crisis had shown the 'failure of our voluntary system'[30] But how widely did the party concur with this assessment? And what should the response be?

But matters were being complicated by the involvement of the foreign policy sceptics, who saw national service as the logical progression for the rearmament programme. For example, a parliamentary amendment tabled in early December 1938 urged a compulsory register and was notable for the support given it by foreign policy dissidents. The unintended effect was to tar the matter with the suggestion of disloyalty. This was apparent when the sceptics tabled a motion in March 1939 which called for national service. It secured only limited support. This was most probably because it also urged the creation of a truly national government and therefore carried the disloyalty stigma.[31]

The November executive meeting of the Winchester association typically demonstrated the complexities of the national service debate following Munich. A resolution of thanks for Munich was discussed which a portion of the executive felt ought to be amended to mention their concern at the position of rearmament. Following the chairman's intervention it was agreed to move this as a separate resolution. This was done by Lieutenant-Colonel Savile, who protested at the inadequate steps being taken to fill the gaps in Britain's defences and urged the immediate introduction of both a compulsory register and a system of compulsory training. For him 'the voluntary scheme had failed'. Savile's resolution was defeated fifteen to nine, but why? The association's previous AGM had already overwhelmingly passed a motion urging conscription. The reason for the association's apparent change of heart was multifaceted. In part it may be explained by the political climate. Disaffected Conservatives were increasingly making their criticisms heard. To loyalists, *any* attack on Munich was a personal attack on the Prime Minister. Indeed, the sensitivity within the association towards such criticism was demonstrated in March 1939 when one speaker addressing the AGM was greeted with cries of derision from the floor for suggesting that Munich had caused national humiliation. The influence of the MP also played a part. In advance of the executive meeting Savile had raised the matter with the finance and general purposes committee. At that meeting Gerald Palmer had indicated his opposition to a register. His opinion undoubtedly carried weight with some activists. At the executive meeting concern was expressed about the likely cost of training and the impact this would have upon taxation whilst diverting resources away from other aspects of defence. It was also pointed out that the government was known to be giving consideration to the matter and, in deferrence, some activists thought they should not attempt to second-guess the government.[32] Undoubtedly, some people felt that a new era of international understanding had been inaugurated at Munich and were anxious that Chamberlain's methods be followed up; the introduction of national service would be interpreted in Berlin as an aggressive action. Moreover, it might be seen, as Chamberlain feared, as an admission of the inevitability of war and therefore of the failure of his foreign policy.

Debates of the nature of Winchester's concerned advocates like Amery about 'the whole thing sliding back before Christmas into general complacency and inertia'.[33] But this was an unduly pessimistic analysis. As illustrated by Tables 5.1 and 5.2, the matter was ascending the party structure. Debate had progressed from constituency to regional to national level. The National Union's central council approved by a large majority a motion from Norwood association demanding compulsory registration.[34] The annual National Union conference, scheduled for September, would in all likelihood have debated the matter had not cancellation been obliged by the inter-national crisis. In early November Chamberlain was forwarded by the National Union executive a number of resolutions urging a compul-sory register, complete with covering letter which whilst noting the matter was under government consideration, observed, that 'there was a strong feeling that some system of registration should be

Table 5.2 Examples of associations debating national service,
October–December 1938

Association	Date	Summary of Debate
Cannock	29/10/38	Urge compulsory register. Forwarded to National Union.
City of Leeds	13/10/38	Chief Agent writes upon behalf of Association's officers telling City's MPs of their support for a compulsory register.
Midland Union	14/10/38	Motion urging compulsory service. Forwarded to National Union.
Inverness	20/10/38	AGM urges immediate introduction of universal service scheme.
Aldershot	22/10/38	Motion proposed urging universal national service. Amended to two separate motions including one pledging support for government with whatever measures it introduces. Carried 33-25.
Winchester	25/10/38	Finance and general purposes committee discuss register. Motion forwarded to National Union. MP indicates opposition, but agrees to support scheme if introduced.
Cambridge	29/10/38	Pass motion on registration. Forwarded to National Union.
Hereford	Nov. 1938	Central Council told by MP of need for compulsory register and Ministry of Supply.
Chelmsford	04/11/38	Full discussion on matter of compulsory service initiated by women's president. Agreeing that this did not mean compulsory military service motion carried by large majority.
North West Area	05/11/38	'Overwhelming majority' pass resolution urging both register and service training.
National Union executive	09/11/38	Forward motions from Midland Union, Winchester, Cannock and Cambridge to PM with covering note pointing out level of support.
Brentford and Chiswick	11/11/38	Motion urging national register passed by meeting of Junior Imperial League. Forwarded to PM.
Scottish annual conference	17/11/38	Pass 2 motions on national service. Carried unanimously.
Chelmsford	21/11/38	Motion received from Brentwood women's branch urging national service immediately. Executive decide not the time to introduce conscription but registration of 'vital necessity'.
National Union Women's Advisory committee	24/11/38	Urge 'immediate' introduction of register and service scheme.
Winchester	29/11/38	Motion urging compulsory register and service defeated after considerable debate, 15-9.
Altrincham	09/12/38	Agent reports to MP definite support for a compulsory register.
Scottish Junior Unionist League	17/12/38	Urge compulsory register. Carried 7-2.

inaugurated without delay'.[35] Within the women's division of the Union the matter had reached the highest level. That November the Scottish annual conference unanimously carried two motions calling for national service. The attitude of activists was effectively summarised by the chief agent of Leeds:

> Our officers feel that the situation of this country after Munich and having regard to the situation in other parts of the world and our imperial commitments requires nothing short of national organisation, including compulsory service, to enable us successfully to meet the challenge which may come, and they think will come, at a comparatively early date.[36]

It was apparent that the concept of a register had widespread support. What is more, the principle of national service had been conceded: the debate was whether it should be compulsory or voluntary.[37] Over this, opinion was evenly divided, reflecting the virtual split of a *Daily Mail* readers' poll on the same question.[38] The 1922 Committee had already swung in favour of compulsion.[39] Critical in the transformation was the realisation of the genuine threat nazism posed. A gradual realisation had emerged that terms had been dictated by Hitler at Munich and it was unlikely that he would stop with this agreement. Further events like *Kristallnacht* highlighted the deprivation of liberty an individual could experience under German rule and emphasised the need for Britain to be able to stave off the threat successfully.[40]

In early December the decision to compile a voluntary national register and to introduce a voluntary national service scheme at the end of January 1939 was announced by John Anderson, Lord Privy Seal and Minister charged with Civil Defence. He argued 'that there is no scope for compulsion in peacetime when the manpower available is so much in excess of actual requirements and when the selection that has to be made can best be effected by relying on voluntary efforts'. Further, ministers considered there to be little likelihood of uniting the country behind compulsion when there was no necessity for such a measure.[41] It was clear that those Conservatives called in the debate were less convinced by the government's rationale, with most of them urging the adoption of varying forms of compulsion.[42] Amery thought the proposals were 'really feeble' and felt that Anderson's dismissal of compulsion 'showed that he had never even given the matter serious thought'. But the debate highlighted the key weakness of the national service lobby: the diversity of interpretations which made the coordination of strategy awkward. Amery found this especially frustrating when Grigg disclaimed the need for compulsory service training: 'After all these months in which he has shown courage enough to press for national service he now runs away from it'.[43]

WHO WERE THE SUPPORTERS OF NATIONAL SERVICE?

It is clear from analysing the parliamentary Conservative support for national service that it reflected all aspects of the political right. An assessment of the signatories of motions on the subject tabled between July 1938 and April 1939 shows that 200 Conservatives (over half the parliamentary party) were willing to support the introduction of such measures. That these supporters were representative of the party is shown in a number of features. The ratio between MPs representing borough and county seats mirrored the party's actual constituency distribution. The average age and age distribution of the supporters reflected those for the whole parliamentary party. Nevertheless, it is clear that the constituencies represented were concentrated in London, south-east England, the Midlands and north-east England – those areas considered to be at most risk from a German aerial assault. A common feature amongst the signatories was military service, although most male contemporaries had seen service in the 1914–18 conflict. The discipline of military service, the sense of national pride it instilled, the improved fitness of recruits, and the opportunies presented for 'seeing the world' were considered to be some of the beneficial consequences of service. It is certainly evident in the post-1945 debates about conscription that Conservatives who had experienced active service saw these factors as powerful arguments for its retention.[44]

The frequency of signatures suggested three general categories of advocate. The first grouping should be seen as the 'advocates'. These MPs had been favourable to national service, and particularly registration, for several years and articulated this support by signing at least three of the four 'key' motions on the issue, as illustrated by Table 5.3. Many of this grouping were senior backbenchers. This was reflected both in terms of their average age being fifty-six years and because most had entered parliament in the early 1920s. Furthermore, many sat on the 1922 Committee's executive or held official positions on other party committees. A significant proportion of this grouping, such as Keyes, Knox and Wilson, had pursued a professional military career before entering parliament. Historians of the Edwardian debate have noted the support professional soldiers gave to compulsion during that period. Over two decades later, some of these former officers perhaps still retained their favourable disposition for such measures.

Table 5.3 National service 'advocates' – supporters of three or more motions

Name	Constituency	Age[a]	Military Service[b]?	July[c]	Nov.[d]	Dec.[e]	Apr.[f]
					Motions on National Service		
Glyn, Ralph	Abingdon	53	Yes	Yes	Yes	Yes	Yes
Grigg, Edward	Altrincham	59	Yes	Yes	Yes	Yes	Yes
Knox, Alfred	Wycombe	68	Yes	Yes	Yes	Yes	Yes
McEwen, John	Berwick	44	Yes	Yes	Yes	Yes	Yes
O'Neill, Hugh	Antrim	55	Yes	Yes	Yes	Yes	Yes
Wilson, Arnold	Hitchin	54	Yes	Yes	Yes	Yes	Yes
Amery, Leo	Sparkbrook	65	Yes	Yes	No	Yes	Yes
Braithwaite, A.N.	Buckrose	45	Yes	Yes	No	Yes	Yes
Carver, William	Howdenshire	60	Yes	Yes	No	Yes	Yes
Emrys-Evans, Paul	South Derbyshire	44	Yes	Yes	No	Yes	Yes
Keyes, Roger	Portsmouth North	56	Yes	Yes	No	Yes	Yes
Loftus, P.C.	Lowestoft	61	Yes	Yes	No	Yes	Yes
Patrick, Mark	Tavistock	45	No	Yes	No	Yes	Yes
Peake, Osbert	Leeds North	41	Yes	Yes	No	Yes	Yes
Ponsonby, Charles	Sevenoaks	69	Yes	Yes	No	Yes	Yes
Somerville, A.A.	Windsor	80	Yes	Yes	No	Yes	Yes
Wardlaw-Milne, J.	Kidderminster	59	Yes	Yes	No	Yes	Yes
Astor, Nancy	Plymouth Sutton	59	No	Yes	Yes	Yes	No
MacDonald, P.	Isle of Wight	43	Yes	Yes	Yes	Yes	No
Reed, Stanley	Aylesbury	66	No	Yes	Yes	Yes	No
Hannon, Patrick	Moseley	54	No	No	Yes	Yes	Yes

a. Age in 1938.
b. Military service whether professionally, during the First World War or in Territorials or Reserve services.
c Private motion given to Chamberlain 28 July 1938. Secured 174 signatures: 'That measures should be taken at once to compile a national register of adult citizens in order to facilitate the voluntary employment of men and women in those duties for which they are best qualified, without delay, confusion or waste should war be forced upon us.'
d. Amendment to the address, 10 November 1938: 'But humbly regret that the Gracious speech contains no declaration of your government's intention to establish a compulsory national register in order to facilitate the voluntary employment of men and women in those duties for which they are best qualified.' Secured 20 signatures. Speaker refused to accept it, therefore Grigg urged people to support it as an indication of the weight of opinion.

e Amendment to notice that approved the government's national voluntary service proposals, 6 December 1938. 54 signatures. 'add after "service": but in view of the Lord Privy Seal's statement that a compulsory register will be desirable for the rationing of food and indispensable for information as to our resources and for critical decisions of policy in the first stage of a war, considers that such a register should be compiled without delay, as soon as the necessary arrangements are complete.'

f. Early Day Motion tabled 18 April 1939. Secured 65 signatures: 'That this House is in favour of the immediate acceptance of the principle of the compulsory mobilisation of the man, munition, and money power of the nation.'

The second grouping, but by far the largest, has for the purposes of generalisation been named the 'occasionals'. The vast majority of these were obscure backbenchers, never destined for high office, but who could be relied on to follow the government line in divisions and yet were prepared occasionally to add their support to the calls for national service. Such examples were Somerset de Chair, the twenty-seven-year old member for Norfolk South West, John Eastwood, who sat for Kettering, and Louis Gluckstein, MP for Nottingham East. It is apparent that the 'occasionals' had accepted the need for registration by the summer of 1938 and by late 1938 or early 1939 had moved to a position of recognising the necessity for some form of service. Many were signatories to the private July motion sent to Chamberlain. The organisers deliberately framed this for private consumption and no doubt attracted greater support from MPs as a consequence. It enabled them to give private vent to a matter that was politically sensitive without gaining negative media publicity and risking political fallout from the electorate. Significantly, Conservative women appear to have favoured national service. Four of the seven female Conservative MPs, Nancy Astor, Irene Ward, Mavis Tate and Katherine Atholl, were signatories for at least two of the four motions. Although there were too few female Conservative parliamentarians to make this statement irrefutable, one finds further evidence to support the supposition at the activist level. In the constituencies, women were often the prime instigators, or most vocal supporters, of resolutions concerning national service. The example of Mrs Western, Chelmsford association women's president, was a well-documented one, whilst the National Union women's advisory committee had added its voice to the calls for national service in November 1938.[45]

The third grouping were the 'foreign policy sceptics'. Critical of Chamberlain's foreign policy towards the dictators, they became involved in the national service debate following Munich for political expediency, perhaps recognising activist support for the issue. For many of these individuals, the failure of the government to act with resolution was further evidence of the malaise gripping the cabinet. As with issues of foreign policy, where it was evident that dissidents acted with ambiguity and inconsistency, the same applied to their actions over national service. This is illustrated by Table 5.4. What is more, the leading sceptics, Eden and Churchill, appeared unwilling to sanction such measures. This failure to lead by example was frustrating to many. Eden's closest political friends unsuccessfully sought to persuade him of the benefits, both politically and nationally. J. P. L. Thomas felt Eden ought to 'crack right out on national service and home defence', believing that 'none of these things can bring you anything but good from the Tory party'.[46] This unwillingness to act bore a great similarity to Eden's response to foreign policy after his resignation in February 1938 as Foreign Secretary, whereby he went to great lengths not to appear disloyal to the government. Certainly, Eden's unwillingness to act disappointed Amery, especially when he refused to add his signature to an open letter to *The Times* urging such measures.[47] Equally, Winston Churchill remained remarkably quiet upon the issue. Even post-Prague when the 1922 Committee called for compulsory service Churchill 'never said a word'. Detractors suggested this owed much to Churchill's desire not to prejudice any possible return to ministerial office.[48]

That national service became a parliamentary issue owed a considerable amount to the tenacity of Amery and Grigg, and a comparision of the two men is revealing.[49] Edward Grigg, having briefly sat as Liberal MP in the 1920s, re-entered parliament in 1933 as a 'National' Conservative. He took an immediate interest in defence matters and supported the policy of appeasement.[50] By contrast, Amery had been in parliament since 1911 and was no stranger to the battle for national service, having been a leading proponent before the First World War. He was not averse to appeasing the Italians, but found it increasingly difficult to justify the same of Germany. Amery consequently found it necessary to abstain from the Munich divisions.[51] The common ground between the two men was their interest in imperial matters. Grigg had been governor of Kenya before his return to politics and Amery was a former dominions secretary and a leading figure in the imperialist wing of the party. One wonders about the extent to which concerns about imperial defence and fears of overstretch encouraged their support for national service. This had been fostered by their association before the First World War with Lord Milner and the Round Table movement. Milner was a leading activist in the Edwardian National Service League and both men were clearly influenced by him.[52] Both men sought to publicise the cause outside parliament by

162   *The call for national service*

Table 5.4   Foreign policy sceptics [a] and national service

Name	Constituency	National Service Motions [b]				
		July	Nov.	Dec.	Mar.[c]	Apr.
Edenites:						
Amery, Leo	Sparkbrook	Yes	No	Yes	Yes	Yes
Duff Cooper, Alfred	St George's	Yes	No	Yes	Yes	Yes
Emrys-Evans, Paul	Derbyshire South	Yes	No	Yes	Yes	Yes
Patrick, Mark	Tavistock	Yes	No	Yes	Yes	Yes
Gunston, Derrick	Thornbury	Yes	No	Yes	Yes	No
Bower, Robert	Cleveland	Yes	No	No	Yes	Yes
Cartland, Ronald	King's Norton	Yes	No	No	Yes	Yes
Macnamara, J.R.J.	Chelmsford	Yes	No	No	Yes	Yes
Cranborne, Viscount	Dorset South	No	No	Yes	Yes	Yes
Crossley, Anthony	Stretford	No	No	Yes	Yes	Yes
Duggan, Hulbert	Acton	No	No	Yes	Yes	Yes
Nicolson, Harold	Leicester East	No	No	Yes	Yes	Yes
Wolmer, Viscount	Aldershot	No	No	Yes	Yes	Yes
Tree, Ronald	Harborough	Yes	No	No	Yes	No
Thomas, J.P.L.	Hereford	No	No	Yes	Yes	No
Joel, Dudley	Dudley	No	No	No	Yes	Yes
Law, Richard	Hull South West	No	No	No	Yes	Yes
Macmillan, Harold	Stockton	No	No	No	Yes	Yes
Spears, Edward	Carlisle	No	No	No	Yes	Yes
Herbert, Sidney	Westminster Abbey	Yes	No	No	No	No
Eden, Anthony	Warwick	No	No	No	Yes	No
Fellow Travellers:						
Makins, Ernest	Knutsford	Yes	No	No	Yes	Yes
Adams, Vyvyan	Leeds West	No	No	Yes	Yes	Yes
Atholl, Duchess of	Kinross	Yes	No	lost by-election Dec. 1938		
Neven-Spence, B.	Orkney	Yes	No	No	No	No
Stourton, J.J.	Salford South	Yes	No	No	No	No
McConnell, Joseph	Antrim	No	No	No	No	No
Ropner, Leonard	Barkston Ash	No	No	No	No	No
Withers, J.J.	Cambridge University	No	No	No	No	No
Churchill Group:						
Keyes, Roger	Portsmouth North	Yes	No	Yes	Yes	Yes
Boothby, Robert	Aberdeenshire East	No	No	Yes	Yes	Yes
Sandys, Duncan	Norwood	No	No	Yes	Yes	Yes
Churchill, Winston	Epping	No	No	Yes	Yes	No
Bracken, Brendan	Paddington	No	No	No	Yes	No

a   Names as defined in appendix 1.
b.   For details of motions see notes to Table 5.3
c   Early Day Motion, 28 March 1939: 'National effort to meet present dangers – In view of the grave dangers by which Great Britain and the Empire are now threatened following upon the successive acts of aggression in Europe and increasing pressure on smaller states, this House is of opinion that these menaces can only successfully be met by the vigorous prosecution of the foreign policy recently

outlined by the foreign secretary; it is further opinion that for this task national government should be formed on the widest possible basis and that such a government should be entrusted with full powers over the nation's industry, wealth and manpower, to enable this country to put forward its maximum military effort in the shortest possible time.' Secured 35 signatures.

publishing books, pamphlets and articles, writing to the press and through involvement in public rallies.[53]

Whilst the advocates were seeking to harness public and parliamentary support, it is evident that a substantial element of the party was willing to support the government line. But after Munich it was accepted that this was voluntarism's last chance. For this reason parliament heard the Member for Thirsk and Malton appeal to Britain to 'show the world in the third week of January that we in this country, as a free democracy, are willing voluntarily to offer our services to the nation'.[54] The national service lobby conceded the difficulties the government would face should it introduce peacetime compulsion, but nevertheless believed public opinion was 'really anxious' for such measures.[55] Constituency correspondence retained by MPs reveals the growing popular support compulsion received from December 1938 onwards.[56] At the same time, by the new year a sizeable portion of party opinion concurred with the judgement of one junior minister that the measures as they stood were simply 'not good enough'.[57]

THE FAILURE OF VOLUNTARISM

It became apparent throughout February and March 1939 that the national service appeal was not attracting enough volunteers, especially for the Territorial Army. The initial enthusiasm of the press was soon tempered, and the government's attitude appeared ambivalent. The national service appeal handbooks, which were supposed to have been sent to every household to coincide with the launching of the campaign by Chamberlain on 23 January, were not dispatched until days after. Similarly when the reserve occupations list was published, it was found that *chefs de cuisine* and sleeve link makers were amongst those deemed 'essential to the war effort'. By mid-February the appeal was failing to attract much media attention and was subject to sustained criticism from the *Daily Telegraph*.[58] A Mass-Observation survey in West Fulham conducted in April 1939 concluded that politicians had 'conspicuously failed' to impose their political agenda on the minds of 'public opinion' and suggested that they ought to learn to communicate their messages 'in a language everyone can understand. Not the formal prose of the national service handbook, or Anderson's scholarly introduction, or Chamberlain's aldermanic broadcasts'. A further survey undertaken in this London borough between April and July 1939 noted only a 'small' peak between January and February in ARP recruitment.[59]

The government was temporarily able to deflect those demanding the adoption of compulsion and the increasing critics of limited liability with Hore-Belisha's second army estimates. These marked a radical departure from the guiding principle of limited liability whilst reinforcing the vital role of home defence that had been the cornerstone of this doctrine. In his speech Belisha argued that the greatest threat facing Britain was the danger of air attack. He proposed to increase the number of Territorial AA divisions from five to seven. At the same time a continental expeditionary force comprising nineteen units was proposed. Nevertheless, Belisha's speech appeared to rule out the possibility of peacetime national service because although 'providing a larger army now, may be argued in grounds of physical and moral well being, it would not necessarily effect in the degree sometimes imagined the dimensions of our initial military contribution'.[60] It was not a view accepted by those backbenchers called in the debates.[61] One week later German troops entered Prague.

As a consequence of this German belligerence, Chamberlain came under a 'good deal of Conservative pressure' to introduce conscription.[62] It reminded Conservatives that 'there is one argument . . . alone that the dictator states respect, and that is the argument of force'.[63] Prague accentuated the calls for compulsion from both backbench MPs and activists as well as some cabinet ministers. As has already been observed, Hitler's action was in flagrant violation of Munich and resulted in Chamberlain's abandonment of appeasement with the guarantee of Poland's integrity. As one association chairman pointed out, 'the senior partner of the Berlin-Rome axis had shown his true colours', which compelled the immediate introduction of compulsory universal training.[64] Halifax, Simon and Hore-Belisha were now advocating conscription, whilst backbenchers Harold Macmillan, Patrick Hannon and George Mitchenson wrote to *The Times* announcing their conversions to the issue. At two meetings of Conservative backbenchers, first with the Foreign Affairs Committee in the immediate aftermath of Prague and then with the full 1922 Committee a week later, national service was discussed: 'a few were critical but the great majority at the meeting[s] were determined that some form of compulsory service ought to be introduced and that the government should one way or another get ahead with the matter'.[65] In an attempt to try and stifle the growing calls for conscription, Chamberlain seized upon Hore-Belisha's off-the-cuff suggestion of doubling the size of the

Territorial Army, and this was shortly announced as government policy on 29 March.[66] Once again the government appeared to Conservatives to be shirking conscription. Cuthbert Headlam considered the measure 'a ridiculous step' unless it was a prelude to conscription. He could not believe that either enough men could be found or that such a force could be maintained for particularly long.[67] This measure was a last-ditch effort by Chamberlain to avoid the introduction of peacetime compulsion. But the pressure continued to mount over the following weeks. Thirty backbenchers, including Churchill, Eden and Duff Cooper, tabled a motion that called for the immediate formation of a truly national government and the immediate introduction of conscription.[68] The foreign policy sceptics had in fact spent several days wrangling over the wording of the motion. Eden had been 'sticky' about coupling the calls for a national government with a demand for universal service and had favoured a more general reference to manpower, whereas Amery believed linking the two points would 'justify' themselves to both the House and the country. Ultimately, the final draft left out direct reference to universal service, leaving Amery hesitant about signing.[69] What is more, the reference to a truly national government discouraged many backbenchers from supporting the motion, and provoked an amendment affirming confidence in the Prime Minister. This amendment secured the support of 200 backbenchers, including many of those who would normally have considered supporting a motion on national service.[70] The proponents of universal service were not to be discouraged. Grigg, Amery and Wolmer then tabled a parliamentary motion urging 'the immediate acceptance of the principle of the compulsory mobilisation of the men, munition and money power of the nation' which secured sixty-five signatures.[71] At the same time, as Table 5.5 demonstrates, associations were passing resolutions demanding compulsory service.[72] Chamberlain eventually bowed to the pressure and introduced limited measures of conscription on 26 April. In the debate the following day one Conservative MP after another rose to add support for the bill.[73]

SOME CONCLUSIONS

The government's decision to introduce conscription was a signal victory for those activists and parliamentarians who had lobbied so vigorously for the measures. It showed that the party could impose a policy reversal on the leadership. Such demands reflected a belief that the mistakes of the 1914–18 conflict must not be repeated and that preparation was essential in an age when the advances of technology

Table 5.5 Examples of associations debating conscription following Prague

Association	Date	Summary of Outcome
Chelmsford	20/03/39	AGM agree to inform National Union of need for compulsory universal training.
Winchester	25/03/39	Motion urging compulsory national register carried.
Altrincham	31/03/39	Pass motion urging universal registration. Forwarded to MP.
Aldershot	15/04/39	Unanimously carry resolution urging compulsory register and service 'without delay'. Forwarded to PM.
Horncastle	17/04/39	Discussion on conscription– general favour.
North Wiltshire	21/04/39	Amended motion calls for compulsory national service. Carried with two dissentients.
City of Leeds	21/04/39	AGM 'overwhelming' majority urge compulsory military service without delay.
Glasgow	24/04/39	Chair urges support for voluntary scheme.
Accrington	25/04/39	AGM urged to 'volunteer'.

meant that war could be brought to the civilian population within hours of the commencement of hostilities. It is important to note that Conservatives tended solely to think of the issue in terms of the 'conscription of manpower'. Chamberlain's 1937 attempt at a limited measure of 'conscription of wealth', with his ill-fated National Defence Contribution tax, was brought down through party pressure and can be interpreted as a warning not to allow the resourcing of war to interfere in the world of business, traditionally a bastion of Conservative support. Of course the deteriorating international situation had a direct bearing upon attitudes to defence. Rearmament was an integral part of foreign policy – the idea of negotiating from a position of strength. Whilst the necessity of rearmament was not in question, there was considerable debate about the extent, nature and pace of the programme. The calls for national service must be seen in this context.

Practioners of Conservative history have observed the difficulty that may exist in pursuing a single issue through constituency minute books. The frequency with which national service arose in 1938–9 clearly highlights the importance attached to the matter. It is possible that the considerable number of persons holding a military rank within the local organisation structure might in part explain the interest, but it still begs the question of why national service and not supply? The preoccupation with national service was based on the belief that it was likely to have the more profound and obvious impact on activists and voters. Although it was evident that activists feared an electoral back-lash, these doubts were overcome by the desire to be able to resist any aerial assault, and in the aftermath of Munich because service appeared to offer the best means by which to plug the holes in Britain's air defences.

6 The prosecution of the war, September 1939 to May 1940

In May 1940, eight months after Britain's declaration of war on Germany, Neville Chamberlain resigned as Prime Minister after his parliamentary majority of 281 was reduced to eighty-one in a vote of confidence on his government's prosecution of the Norway military campaign. In fact the Norway debate was more than simply a deliberation on the failure of one military campaign; it was seen as a referendum on the Chamberlain government's whole war conduct. It proved to be the first twentieth-century example of a majority administration being forced out of office by a parliamentary vote. This chapter will consider how the Conservative party reacted to the Chamberlain government's handling of the war effort between September 1939 and the German invasion of France in May 1940. An examination will be made of the mechanisms available within parliament and the party for its membership to communicate their concerns to the leadership. This period, which became known as the 'phoney war' or the 'strange war' because of the failure of allied forces to engage the axis enemy actively, was to prove crucial in the fall of the Chamberlain government.[1] After an initial show of unity immediately following the declaration of war (because of their belief that it was their patriotic duty), many Conservatives soon expressed disquiet with the prosecution of the war. This chapter analyses those areas of policy that caused Conservative disgruntlement, and asks to what extent Chamberlain's fall from office was inevitable.

MAINTAINING NORMALITY?

War had immediate implications for the continued functioning of the party organisation and the pursuit of party politics. Hacking, the party chairman, sent a circular to all constituency associations requesting on behalf of the authorities that they close down for the duration of the war 'in the interests of the economy'. In fact, this left Hacking feeling 'greatly worried about the party's position'. He believed that

> whatever the duration of the war may be, it will be disastrous if, when hostilities have ceased, we find ourselves confronted with a situation where the other parties are in possession of their organisation and ours has ceased to exist.[2]

This letter from Hacking was followed by a circular from Sir Eugene Ramsden, chairman of the National Union, to all associations, pointing out that the executive had passed a motion urging the continuation of activities during the war and the 'disastrous' consequences for the party if activities were 'seriously impaired'.[3] Many associations did cease activities for the war's duration, feeling that party politics could not be continued when national unity was of the utmost importance. Some cooperated with the creation of Local Information Committees established under the auspices of the Ministry of Information.[4] Others attempted to continue functioning, if on a somewhat reduced scale, arguing that since the Labour party had not yet seen fit to join a war coalition government, Conservatives could not afford to rest on their laurels. Agents were released so that they could participate in the war effort, women's branches merged with the main association and expenditure was limited.[5] Other associations like Edinburgh North women's decided that with party politics in abeyance 'it would be a means of keeping in touch with our people, if a party or work parties could be arranged to do some war work, probably knitting war comforts for the troops'.[6] Ultimately, many associations managed to maintain activities until shortly after the invasion of France in May 1940. After this point most appear to have ceased all political undertakings. As one chairman explained:

> we do not think it would be any good having a divisional council now. So many of them are doing war work . . . and the women are working too that we think it would not be worth calling them and at the same time we feel sure nobody wants to think of politics now.[7]

The war also affected the activities of MPs. Attendances at the House of Commons were reduced, as many MPs felt it necessary to participate in the war effort. By January 1940 some sixty-two government backbenchers were on active service with the army, a further sixteen with the RAF and seven with the Navy.[8] Members such as Ronald Cartland, Christopher York, John Mills, Somerset de Chair and Maurice Petherick joined up with their regiments on the declaration of war.[9] Others divided their time between home defence service and parliament. Victor Cazalet served with an anti-aircraft battery in Kent which he had formed, but continued to attend important parliamentary debates, whilst Ruggles-Brise, the Member for Maldon, would only turn 'up for his agricultural c[ommi]ttee on Tuesdays and home again the same evening to run the L[and] D[efence] V[olunteers]'s of Essex'.[10] For those MPs who joined up for active service there were problems for the continued representation of constituency affairs. Buchan-Hepburn arranged for a secretary to respond to his East Toxteth correspondence and for another older MP to handle any issues that required pursuit. Ronald Cartland, on joining his regiment in September 1939, notified his King's Norton constituents through local newspapers to address all correspondence for him via the House of Commons. Then on being posted to France in January 1940 he arranged for his secretary to reply on his behalf.[11] Other MPs participated in the war effort in different ways. Ronald Tree joined the Ministry of Information, and within three weeks of the war's declaration had been seconded to America to set up an information service. He returned to Britain the following January and worked thereafter at Senate House under Lord Reith.[12] Duff Cooper was absent owing to an American lecture tour, only returning to Britain in March 1940.[13] Others such as Richard Law were away from Westminster because of work – in Law's case running a steel mill in Wales – or like Cranborne because of ill health.[14] Those MPs too old for active service and unable to secure other wartime work, remained at Westminster. But not all were happy in their role. Frank Fremantle complained that 'we MPs are acting as postmen between constituents and gov[ernmen]t dep[artmen]ts; and as a safety valve for the former – as a body guard, guide and sometimes to kick the latter'. As the war continued, this same Member felt increasingly despondent, confiding in a former colleague that

> the House is changing fast, through resignations, deaths and service; and many feel there is no object in their attending, where there are no divisions and awkward questions are passed. . . . I have lost all my old friends. The lads – up to fifty – naturally look on a 68-er as 'an old buster'.[15]

Another MP, Channon, thought about taking 'some semi-military occupation' but decided to remain at Westminster. He excused himself, joking of flat feet, unfitness, 'inefficiency and loathing of drill, exercise, discipline and danger'. But he recognised that at forty-two he was too old for military service: 'Old enough not to have to do anything, yet occasionally embarrassed and envious of people in uniform'.[16] It was in this rather strange atmosphere of political suspension that the debate about Chamberlain's suitability as a war leader was to be conducted.

EXPECTATIONS OF VICTORY?

The declaration of war by Britain and France on Germany was greeted with sombre resignation by the British population. Observers noted the difference in reception between this declaration of hostilities and that of July 1914.[17] It was seen as ironic that within hours of the declaration of war the air raid sirens should be wailing. The long expected knockout blow was being unleashed.[18] Ultimately it proved to be not only a false alarm, but also a false theory. That British land forces failed to commence battle for a further six months after the fall of Poland created a rather unusual situation.[19] Inskip, now elevated to the House of Lords as Lord Caldecote, admitted it was 'an odd affair' and noted the bemusement of one allied foreign minister who 'had heard of wars waged without a declaration of war but never of a war not waged after a declaration'.[20] As this chapter will show, the standoff between the allies and axis was to prove crucial in the fall of Chamberlain's government in May 1940. The failure of British forces to engage the enemy immediately, particularly the RAF who merely dropped propaganda leaflets over Germany, provoked considerable criticism from Conservatives.[21] Critics noted the discontent and were left wondering 'whether we are trying to win the war, or whether we are waiting for the German people to do it for us?'.[22] During the Norway debate, Earl Winterton, formerly a cabinet minister, attacked the government for this attitude, suggesting it was 'one good example of our wrong approach'. He felt the German people

> follow Hitler with a fanatical devotion comparable only to the followers of Genghis Khan or the Prophet Mohammed in days of Moslem ascendancy. . . . You cannot appeal to such people by moral exordiums. Right or wrong mean nothing to them; only superior force and its effective use.[23]

Unlike in 1914, many contemporaries did not expect a quick and victorious war. Conservatives in one Norfolk constituency during November 1939 were asked how long the war would last: one-third believed it was a matter of months; another third thought it would continue for years; and the remainder were unable to decide.[24] Cartland, serving with the 53rd Worcestershire regiment, wrote to his sister at the end of September indicating that he did not expect the war to end until 1946, but at least it would enable him to get his 'red tabs or two rows of medals!'.[25] Not every Conservative perceived the failure to engage the enemy as a sign of weakness. Indeed one survey of civilian morale noted that people regarded 'the slow movement of this winter as a sign of our superiority and Germany's inability to face up to a real equal'.[26] The secretary of one Norfolk association branch considered that Hitler was 'waiting for something to occur to save him'. This the secretary felt to be 'strange', because without fighting 'we must be increasing our strength in men, arms and position at a far greater rate than he'.[27] For others it suggested that the government at least appreciated the likelihood of a long war and therefore possessed some understanding of the realities of the military situation.[28]

THE CRITICS: THE AMERY GROUP, DAVIES ALL-PARTY GROUP AND THE WATCHING COMMITTEE

For the present those Conservatives who had been disaffected during peacetime were prepared to keep private their doubts about Chamberlain's suitability as a war leader, since two of their principal pre-war objectives had been achieved, namely the return to office of Churchill, as First Lord of the Admiralty, and of Eden, as Colonial Secretary.[29] Not surprisingly a view prevailed that it was almost disloyal to express strong antagonisms about government leaders, at least publicly during wartime. This view was reflected by the fact that until the Norway debate Conservatives kept their public criticisms muted and were only prepared to express these in the private sessions of parliament or in private discussion groups. Leo Amery, himself disappointed at having not been recalled to office, assumed the unofficial chairmanship of the formerly named Eden group. The Amery group, after an initial truce, soon began expressing concerns about the handling of the war at its weekly gathering in a private function room at the Carlton Hotel – numbers were slightly diminished in view of the fact that a number of former attendees, such as Cartland, were on active service, or like Law, working away from Westminster. J. P. L. Thomas continued to attend despite once again being Eden's PPS, whilst Brendan Bracken, who had become Churchill's PPS, began maintaining a presence. Consequently both Eden and Churchill were aware of how dissident Conservative opinion continued to operate. However, when it came to the Norway division both PPSs were instructed to vote with the government. Neither wished to follow such a course of action. Nevertheless, they realised that their rebellion would be taken as the 'private views' of their chiefs and might prejudice both ministers' futures.[30]

In addition to the Amery group, several other groupings of Conservative supporters emerged in criticism of government prosecution of the war. The second grouping was centred around the Liberal National, Clement Davies, and was all-party. The independent Eleanor Rathbone acted as secretary. The all-party group began meeting in September 1939. Davies resigned the National government whip in December because there were 'so many instances of failure on the part of the government to take the necessary measures for the vigorous prosecution of the war, that the government has not the resolution, policy or energy demanded by the country'.[31] From the Conservative party, Boothby and Amery were associated.[32] Boothby chaired the economics sub-committee, and it was the issue of economics that drew Amery's interest in the group.[33]

The third group of critics was the Watching Committee. Formed around the Cecil family, and comprising members from both Houses of Parliament, it held its first meeting on 4 April 1940, just days after another cabinet reshuffle had been badly received. Its purpose was 'to watch the conduct of the war. . . . to make representations to the government where they consider there is a risk of mistakes being made or where it seems that the trend of public opinion is not appreciated'.[34] At their inaugural meeting, the topics under discussion were the war cabinet, strategy, economics and the home front. As Table 6.1 illustrates, many of the Amery group were associated with the Watching Committee. In addition to these potential critics a number of government loyalists and technical specialists were affiliated to the Committee. The blend of critics and loyalists was deliberately created so that all sides of party opinion would be represented.[35] This would of course make any representations to government more acceptable. However, the numbers 'selected' to join the Committee were deliberately limited on the grounds that 'it would only lead to misunderstanding if our other colleagues were troubled with this suggestion'.[36] The Committee was chaired by Salisbury with Emrys-Evans as honorary secretary. The Committee was also divided into sub-committees, each responsible for assessing a particular aspect of the war.[37] Owing to the seniority of many of the Committee's members, they would pass on their recommendations and concerns to government ministers. Of these, Halifax was their most regular contact – perhaps this was because he was perceived as the minister mostly likely to listen and because of his sympathies for a broader national

Table 6.1 Composition of the Watching Committee (April 1940)

Peers	MPs	
	Critics	*Loyalists*
Lord Salisbury* (chairman)	Leo Amery*	Patrick Spens
Lord Trenchard*	Harold Nicolson	Joseph Nall
Lord Swinton*	Richard Law*	Geoffrey Ellis
Lord Cecil*	Derrick Gunston	Nancy Astor°
Lord Hailsham	Viscount Wolmer*	J. Henderson Stewart
Lord Horne*	Louis Spears*	Stuart Russell
Lord Lloyd*	Ronald Tree	Mavis Tate
Lord Londonderry	Duff Cooper	
Lord Trent	Edward Winterton	
Lord Macmillan*	Paul Emrys-Evans* (honorary secretary)	

* From 1 May these individuals agreed to be available to meet each morning if circumstances insisted.
° Although Astor had been a vocal supporter of Chamberlain in peacetime during the months of the phoney war she became dissillusioned.

government, but also because he was considered as the likely successor to Chamberlain.[38]

TOWARDS A NEGOTIATED PEACE?

The inactivity of military forces in the opening weeks of the war fuelled the suspicion held in some quarters that Chamberlain may have been seeking a peace accord with Germany. The delays in declaring war were taken as proof that the appeasers were trying for another Munich. The reality was somewhat different – the delay being necessary because of the British government's desire to declare war in unison with the French and not because they were giving serious consideration to Mussolini's proposal of an international conference.[39] Some Conservatives felt that the delay was 'good moral propaganda'.[40] Fears were again heightened of a negotiated settlement when

Hitler offered peace terms on 6 October, but Chamberlain publicly rejected these six days later.[41] But the belief that elements within the government favoured coming to terms with Germany was not helped by the declarations of a defeatist element within the party comprising several Conservative peers, Arnold, Brocket, Buccleuch and Westminster, and a number of MPs, Culverwell, Southby and Ramsay. Westminster, an old personal friend of Churchill, allegedly told a private meeting in early October 1939 that Britain need not be at war with Germany at all, it all being part of a Jewish and Masonic plot to destroy Christian civilisation. The speech was reported to the war cabinet the following day and earned the Duke a rebuke and warning from Churchill: 'When a country is fighting a war of this kind, very hard experiences lie before those who preach defeatism and set themselves against the will of the nation'.[42] Contemporary wits suggested the Duke's desire for peace stemmed from economic sensibilities: he owned considerable tracts of property in London, and a German aerial assault was likely to inflict considerable material damage to these assets! One proponent, the Duke of Buccleuch, was still in February 1940 trying to persuade officials from 10 Downing Street of the advantages of a negotiated peace. His argument was that Britain would eventually have to sue for peace and the Nazis would still be in power, so 'why not do so now, when comparatively little damage has been done and when there is still time to avert economic ruin?'[43] The concern was that economic collapse would then provide a fertile breeding ground for bolshevism and revolution.[44] Similar concerns had privately been exercising Lord Rothermere. He had even drafted a letter to Chamberlain putting forward the arguments for peace, but drew back at the last moment from sending it, correctly judging that such a letter could damn a man.[45]

The attitude of surrender adopted by some Conservatives was of considerable concern to others in the party. Amery considered this 'sorry defeatism' to be only confined to a few persons, but was ready 'to rally all forces to scotch it' should it become serious.[46] It had emerged during a debate in a secret session of the 1922 Committee on 4 October. The minutes of this meeting reveal that Cyril Culverwell felt Britain was heading for disaster since

> the country, in his view, had been stampeded into war by the press, opposition and right-wing Conservatives. Poland would never be restored, nor would we break through in the west, and the defeat of Germany would mean that Europe would become bolshevik. It was

folly to pursue the war and we should make peace, recognising Hitler's claim to Poland if he offered reasonable terms.[47]

Concerned that this 'miserable effort seemed to meet with some approval from various quarters', Amery intervened, and counter-argued that to make peace with Hitler now was 'sheer madness and would have a deplorable effect on the neutrals'. Culverwell was supported by Southby but rebuked by Lamb and Raikes before Wardlaw-Milne 'urged' the Committee not to waste time even discussing the matter and proposed adjourning the debate.[48] Culverwell's enthusiasm for the Nazi regime had been a matter of public record since the time of the Czech crisis. During the Munich debate he had denied German 'war guilt' for the 1914–18 war and argued that the regime was only seeking 'her just rights', which had been deprived by 'the stupidity of the allies'. This had been followed by a newspaper article accounting for his impressions of a visit to Germany where he had found many of the regime's features 'commendable'.[49]

Culverwell continued to advocate the benefits of a negotiated settlement outside the 1922 Committee, consequently incurring the wrath of his local Bristol West association. At a specially convened executive meeting, Culverwell was called to account for his opinions. He 'refuted the charge of being a pacifist, pro-Nazi, or pro-German' and claimed himself to be 'a strong and consistent supporter' of Chamberlain. When questioned by members of the executive who doubted if any guarantee given by Hitler as part of a peace deal could be trusted, Culverwell replied that 'he was only trying to correct the impression . . . that it was possible to build up a utopian Europe after the war'. He further explained that 'the only peace worth while is by negotiation, coupled with guarantees, disarmament etc.'. Although Culverwell appeared to have secured the support of a few of the executive, the majority of members, led by the chairman and vice-chairman, were openly hostile. It was urged that Culverwell 'be severely reprimanded' and that the association do 'something definite' about his position. This led to the acceptance of a resolution which expressed its disagreement with his views, and a further resolution being passed warning Culverwell not to expect reselection.[50] In fact he was deselected in 1944.[51] Once more, the importance of keeping the support of constituency officials had been highlighted. It is evident that activists were unprepared to tolerate defeatist talk. In December, Scottish Conservatives urged 'greater efforts . . . to counteract pacifist and subversive elements, and to keep up morale "on the home front" '.[52] In

Barkston Ash members were exhorted 'to quash defeatist talk'.[53] Maidstone association at their March 1940 AGM passed a resolution that 'strongly' protested at the activities of the pacifist Peace Pledge Union, considering their undertakings to be 'an insult to the great mass of British people', and therefore demanded 'that steps be taken drastically to curtail the potentiality for evil'.[54] For the political right, these quasi-pacifist organisations were deemed to be fronts for bolshevism which threatened the very fabric of society. But the patriotism of most Conservatives prevented them from conceding the arguments of Culverwell *et al.*. To submit to a fascist regime would entail the loss of the same liberties threatened by bolshevism.

From the perspective of the authorities it is clear that the 'defeatist' element of the Conservatives posed little direct threat to security. The exception was the obscure and eccentric Conservative MP Captain Ramsay, who sat for Peebles. In May 1940 he was imprisoned for the remainder of the war under regulation 18B.[55] This emergency legislation had originally been passed as a means of responding to the IRA terrorist threat, but was invoked to arrest a number of leading fascist sympathisers. It was Ramsay's continued operation of the Right Club and his involvement in the Tyler Kent affair that provided the authorities with the excuse for the roundup. According to MI5 Ramsay had been shown copies of highly secret and sensitive correspondence between Churchill and Roosevelt by Tyler Kent, a cypher at the American embassy.[56] In the view of the Home Office, the Right Club, which in September 1939 could claim among its members a vice-chairman of the Conservative party and two government whips, 'was designed secretly to spread subversive and defeatist views among the civil population of Great Britain, to obstruct the war effort of Great Britain, and thus to endanger public safety and the defence of the Realm'. Ramsay continued to protest his innocence throughout his time in Brixton prison, arguing that the main objective of the Right Club was 'to oppose and expose the activities of organised Jewry'.[57] Ramsay's Germanophile credentials had been evident since early 1939, when he had become associated with 'The Link', an organisation which had sought to avoid war between Britain and Germany by educating the British population about the 'true' nature of nazism and through correcting the 'false' impression cultivated by the press.[58] Like the other 'defeatists', Ramsay believed that the war was a deliberate Jewish plot to secure world domination, but unlike Lords Westminster and Brocket (who were never interned) Ramsay had little, if any, access to the decision making elites and therefore minimal influence and protection when the internment orders were granted.[59]

For the residuum of the party there was concern that this 'defeatism' might spread to the general public.[60] It was a concern shared by the Ministry of Information.[61] This loss of public morale was due to the 'generally negative attitude of things, excessive concentration on "funk-holism", the forbidding of meetings and the discouragement of volunteering', considered Amery. This latter point was particularly ridiculous to Amery, who had long been an advocate of national service, and to others who attended the 1922 Committee. The problem was that although parliament had passed the National Service (Armed Forces) Act on the opening day of the war, the call-up was divided into three age categories between the years of eighteen and forty-one. Registration did not begin until 21 October and then only for the first group aged 18–23. The process of compiling the register was not completed until the beginning of the following year. These delays confirmed the very fears that had been expressed by the peacetime advocates of a compulsory register. Amery considered it 'preposterous' that able-bodied men should be prevented from coming forward for some form of training in a situation of war. This was a view echoed in a 'most secret' memorandum on the 'general British military position' that was circulating amongst MPs. But Amery predicted that 'when the big German push comes it will shake us up quickly enough and almost [certainly] bring most of the peace-mongers to their senses'.[62] There was also a concern that with Conservatives and Liberals volunteering to participate in the war effort it left the arena open for the pacifist and communist factions to go unchallenged. Nevertheless, when the 1922 Committee discussed that matter, it was generally felt that freedom of speech was essential since it was easiest to counter communist and fascist propaganda in the open.[63]

INEFFICIENCY, BUREAUCRACY AND LEADERSHIP

Whilst the desire to secure an early peace with Germany was limited to a minority of Conservatives, the remainder were concerned with issues specific to the war effort and to making the British war machine more effective. The questionnaire de Chair distributed amongst party officials in his constituency reflected the concerns being expressed amongst backbenchers. The questions posed spanned all aspects of the war, enquiring about its expected duration, the reaction to the possibility of fighting bolshevik Russia, the position of agriculture, the health of the Labour party, the success of the government's war prosecution and popularity of ministers and their war aims, to the domestic concerns about ARP and evacuation.[64] Specifically in parliamentary and media circles, the composition of the war cabinet came in for criticism. It was comprised of nine members, including the service chiefs. This latter grouping had originally been excluded until the Liberals refused to join the coalition and the threatened resignations of the air and war ministers warranted their addition.[65] The inclusion of the three service chiefs in the cabinet made it too large and unwieldy to make decisions, and 'in times like these speed does count'.[66] The Watching Committee considered the subject of a smaller, more effective cabinet on 4 April 1940, in a debate led by Amery and Swinton with 'practically all the peers for it, but one or two of the commoners like Spens and Nall, doubtful'.[67] As a result of this discussion, Amery then circulated a memorandum amongst the Committee and to the editor of *The Times*, that put the argument for a 'cabinet which will think ahead in terms of policy and not of routine day to day administration ... like a general staff, free of departmental work'.[68] Two days later *The Times* carried a leader entitled 'Relief for ministers', which urged a smaller and more effective war cabinet.[69] *The Times*, although it had been a staunch supporter of appeasement, during the phoney war became one of Chamberlain's most objective and constructive critics.

A considerable area of concern was the apparent incapability of government departments to overcome bureaucracy and red tape, and the implications this had on supplying the war effort. One area chairman was ever-conscious of the complaints and rumours about the 'futilities and follies of government departments and their inability to get war work commensurate with their claims'.[70] A number of branch secretaries in the Norfolk South West constituency noted the ARP equipment shortages and indicated that these caused 'a good deal of comment'; whilst the York association executive agreed that there 'was a good deal of feeling and dissatisfaction' with ARP organisation.[71] Victor Cazalet, who was serving with an AA Battery, found the situation at the War Office exasperating. He felt there was an 'incredible amount of fuss over everything and such muddle as beggars description'. His own battery was short of ammunition to the extent that they only had enough for seventy-five seconds of firing time.[72] For those Members on active service, the first-hand experiences of bureaucracy and red tape preventing the equipping and supplying of the armed forces must have had an important, if unquantifiable, impact upon their attitudes to the government's prosecution of the war. Their cross-voting or abstentions would prove crucial during the Norway vote. Those members in military service represented the younger elements of the party. As was apparent during the expressions of

dissent over peacetime foreign policy, youth was an important charac-
teristic of the disaffected. During the Norway debate, youth and
military service reinforced each other and culminated in a more
vigorous opposition to Chamberlain than either did singularly. In
February 1940, one service Member wrote from France that 'there are
innumerable scandals out here; we want another Miss Nightingale,
another Lloyd-George, and every soldier I've spoken to wants
Churchill in place of Chamberlain'.[73] For the first secret session debate
that took place in the House of Commons on 13 December, a number
of MPs on active service sought special leave in order to air their
grievances. One such Member was Colin Thornton-Kemsley, who sat
for Kincardine and Aberdeenshire West and was serving in the Royal
Artillery.[74] The situation appeared not to improve during the opening
months of 1940. Cartland, now serving in France, suggested he would
return if there was another secret session, in order to 'revive the
scandal. Believe me there are some too – the colonel said tonight it
might yet be my best war work – forty-eight hours in the House of
Commons!'.[75]

Whilst the military supply matters were causes for concern, the
political inabilities of the government were exacerbating the situation.
The government's performance in the House of Commons also came
in for criticism. Although it was felt that fighting a defensive military
war and an offensive economic one was probably the correct strategic
course of action, critics could not but

> help feeling that it ought to be explained rather more forcibly to the
> British people and neutral countries. The PM's weekly talks are far
> too colourless. Parliamentary language is quite alright in the piping
> times of peace, but a meagre ration of departmental platitudes,
> which have an evasive air, are not adequate in these strenuous days.[76]

Lord Macmillan, the Minister for Information, had in December 1939
urged that 'Britain must be represented as fighting Germany on land,
in the air, and at sea, ceaselessly, without remorse, with all her armed
might, with financial resources, industrial manpower, and commercial
assets, with all her idealism and determination'.[77] Yet, to observers the
government was failing to provide any such image. As one Norfolk
Conservative explained, 'when more is heard of how the war *is* being
won we can tell better if people *are* satisfied! The general feeling is we
know *too little*'.[78] Amery noted a speech Chamberlain gave to a 1922
dinner at the Junior Constitutional, which he could only describe as a
'city councillor's speech': a narrow party speech which gave a 'compla-
cent review' of the situation and which struck Amery 'as lacking real

grip of things as well as platitudinous in diction and wholly without inspiration'. He noted that 'even Nancy Astor who is on the whole a good yes-woman frankly expressed her disappointment'.[79] Astor concurred with Amery's verdict and although sure Chamberlain intended 'a fighting speech . . . its effect on me was to make me wish that Winston was PM (This was only momentary, and I know it was wrong, but that was my reaction!)'.[80] Of more concern was that ministers were also expressing doubts about the PM's inability to provide an inspirational lead.[81]

WAR AIMS?

The lack of leadership and direction itself led to another area of debate and concern, namely, for what purpose was Britain fighting the war? There was a growing awareness of the need to establish the criteria which Britain required to be satisfied in advance of any peace settlement, so that no one side would be under any delusions. Did this mean the restitution of Poland to her pre-September 1939 borders, or was merely her 'independence' enough? Were the liberation of Czechoslovakia and Austria intended goals? Was Britain fighting to destroy Hitler personally or to ensure the total destruction of the Nazi system? A poll taken amongst Norfolk activists in November 1939 about war aims, found that 36 per cent believed Britain was fighting to 'smash Hitler' and a further 28 per cent to 'restore Poland and Czechoslovakia', with 'one or two want[ing] to divide Ger[many] up or restore a monarchy'.[82] Correspondence in the press indicated a desire for more explicit government guidance.[83] When considering the options, the Northern Area chairman thought fighting to destroy Hitlerism was 'simple enough' but if the objective was the restoration of the pre-war east European order 'it may lead to many awkward complications and necessitate a very long war'.[84] Others saw the war as being fought to preserve liberty, both in Britain and Europe. As Buchan-Hepburn told a constituent, the choice was clear, either surrender and be subjugated under nazism or fight to the end to ensure the destruction of nazism and preserve the liberty of the British people. Wolmer was equally clear that it was 'a fight to the finish between the British Empire and nazidom'.[85] Likewise Lloyd in his pamphlet, *The British Case*, believed that

> the people of the British Commonwealth are engaged today in a life and death struggle for a political principle necessary to the liberties and therefore to the prosperity and progress of the peoples of

Europe. It is the principle of national independence. This principle is the sole guarantee of the survival of individual liberty in Europe.

In this work Lloyd sought to present the necessity for war in a manner that drew upon history and Christianity. With a whig interpretation of history that went back to Caesar, Lloyd attempted to play upon the British sense of fair play. Germany was a 'tyranny' determined on world domination. With Austria and Czechoslovakia 'the humanitarian motives of the German government could not be accepted at their face value by a world deeply disgusted by the steady growth of religious, racial and political persecution within the now enlarged political boundaries of the new Reich'. The sole responsibility of securing 'European freedom' rested with Christian Britain.[86] However, to the concern of many, when Halifax addressed the issue at a packed meeting of the 1922 Committee, he was rather vague. He explained that the government was seeking to improve its relations with neutral countries and that efforts were being undertaken to ensure continued Italian neutrality. As for the suggestion of an Anglo-Soviet alliance, Halifax believed this would only be secured if the USSR was given a free hand in the Baltic, which would have 'staltified our whole position with regard to aggression'. It was considered particularly worrying that he concluded by suggesting that Britain should avoid rigidly defining its war aims.[87]

That Britain was now at war with Germany enabled Conservatives to unleash their hostility towards the German nation. Germany was now the enemy, and in war it is almost axiomatic that the individuals of participant nations must hate each other. When Thomas Moore was pictured in the *Sunday Pictorial* shortly after the outbreak of hostilities and described in the blurb as 'Hitler's friend', his Ayr Burghs executive was quick to express disquiet.[88] Conservatives who had been associated with the unease over peacetime appeasement had no difficulty in attacking Germany. They even portrayed Germany and Hitler in a light that suggested it was obvious that Hitler had been planning world domination, thereby justifying their past behaviour and criticisms. 'Poland was not an isolated incident' wrote Wolmer to the *Aldershot News*, 'but the culmination of a whole series of similar attacks on peaceful neighbours ... against such a challenge England must always fight'. This letter was written in October 1939 when Hitler had made his alleged 'peace offer', and Wolmer in common with other sceptics was keen to quash any suggestion of a negotiated settlement. For this purpose the ghost of Munich was resurrected: 'it is impossible to attach any reliance to any promise made by Herr Hitler or his gang.

Before peace can be considered we must have something more reliable to go on than "scraps of paper" '.[89] The inference was clear: Wolmer did not have to mention Munich by name, for that would have implied disloyalty at a time when national unity was required. The reference to the 'scraps of paper' was enough of a connotation, but with the emphasis of blame being laid on Hitler, the enemy. In a similar vein Leonard Ropner addressed his Barkston Ash association AGM in April 1940.[90] He concluded with a robust declaration 'that Hitler would be crushed, and that millions of slaves living under his tyranny would be liberated. No sacrifice was too great to accomplish that'. The use of highly emotive words and loaded phrases such as 'slaves' and 'tyranny' was a typical exercise in order to rouse audiences against the Nazi threat. Churchill was a prime example of this phenomenon. Although the emotive nature of his oratory had discredited the value of alarmism during peacetime, in war Churchill's mastery of the English language made him a powerful speaker. During his first wartime radio broadcast, which earned him considerable praise, Churchill spoke of the allies' intention to prevent the 'Nazis carrying the flames of war into the Balkans and Turkey'. He confidently predicted victory against Hitler 'and his group of wicked men, whose hands are stained with blood and soiled with corruption', and was convinced that the British were 'the defenders of civilisation and freedom'. In another broadcast, Churchill defiantly declared:

> The whole world is against Hitler and Hitlerism. Men of every race and clime feel that this monstrous apparition stands between them and the forward move which is their due . . . Even in Germany itself there are millions who stand aloof from the seething mass of criminality and corruption constituted by the Nazi party machine.[91]

Some observers were inclined to feel that at times these Churchillian speeches were over the top, which lessened their intended impact. Indeed the BBC Director of Talks was concerned that these broadcasts were making the wrong impression on dominion opinion, which 'makes one more doubtful than ever about the value of Mr Churchill's broadcasts. In addition of course he has managed to offend both Italy and the US in successive talks'.[92]

That nazism was the enemy was not in question. The real problem lay in defining the expected aims once nazism had been defeated. Some Conservatives saw a risk in emphasising the crusade as purely against Hitlerism, for fear that he might be replaced by another Nazi government (and thereby invalidating the legitimacy of continuing a war, especially to American and dominion opinion). Winterton believed that since the German people accepted that Hitlerism and the German nation were one, it had to be made clear that Britain intended

> to smash both in overwhelming force. Then and then only can we both settle down . . . in peace in Europe. We do not want permanent enmity between us [and Germany], but we are going to make it impossible for [her] to make another war of aggression.[93]

But such an interpretation was not accepted by the government until the withdrawal from Norway.[94] The difficulties of the British position were summarised by Alec Cadogan, permanent secretary at the Foreign Office, when at the end of September 1939 Halifax asked for his assessment of war aims:

> I told him I saw awful difficulties. We can no longer say 'evacuate Poland' without wanting to go to war with Russia, which we don't want to do! I suppose the cry is 'Abolish Hitlerism'. What if Hitler hands over to Göring?![95]

The apparent conclusion of the war cabinet was the generally vague idea that the purpose was to free Europe from its fear of German aggression and enable these peoples to preserve their liberties and their independence. This basically meant the removal of Hitler. As Halifax wrote, he

> wished to fight long enough to induce such a state of mind in the Germans that they would say they'd had enough of Hitler! And that point is not really met by talking about CZ[echoslovakia], Poland and all the rest of it. The real point is, I'm afraid, that I can trust no settlement unless and until H[itler] is discredited. When we shall achieve this nobody can say, but I don't think any 'settlement' is worth much without![96]

In other words, whilst Chamberlain persisted as Prime Minister and the war was confined to eastern Europe, the British government laboured with the misconception that Germany was like some juvenile offender who could be brought to their senses by a short sharp shock. Such an attitude did not resolve the debate, and these criticisms and concerns were to persist throughout the months that Chamberlain remained Prime Minister. Indeed, Reith, the Minister for Information from January 1940, was longing during mid-March for a 'concrete indication . . . of the precise policy they intended to pursue to defeat Germany', which would enable him to counter the 'general atmosphere of anxiety in regard to high policy and the conduct of the war in general'.[97] Nevertheless, these doubts were kept private. The public utterances of Conservative individuals, and associations, with the use of phrases and words such as 'liberty', 'defeat Nazi aggression in Europe' and 'lasting peace', suggested that at least for the sake of national unity, they were prepared to accept the government's aims.[98] By the time Churchill succeeded to the premiership the immediate war aims were much clearer, having been narrowed specifically to military issues of survival or surrender.

PERSONALITY AND LEADERSHIP

Despite the debates about Britain's war aims and war prosecution, these did not make Chamberlain's defeat and Churchill's succession to the premiership in May 1940 inevitable. What would prove crucial was the perceived suitability of a minister for conducting a war. Chamberlain had once commented that the nearer war came then the better Churchill's chances of returning to office and vice versa.[99] Indeed once war broke out, Churchill's standing improved. The transformation in fortunes was quite astonishing; just a few months earlier, in July 1939, it was reported that four out of five backbenchers would not tolerate his inclusion in the cabinet. Churchill's hostility to Indian reform and his role in the abdication crisis had left him isolated on the fringes of the party. But by the end of 1939 he, along with Halifax, was talked of openly as successor to Chamberlain. To some it was inevitable.[100] This support appears to have begun filtering down to the activists. Branch secretaries in North West Suffolk were canvassed in November 1939 as to whom they considered to be the four most popular ministers. Churchill's name was listed by 63 per cent and Chamberlain's by 53 per cent.[101] From mid-September onwards, sections of the press, principally the *Sunday Pictorial* and *Daily Mirror*, began canvassing for Churchill's succession.[102] In contrast to Chamberlain's ineffective performances on the radio, Churchill seemed to revel in this medium.[103] Ernest Makins heard a 'good fag' that when the Prime Minister broadcasts 'he thinks he is on the National, but it is only the Midland Regional'.[104] In contrast Churchill's first radio broadcast on 1 October received all-round praise, with one senior minister noting how 'the press talked of him as Prime Minister'.[105] Likewise, Churchill seized every opportunity to improve his standing by some impressive parliamentary performances. As one junior minister observed in the opening weeks of the war, little had roused the House of Commons until Churchill spoke on the naval situation, a speech with which he took 'a long step forward towards being a future

Prime Minister'.[106] Churchill was also adept at ensuring that he was associated with positive news about the war effort which boosted national morale (the *Altmark* incident, whereby the navy intercepted a German ship carrying British prisoners of war, and the *Graf Spee* scuttling in December 1939 being the most spectacular). One lobby correspondent observed Churchill's growing confidence in April 1940:

> Winston left the Chamber and crossed the Lobby. He is a great showman. He stood in the porchway talking to Admiral Keyes, while he took snuff with the attendant. (There has always been a convention of snuff taking with the attendant and his predecessors.) He then moved slowly across the Lobby, looking bent and tired, and like a man who was getting no sleep – but smiling.[107]

There is some evidence to suggest that Churchill was encouraging newspaper criticism in order to stiffen the war effort, but whether these were deliberate attempts to undermine Chamberlain's position for his own benefit is less than certain.[108] Having only recently returned to office, he could not risk being implicated in the fall of an administration of which he was a member. The party would never forgive this ultimate sacrilege.

In accordance with a growing awareness of the improved standing of Churchill was a mounting consciousness amongst backbenchers of the potential threat Labour would pose after the war. Although for Conservatives, their concern was the prosecution of the war, backbenchers had occasion to notice the manner in which the opposition conducted themselves. The Labour leadership followed a policy of 'constructive opposition' which was underlined by the electoral truce agreed on 5 September 1939. At a parliamentary level various Labour frontbenchers took up official contacts with particular ministers and departments. That this growing stature for Labour became apparent to a number of Conservatives once Labour joined the Churchill coalition in May 1940 cannot be disputed, but what is interesting is that there were limited signs of this realisation during the period of the phoney war.[109]

After the initial few months of the war Chamberlain asserted his leadership at least over the government and the party, though it is by no means clear that this confidence extended any further. The government's popularity was rather volatile, and certainly by December 1939 it was ill-regarded once again. The appointments of Morrison, as Minister for Food, and Dorman-Smith, as Minister for Agriculture, were unpopular and deemed a weakness for the government.[110] To critics, these appointments were taken as evidence of the undue influence wielded by Horace Wilson and David Margesson, the chief whip. But Margesson saw the problem of personnel from a different perspective. He recognised that Chamberlain was experiencing difficulties in finding men and women of sufficient quality for ministerial appointments, therefore 'it was considered that some accession of strength to the government might be found by importing one or two people from outside'.[111] This was not a new concern for Chamberlain, for even in peacetime he had lamented the lack of young talent on the government backbenches.[112] Now, under the pressures of war, the necessity for ministerial aptitude was much greater and Chamberlain was forced to look to the world of business for men he deemed worthy. This led to the appointments of the 'super-men', Lord Reith as Minister of Information and Sir Alan Duncan to the Board of Trade, in January 1940. Unfortunately, neither man appeared particularly comfortable in his post, and both would remain in office only until Chamberlain's fall from power. Further, many of the key personnel in the cabinet had been ministers since at least 1935, and this led some critics to suggest that perhaps they were too 'tired' to continue with the strains of office, especially in a time of war.[113] One wonders to what extent Chamberlain's declining health affected the running of the war effort. His private secretary recorded on several occasions that the Prime Minister was too ill to fulfil his duties, to the extent that at the end of 1939 Chamberlain was 'worried at the prospect of not being able to carry on if these attacks increase in number and violence'.[114]

THE DISMISSAL OF HORE-BELISHA

The problems over personnel persisted into the new year. In January 1940 Hore-Belisha was sacked as Minister for War.[115] Belisha, suitably aggrieved by his dismissal, especially since Chamberlain had assured him the previous month of his backing, refused to accept demotion to the Board of Trade. It had been suggested that Belisha be moved to the Ministry of Information, but Halifax had intervened, arguing that this would have a poor impact upon the neutrals and enemy in view of Belisha's Jewishness and methods.[116] Belisha was in no doubt as to why he was dismissed, and he summarised it in two words to a friend, ' "Jew-Boy" '.[117] The press, whom Belisha had been careful to cultivate during his years in office, came to his defence, but Chamberlain stood his ground, arguing that he must be free to make changes in his team as he thought necessary. Observers of the resignation debate felt that the Prime Minister's performance was rather 'lame', whilst the impression Belisha's speech 'left on one was "well, if he and the generals, the cabinet and the PM saw eye to eye on every question of foreign policy, why was he forced to resign?"'. The general consensus was that Chamberlain had handled the whole situation poorly.[118] Belisha had made few friends in military circles. His use of Liddell-Hart as an informal advisor during the early years of his tenure at the War Office had irritated the military establishment. To their detractors, Hore-Belisha was 'just a charlatan out for his own publicity' and Liddell-Hart 'a fanatic about things military about which he really is not an expert'.[119] Belisha had managed to survive the December 1938 under-secretaries' revolt, involving his junior Lord Strathcona, which had demanded his removal, but his doubling of the Territorial Army and support for peacetime conscription during 1939 further angered the military. The phoney war and problems of supplying the British expeditionary force, and particularly the 'pill-box affair', were too much for the senior generals and the Duke of Gloucester. Unprepared to tolerate any more they presented Chamberlain with an ultimatum. Belisha's successor to the War Office believed that he 'was sacked for his insolence to Gort and co. and that the mess he has made will take a lot [of] clearing up'.[120] Lieutenant-General Dill considered Hore-Belisha's passing to be good but felt the manner of his dismissal to be 'clumsy'. He expected it to be some time before the army would be able to recover from the havoc Belisha had wrought and thought it preposterous 'that a man with his record could ever have been instructed with a great department of state'. He suggested his correspondent read the 12 January edition of the journal *Truth*.[121] This was a venomous anti-semitic character assassination in a weekly journal that was secretly controlled by Joseph Ball, director of the CRD, on behalf of the party. Churchill, Eden and Hore-Belisha regularly suffered under the journalists' pen in *Truth*. But it was the latter who received the most extreme condemnation. He was regularly made the subject of jokes through their articles and poem feature. His dismissal provoked a satirical poem, 'Exodus from Whitehall' and the article 'Belisha is no loss'. Numerous copies of this particular issue were posted to prominent persons during the ensuing week, presumably to counter the support the ex-war minister had been receiving from large sections of the press. The article was again reprinted on 19 January, 'by popular demand', along with a further condemnation of the man.[122] Vansittart, who conducted an enquiry into the activities of *Truth* in 1941, concluded that the two articles represented 'a deliberate effort to kill Belisha once and for all as a political force'.[123] One joke circulating amongst Conservative backbenchers concerning Hore-Belisha was the story of Queen Mary asking King George 'Who is this Hore-Belisha?', to which the King replied 'My dear I've never heard of the woman'.[124] The newly acquired significance behind the joke becomes only apparent from the account of the resignation in Channon's diary, which revealed that King George had personally intervened and 'insisted' on Belisha's removal, perhaps being the 'extra pressure' Lieutenant-General Pownall alluded to in his own account of the dismissal.[125]

The cabinet reshuffle that followed failed to inspire confidence, at least among politicians. Oliver Stanley, son of Lord Derby, became Minister for War. Victor Cazalet understood that Stanley had been appointed 'to give [the] W[ar] O[ffice] a period of rest, and as Lord Derby's son it would please [the] French, not two very good reasons'.[126] Headlam, whilst not doubting Stanley's abilities, wondered whether he would be able 'to stand the strain of the W[ar] O[ffice] in war time – still more, whether he possesses the guts to become leader?'.[127] A similar view was held by Emrys-Evans, who considered it an 'astonishing appointment'. Stanley was 'a weak man,' and Evans could not 'help feeling that it is his weakness which has been his chief recommendation in the eyes of the PM. He has proven on so many occasions that he will not resign in the last resort'.[128] Even the usually sycophantic Channon felt it was a 'calamity' that 'a dry stick' like Stanley was taking the War Office.[129]

Nevertheless, Chamberlain gained confidence from dismissing Belisha and during the next month appeared to be at his best.[130] Several speeches to the House of Commons were well received. Although the collapse of the Finnish resistance in mid-February left the House feeling 'rather glum' with 'all the old Munich/Chamberlain doubts rampant again', Chamberlain asserted his leadership with a series of fighting speeches that improved the House's attitude.[131] All of which caused Euan Wallace to remark that parliament was 'really an extraordinarily volatile assembly'.[132]

All was to change during April. Initially, the cabinet reshuffle of that month was very poorly received.[133] Hoare went to the Air Ministry, Wood became Lord Privy Seal, Morrison took the Post Office, Hudson moved to Shipping, De La Warr was given the Office of Works and Shakespeare the Department of Overseas Trade. To Wolmer it was the 'last straw'.[134] It was not coincidental that the Watching Committee began meeting after this failed reshuffle. Chamberlain did not expect the changes to satisfy his critics, but believed that they were necessary for the smooth and efficient running of the government and that in time they would justify themselves.[135] This was followed by the reversals for the British expeditionary forces in Norway and their subsequent withdrawal as German forces overran yet another country. By early May, following the Norway evacuation and the announcement of a debate on the fiasco, it was 'clear that a serious political crisis was developing'.[136]

In the six weeks or so before the Norway debate it had been the AGM season for local associations, or at least those that had over-looked the request of Hacking and continued to function. On the public face, the associations continued to express their confidence in the government. For example, Leeds City association carried 'with acclamation', the day before the Norway debate, a resolution which expressed 'its complete confidence' in the government 'to defeat Nazi aggression'. But the resolution carried an additional sentence 'calling for the prosecution of the war with the utmost vigour', which implied a level of dissatisfaction.[137] Likewise, a month earlier, the Northern Areas council had adopted a resolution which recorded 'its complete confidence in the government to prosecute the war with the utmost vigour and determination until victory is attained and the liberty of the world secured'. This resolution had been proposed by their chairman Cuthbert Headlam, who throughout the period of the phoney war had been expressing increased concern about the govern-ment's handling of the war effort. Once again, this illustrates the ability of Conservatives to express disquiet in private whilst preserving a outward façade of loyalty.[138] That activists felt it necessary to carry resolutions of acclamation for the Prime Minister most probably indi-cated an awareness of the all-round criticism that was being made of the government. These were views that most certainly would have been communicated to local MPs. Indeed, Mass-Observation was noting the increased public dissatisfaction with the government, the Norway reversals having left people 'staggered'.[139]

THE NORWAY DEBATE

The Norway debate took place over two days and was to be the instru-ment that led to Chamberlain's fall from power. Attendance was very high, with many Members on active service gaining leave to return for the debate. The atmosphere was highly charged and 'uncomfortable', with 'even the strongest supporters of the government . . . doubtful about its survival'.[140] Chamberlain opened the debate and made no attempt to minimise the fact that the Norway evacuation had been a reverse. A few days previously Chamberlain had written to his sister setting out his thoughts. He believed that most of his domestic critics were enemies of the government in general [and of himself] in particular, and they will try and use every setback to weaken or if possible to destroy us. But then there are a lot of other critics, not malevolent at all, but merely not very intelligent and it should be possible to answer them effectively. I only wish I did have the answering, but I shall have to lead off.[141]

As the debate would show, Chamberlain's recognition of the significance of the governmental closing speeches was correct.

The debate reached fever pitch when Roger Keyes rose, dressed in naval uniform as Admiral of the Fleet, and in 'the most sensational episode' of the first day, attacked the government. He compared Trodheim to another Gallipoli and told the House that he had daily urged the Admiralty to allow him personally to lead the naval assault. Keyes was not the greatest of orators, but his speech made 'a considerable emotional appeal to the House' which one minister considered 'rather frightening on an occasion of this kind'.[142] Amery's speech was more significant for it openly attacked the government's war record. He argued that wars were 'won not by explanations after the event but by foresight, by clever decision and by swift action'. It was his belief that the government neither 'foresaw what Germany meant to do, [n]or came to a clear decision when it knew what Germany had done, or [had] acted swiftly or consistently throughout the whole lamentable affair'. If Trodheim had been an isolated incident of 'indecision, slowness and fear of taking risks' then it could be excused; however, it displayed similar traits to the Finnish campaign, to the government's wartime economic policies, to the retraining of workers and production of munitions, as well as the handling of agriculture. Recalling Cromwell's words when dismissing the Long Parliament, Amery declared: 'you have sat too long here for any good you have been doing. Depart, I say, and let us have done with you. In the name of God, go!'.[143] Oliver Stanley, the War Minister, was left to wind up for the government. His speech was continually interrupted by Members from all parties.[144] It was judged a bad performance, with the minister not being 'at ease at all'. Worryingly, it was 'idle to pretend that his speech convinced either the opposition, or, more still, the malcontents in our own party'.[145]

The outcome of the debate was by no means settled after the first day. Not all the Conservative speakers had attacked the government. Page-Croft had suggested that the situation had been artificially created by the press, without true reference to the facts. In the opinion of Archibald Southby, Norway had merely been a 'minor setback', and he had rounded on those who sought to destroy the government 'by means of intrigue', for it 'would be a great disservice to the allied cause which might well be irreparable'.[146] Whether such defences impressed other backbenchers was another matter. Margesson, the chief whip, felt that the government had put up a creditable performance under difficult circumstances, and appeared to feel that it would achieve a reasonable majority if forced to a division. By contrast, Macmillan was 'jubilant' at the likelihood of the government's demise.[147] Even so, when the Watching Committee met on the second morning shortly before the debate was to begin, its chairman Lord Salisbury was only prepared to suggest that in the event of a division Conservative critics should abstain. But as the debate reconvened it soon became apparent to Emrys-Evans that a substantial proportion of Conservative MPs, particularly those in the services, were intending to vote against the government. When the Service Members Committee met, all bar one indicated that they would be cross-voting whatever happened.[148]

Table 6.2 Known members of the Service Members committee[149]

Name	Constituency	Service
Anstruther-Gray, John	Lanarkshire North	Army
Cazalet, Victor (chairman)	Chippenham	Army
De Chair, Somerset	North West Norfolk	Army
Hogg, Quintin	Oxford City	Army
Keeling, Edward	Twickenham	RAF
Kerr, Hamilton (secretary)	Oldham	RAF
Medlicott, Frank	Norfolk East	Army
Profumo, John	Kettering	Army
Russell, Stuart	Darwen	Army
Taylor, Charles	Eastbourne	Territorials
Wise, Roy	Smethwick	Army
Wright, James	Erdington	RAF

Emrys-Evans now believed 'that the position had gone too far and that abstention was really impossible'. This view was communicated to Alec Dunglass, Chamberlain's PPS, when he tried to broach a compromise with Evans. Dunglass implied that Chamberlain was prepared to meet his critics, who could 'place any demands' they wished, with the suggestion that the Prime Minister was prepared drastically to reconstruct the government. Evans left Dunglass with no illusions. They were 'thoroughly dissatisfied' with the likes of Simon and Hoare, whilst Horace Wilson's 'intolerable interference in politics and his evil influence on policy' was too much. Evans also criticised the whips, believing they had adopted a 'disastrous' attitude. Nor was it felt that Chamberlain had 'the right temperament' to continue as head of a wartime government.[150] These were certainly not new complaints from Evans. In February he had lamented to the deputy whip, James Stuart, about the failure of the war cabinet to act with speed.[151] It was also clear that personality differences were influencing Evans. In early March he told Eden that certain cabinet ministers lacked both the 'imagination and dynamic energy' to ensure victory, and complained about the persistence of party politics:

> The whips are just as busy . . . They seemed to enjoy keep [sic] up antagonism against the Opposition, and indeed against those of us on our own side who have not seen eye to eye with them in the past.[152]

The problem was that these same sentiments were felt by Conservatives who normally could be relied upon as lobby fodder. Samuel Hammersley retrospectively explained in a letter to *The Times* that he had voted against the government because there had been a failure of the party system and that the leadership was 'not susceptible to the criticisms of its own supporters'.[153] Victor Cazalet, who reluctantly decided to vote with the government, was aware that the

> story of discontent against PM is a long one. It's partly the result of Margesson and whip hostility to all who voted against or criticised gov[ernmen]t at time of Munich. Anyone connected with Winston and Eden was condemned. There was general discontent v. war effort and particularly v. Sam Hoare and Simon.[154]

Roy Wise let it be known to one government loyalist that he intended to vote against the government as 'it was the only way to shock us out of our complacency', whilst Charles Taylor admitted he intended rebellion too.[155] At the suggestion of Dunglass, Cazalet and Wise reiterated all the criticisms to Chamberlain on the evening of 8 May.

They also explained why the Service Members rebelled: 'Gun position of AA Territorials in Norway never fired a shot. Medical services – all we wanted was more guns and ammunition. We had no personal quarrel with him, in fact we were his most loyal supporters'.[156]

It would appear from the previous displays of Conservative rebellion during the Chamberlain premiership that voting behaviour during any particular crisis was conditioned by the immediate circumstances. With the February 1938 Eden censure vote, those who defied the whips were moved by an identification with the policies and principles that Eden represented, whilst the vast majority of the party considered that an expression of loyalty to the Prime Minister was required. Likewise with the Munich votes, the euphoria of peace encouraged many to support the government despite the persistence of private doubts. The rebellion of Members in military service with the Norway division was linked with their relative youthfulness. In peacetime it had been the under-fifties who had been most inclined to question Chamberlain's foreign and defence policies and occasionally to give public expression to these doubts. But war service exposed these MPs to direct and compelling evidence of Britain's ineffectual war effort. Furthermore, active service removed these Members from the rarefied atmosphere of Westminster and the scrutiny of the whips, and placed them in situations whereby they were potentially expected to sacrifice their lives in defence of their country. Perhaps not surprisingly then, the normal bonds of loyalty were weakened.

The sense of crisis, even panic, gradually filtered through to the government. At one point on the second day Margesson was worried that the government would actually be defeated. This was probably reflected by the continual interruption of speakers in the opening half of the day's debate.[157] Channon refused to take a bet with Hamilton Kerr that a hundred of the government's supporters would rebel. Nevertheless, he agreed a five-pound bet with Mavis Tate that fifty would defy the whips.[158] Chamberlain bullishly fought on. But he made a crucial error when responding to Labour's calls for a division. In reply, Chamberlain made the division one of a motion of confidence which he believed his 'many friends' would assist him in defeating.[159] This was the final straw for many backbenchers. It suggested that Chamberlain was too concerned with party politics and personalities at a time when the gravity of the war situation demanded national unity. Duff Cooper rose to declare that

> in the three speeches that we have already heard from the front
> bench, there has not been the slightest admission that something is

fundamentally wrong with the machinery of government, that there is something rotten in the state.[160]

As the House divided, Channon and fellow loyalists shouted insults from the aye lobby at the rebels filing out of the opposition lobby.[161] When the result was announced, Chamberlain's normal majority of 281 had been reduced to 81. In the end forty-four Conservatives had cross-voted and sixty abstained. Although the majority of Conservative backbenchers had supported Chamberlain, the defection of over one hundred supporters was a very serious and humiliating reversal.

THE REPERCUSSIONS

The following day, news reached Britain that the German attack on western Europe had begun. Negotiations behind the scenes attempted to create a new coalition government. For a while Chamberlain appeared to harbour ideas of remaining in office, but when Labour rejected outright all offers of joining a coalition with him as leader, he resigned. Charles Waterhouse, a former whip, admitted Chamberlain had no course but resignation: 'he cannot stand the strain of war against half the world, two opposition parties and a considerable section of his own'.[162] Halifax, who had widely been seen as the possible successor, refused the job and Churchill became Prime Minister, although Chamberlain retained the party leadership. This he felt was 'essential, if Winston was to have whole-hearted support', as many Conservatives were wary of Churchill reflecting that perhaps they had been rather harsh on their leader.[163] Indeed, following Hitler's invasion of the Low Countries, the secretary to the 1922 Committee, Hely-Hutchinson, told Rab Butler, 'you must not underestimate the great reaction which has been caused among Conservative Members, among whom you will find over three-quarters are ready to put Chamberlain back'.[164] Indeed, the divisions and ill-feeling ran deep, as one of the rebels, Ronnie Tree, discovered. He had been due to be elected to the Royal Yacht Squadron the day after the Norway division, but was surprised to find himself blackballed. Apparently, it transpired that this was the 'childish revenge' of one of the whips who had been heard to say 'I'll cook Tree's chances'.[165] Chamberlain must have been gratified with the reaction he received on his return to the Commons for the first time following his downfall: whilst Churchill was 'greeted with some cheers [on Chamberlain's entry] MPs lost their heads; they shouted; they cheered; they waved their order papers, and his reception was a regular ovation'.[166] To some this was disquieting, and for about a month, some observers were concerned about divisions in the new Churchill administration, with some elements 'fighting war on two fronts, against Hitler and against enemies much nearer home'.[167] Nevertheless, the Conservative activists, acutely conscious of the need for national unity at such a grave time, fell in behind the new premier with pledges of loyalty.[168] This did not prevent some associations from rebuking their Members if they had rebelled.[169] Chamberlain later filed amongst his papers a memorandum from the party's general director to the chairman, which noted that

> there has been serious anxiety in the party with regard to the change of government and the utterances of our political opponents before and since the change took place. While members of our organisation are willing and anxious to give support to the new Prime Minister and his government, there is great resentment at the criticism of Mr Chamberlain and the other members of the previous government who have accepted office in the new administration.[170]

Nevertheless, by July it appeared that Churchill, 'the war leader' had won the confidence of both the Conservative party and the nation. As one Chamberlainite backbencher noted, with 'every week that passes, the more does one appreciate Winston's astonishing power and statesmanship. He keeps his team and the whole House together, in spirit as in fact'.[171]

SOME CONCLUSIONS

There was no inevitability about Chamberlain's fall from power. He was under no obligation constitutionally to resign after the Norway division for he had secured a majority vote. If the failed Norway expedition had been an isolated incident then it would have been unlikely to cause the fall of a government. Nevertheless, many Conservatives perceived it as yet another example of indecision, weakness and ineffectiveness. From the outbreak of war, Chamberlain appeared to act on the assumption that the National government would be able to continue running the country through a limited war, without major upheavals in the pre-war *status quo*. Major differences with the unions on the questions of wages, as inflation increased, and the severe shortages of skilled labour were left unresolved for months. When combined with the disgruntlement concerning the war cabinet and its personnel, and the supposed unwillingness of the government to take the war to Germany, these ingredients provided a molotov cocktail only requiring its fuse to be lit. The discontent that had been simmering beneath the surface since October 1939 spontaneously combusted in May 1940. War no longer required party politics but necessitated national unity – a realisation that had dawned upon many of the younger MPs, especially those on active service. It would appear that Chamberlain had failed to recognise the flammability of the situation. In part this was due to his character, with its combination of vanity and shyness. 'Ungregarious by nature', wrote Duff Cooper, Chamberlain 'never frequented the smoking room of the House of Commons, where Stanley Baldwin and Winston Churchill were familiar figures, often in the centre of groups which included political opponents'.[172] This failure to mix freely with his own backbenchers had by 1940 created the belief that the leadership was no longer receptive to criticisms. Chamberlain's own conservative conviction combined with his reserved nature tended to divorce him from many of the younger minds in the party whom he was inclined to dismiss as a disappearing lot. All this must have emphasised the generation gap within the party. Defeat also represented a failure in the whips' system, which left Chamberlain ignorant of the extent and intensity of dissatisfaction within the party. Many of those who were to rebel over the Norway vote were the foreign policy sceptics of the peace years and their fellow-travellers – their sense of national duty under the pressure of war meant they could no longer keep their criticisms private. The significance of the Norway vote lies in it being the only twentieth-century instance of a majority government being forced out of office by a House of Commons vote. But further it is an illustrative example of the temporary suspension of the shackles of loyalty. The younger MPs who rebelled felt unconstrained by normal obligations to the party whip. Such behaviour would have been inconceivable in peacetime. MPs on war service attended the Commons infrequently. This denied them the normal channels of communication through which to express concerns over a period of time and lobby for a particular issue. If an MP was only attending for one special debate then a public registration of protest must have been perceived to be a most profitable exercise. At one extreme there were some young Conservatives, like Richard Law and Ronald Cartland, who were so disillusioned with the state of the party that they were contemplating never returning to politics, which meant that the action of cross-voting or abstention and its expected censure carried no risks. Therefore, whilst the Norway debate is significant because it brought down a government, it perhaps should be viewed as an untypical example of the breakdown of a party system, but one which nevertheless carried important lessons for the future party leadership.

Conclusion

This study has been both an analysis of how the Conservative party responded to the deteriorating international situation from 1935 and a consideration of how the party sought to influence the responses of its leadership. It is apparent that contemporary Conservatives perceived both diplomacy and rearmament as the tandem mechanisms by which to respond to the dictators' increased belligerence. The fascist regimes were like a lintel being prevented from smashing down on the foundations of the British Empire by the twin pillars of diplomacy and rearmament. If one of these supports failed then the remaining one was expected to shoulder the entire burden. A strong defence programme would enable the government to negotiate, whilst if that negotiation languished, an adequately prepared defence scheme would repel the initial aerial assault and ultimately ensure military victory. The doubts about the ability of diplomacy to restrain the dictators became privately evident from September 1938. However, by the end of that year the party's concerns about defence were proving more divisive and potentially damaging than those concerning foreign affairs – purely because this debate was being conducted with greater publicity.

In theory, policy issues are decided by the leader and handed down to the party.[1] But this classical analysis of the party structure places too great a stress upon the written constitution. In reality, although the party is based largely upon deference, it is accepted that the evolution of policy is subject to unwritten constraints. The leader is reliant on the support and goodwill of the party, and as a consequence the attitudes and preferences of four sectors of the organisation have an input into policy formulation. The leader needs to carry the front bench if a particular policy is to be successfully advocated. The views of the wider parliamentary party need to be accounted for. If not, there is a risk of presenting an image of disunity to the electorate and of damaging the leader's prestige if a reversal is obliged. The party at large is not overlooked either. Activists are at the forefront of the electoral battle. At each general election the party's parliamentary candidates rely upon the grassroots to ensure reselection, to help canvass and fund-raise, and between elections guarantee the maintenance of the local organisation. The leadership cannot afford to ignore the rank and file. This had revealed itself in 1922 when the discontent in the constituencies clearly influenced the voting behaviour of the middle-ranking MPs in the infamous Carlton Club revolt.[2] The National Union is the final sector that must be accounted for. It is the mechanism that the constituencies can use to articulate their views. Its officers have regular and unpublicised contacts with the chairperson and leadership. Although essentially an advisory body that can only draw attention to problems, it would be a foolish leader who regularly ignored its advice.

Having taken the debates about foreign policy and defence as the chronology for this study, it becomes evident that the ability of these four sectors to influence ebbs and flows. The only discontinuity during the period was the changeover in leader between Baldwin and Chamberlain. This would suggest that the explanation can be found in the style of leadership. Opportunities will be exploited by each of the groupings identified above to improve their position. Baldwin's tenacity in holding onto the leadership despite concerted efforts to oust him was not in doubt.[3] But upon assuming the premiership in June 1935, his administration appeared imbued with a sense of drift. By nature a politician of consensus, his desire to occupy the middle political ground left him vulnerable to criticism from both left and right. As leader of a party so recently and so bitterly divided over the passage of the Indian reform act, Baldwin was anxious to heal the divisions, but this also made his government extremely sensitive to the shifting opinions of the parliamentary party. Backbenchers had been given an experience of influencing and had no intention of giving up their new-found status. Although the opportunities to influence as an individual backbencher were minimal, it was accepted that collectively the chances were much greater, and in the realm of foreign policy, the Foreign Affairs Committee was the vehicle. Its combination of senior figures – Austen Chamberlain, Leo Amery, Edward Winterton and Winston Churchill – and foreign policy specialists warranted the respect it was given by ministers and whips. Its role in the dismissal of Hoare in December 1935, when many MPs listening to the views of their activists decided to abandon the Foreign Secretary, and the fact that cabinet was regularly appraised of its views, indicated its influence. Essentially, the committee system enables the parliamentary party to define the parameters within which policy must fall and on occasion determine whether or not a particular policy is acceptable. From the perspective of the front bench, Baldwin's lack of interest in foreign affairs and the problems associated with defence led to questions being asked about his leadership qualities. The indecision experienced in cabinet over whether to abandon sanctions in 1936 evidently exasperated Chamberlain, whilst younger cabinet members saw opportunities to reflect the nation's moral sentiment with their decision not to accept the Hoare-Laval plan. Although it was frustrating, especially for Chamberlain who been patiently waiting as heir-apparent since 1931, there existed no formal mechanism to seek Baldwin's removal and all they could do was wait for his expected retirement.

When Chamberlain took over in May 1937 there was a determination not to repeat the mistakes of Baldwin. At the meeting formalising his adoption as leader, he had sounded a warning: 'No major point of policy can be decided, no real fateful step can be taken without the assent, either active or passive, of the Prime Minister'.[4] Indeed, Chamberlain had no intention of allowing his ministers to forge ahead unsupervised. They were told 'to be in the closest touch with him, to tell him their difficulties, to inform him not only about their immediate plans in their departments but what they were planning for the future'.[5] He further validated this declaration by taking the chair, from the start, of all the cabinet committees which had to make recommendations on matters of major domestic policy. In the aftermath of Eden's resignation, Chamberlain rationalised the views of his party and cabinet colleagues:

> there is no wish to have any other leader and the differences such as they are arise from the fact that a few colleagues always think first of my proposal not 'is this' right but 'how will this' affect the H[ouse] of C[ommons], or my constituents.[6]

Just prior to taking over the leadership Chamberlain had been warned of the potential of the parliamentary party to inflict a policy reversal. The furore over the National Defence Contribution tax indicated the necessity of carrying the support of the party. As a pragmatist, Chamberlain believed in his ability to solve obvious problems. This again was in contrast to Baldwin, who had felt that efforts to resolve issues merely diverted or weakened the forces that had caused the problem in the first place. It is evident that under Chamberlain the influence of the Foreign Affairs Committee waned. Circumstances and luck explain this in part. Austen Chamberlain was dead and Churchill isolated and discredited following his stance on the Abdication. The officers of the Committee did not carry the same political stature in the corridors of Westminster, despite being foreign policy specialists. The lack of influence was also very intentional. In the aftermath of Eden's resignation Chamberlain brought Winterton into the cabinet, which deprived the backbenches of a vocal and senior critic, but also the whips began taking a close interest in the affairs of the Committee. The events surrounding Hoare's resignation in 1935 had not been forgotten by Chamberlain. To ensure that the Committee could not provide a useful platform for Eden's supporters, the whips neutralised it by engineering the election of 'sound' backbenchers to the chair. Despite indicating in 1937 his desire to avoid overtly party political approaches to office, Chamberlain's premiership saw an escalation in party warfare. It was recognised that the more partisan the issue between the parties the greater the pressure on the disaffected within the party to conform. Chamberlain's distinctive leadership style dismissed opposition, personalised debate and stressed loyalty. His parliamentary majority, marshalled by Margesson, followed him stirred by appeals to their loyalty as well as to their fear of political ostracism.

The role of the National Union and constituency parties remained relatively constant between the two leaderships. Once the 1935 general election was over, the influence of activists upon their MP was considerably greater; but by late 1938, with thoughts turning towards a general election, MPs began seeking to broaden their appeal to the wider electorate in their constituency. During this period, with the two themes that particularly exercised the activists, colonies and national service, their views clearly influenced the leadership. The hostility to returning the mandates to Germany was consistently strong throughout the period 1936–8. The 1936 Margate conference particularly indicated the vexation felt. The platform found its own motion being overturned and amended in an atmosphere of considerable passion. This opposition was being marshalled by parliamentarians, and without this combination campaigns from the constituencies risk faltering. Again the parliamentarian/activist alliance was significant in the national service debate. This time the activists took the proactive role, forwarding motions up through the National Union and encouraging MPs to support the cause. That they increasingly did so during 1938 and because the debate was being publicly conducted illustrates that it was understood that 'national' issues could be discussed more openly. The debate reflected the party's concern about the position of

Britain's defences and especially against an aerial assault. The episode indicated that the activists could be responsible for initiating policy decisions.

Although activists could feel that their views were being accounted for, the style of Chamberlain's leadership deprived disaffected MPs of an opportunity to influence. With no effective platform to propagate their doubts, and lacking leaders, either willing or trusted, to direct their energies, the disaffected who grouped around Eden from September 1938 found they had little impact. Earlier in 1938 Churchill had sought to launch an extra-parliamentary campaign 'Midlothian'-style, urging rearmament, but it failed to capture the nation's imagination. If one distinguishes between the public façades and the private observations, it becomes clear that there was a far larger section of the party uneasy with the position *vis-à-vis* the dictators. These doubts first emerged in September 1938 and gained increased currency during the autumn of that year as the Nazi regime revealed its potential for brutality with *Kristallnacht*. The implication to be drawn from this is that had it not been for the constraints of public loyalty then Chamberlain might have been persuaded before March 1939 to pursue a different line in foreign policy. But no-one sought to provide a lead or to give a 'mid-summer of madness' speech as Chamberlain did to Baldwin in 1936. Indeed it can be argued that this belief in maintaining an image of public unanimity prevented a fuller debate about the wisdom of conciliating the dictators. From 1938 the sceptics increasingly emphasised the need to rescue the League of Nations, and when it was apparent that this had failed, they moved towards demanding 'collective' resistance to fascism (whereas the residuum of the party asserted the ability of other methods of securing peace). Both had the same aims, namely peace and international stability, but the means of securing this intent were disputed.

The need for unity was favoured by the constituencies, who responded in typical fashion to each of the crises with displays of solidarity. The local party chairperson plays an important role in the promotion of unity. It is a pivotal position, obliging them to act as an intermediary between the MP and the rest of the association. Providing the chairperson and MP respect each other then the chairperson acts as a form of buffer zone. This role was especially important if the Member was ever considered to have acted disloyally towards the leadership. The chairperson could be crucial in restraining the more vigorous censors. During the 1930s it would appear that the relationship between a Member and his association was undergoing a transformation. Disquiet was being expressed by both parties concerning the financial relationship between the two, and about the extent to which an MP felt able to assert the right for independence of action. The role associations played in censuring the activities of MPs who criticised the government's foreign and defence policies reveals the importance of the association's role in the party's structure. Loyalty at the grassroots tends to be at its most exuberant, and association executives assumed a role as second-line whips. The backlash against the Munich rebels in the constituencies revealed the activists' belief that a public façade of loyalty was crucial. It suggested that the grassroots were aware of the uneasiness within the party over post-Munich foreign policy, and that they considered the situation best quelled by demonstrations of party unity.

These demonstrations of loyalty, whilst providing the party with a useful electoral tool, have also perhaps restricted the party's development. Certainly, the media have always been keen to seize upon the slightest sign of dissension and portray it in terms often out of proportion. At the same time, the need to restrain criticisms prevents open debate on policy, and can cause the build-up of resentment. Images of loyalty often mean that the Conservative party is presented as a block of unwavering followers of the leader. Indeed, Chamberlain's critics within the party were apt to make such accusations.[7] Constructive criticisms made privately, through the party structure, have enabled members to communicate their concerns with the leadership. It is recognised that this private debate is more productive than public expositions of doubt, which usually provoke retribution and hostility from the whips' office and local associations.

Ultimately, Chamberlain's control of the party system backfired during the opening months of the war. During the years of peace there was no real doubt about Chamberlain's suitability as leader. Foreign and defence policies, though increasingly dominating people's attentions, were not the only areas of government policy. In domestic policies, the Chamberlain administration's achievements were considered sound. Certainly by 1939 Central Office (or more specifically the CRD) had detected a change in public opinion that desired a greater emphasis on domestic reforms.[8] This trend suggested that if the government expected to be returned convincingly at the next election then a revised domestic policy was required. It would only be in the atmosphere of war, when all aspects of life and governmental policy were subjugated to the war effort, that doubts about Chamberlain's leadership abilities arose. Although Conservatives are strong on the idea of pulling together in a crisis, a significant proportion of the party felt alienated from the decision making process by May 1940.

The impression that Chamberlain and his closest advisors were impervious to backbench expressions of concern persuaded a small but significant number that it was necessary to give the leadership a jolt. It was not the intention to bring down the government. For those Conservatives who had been foreign policy sceptics during the years of peace, Chamberlain's weaknesses were already apparent, and the lingering suspicion that Chamberlain was only half-hearted about his desire to pursue the war was not easily dispelled. The apparent inability of the government to adopt a positive and constructive approach to various areas of the war effort, especially the economy and agriculture, when combined with the reverses of Finland and Norway in early 1940, created an atmosphere of despondency. This was compounded by Chamberlain's personality and the personnel problems of his cabinet. Although one speaker suggested during the Norway debate that these problems, if true, would have been reflected in his constituency postbags and they were not, many Conservatives were not so convinced.[9] Public opinion polls suggested also that civilians had been shocked by the Norway reversals and were increasingly critical of the government's war prosecution and of Chamberlain in particular. A number of Conservatives such as J. P. L. Thomas, Victor Cazalet and Brendan Bracken, only gave their support to the government reluctantly, whilst crucially the younger MPs on leave from active service (who had been experiencing first-hand the equipment shortages and bureaucratic red tape) felt able to disregard the party's conventions on loyalty, and free either to abstain or cross-vote. Chamberlain feared that history, written by those who replaced him, would judge him harshly, and he was correct.[10] In the fifty years since Chamberlain resigned the seals of office, the reputation of appeasement, and the Conservatives' role in its propagation, has undergone a series of metamorphoses. Only in recent decades have historians been capable of a more dispassionate assessment.

Appendix I
Conservative groupings

EDEN/AMERY GROUP

Amery, Leo	Sparkbrook
Bower, Robert	Cleveland
Bracken, Brendan	Paddington (from September 1939)
Cartland, Ronald	King's Norton
Cranborne, Viscount	Dorset South
Crossley, Anthony	Stretford
Duff Cooper, Alfred	St George's
Duggan, Hulbert	Acton
Eden, Anthony	Warwick
Emrys-Evans, Paul	Derbyshire South
Gunston, Derrick	Thornbury
Herbert, Sidney	Westminster Abbey
Joel, Dudley	Dudley
Lancaster, C. G.	Fylde (from January 1939)
Law, Richard	Hull South West
Macmillan, Harold	Stockton
Macnamara, J. R. J.	Chelmsford
Nicolson, Harold	Leicester East
Patrick, Mark	Tavistock

Spears, Edward	Carlisle
Thomas, J. P. L.	Hereford
Tree, Ronald	Harborough
Wolmer, Viscount	Aldershot

FOREIGN POLICY SCEPTICS FELLOW-TRAVELLERS

Adams, Vyvyan	Leeds West
Atholl, Duchess of	Kinross
Makins, Ernest	Knutsford
McConnell, Joseph	Antrim
Neven-Spence, B.	Orkney
Ropner, Leonard	Barkston Ash
Stourton, J. J.	Salford South
Withers, J. J.	Cambridge University

CHURCHILL GROUP

Boothby, Robert	Aberdeenshire East
Bracken, Brendan	Paddington
Churchill, Winston	Epping
Keyes, Roger	Portsmouth North
Macmillan, Harold	Stockton
Sandys, Duncan	Norwood

Lords

Cecil

Lloyd

Horne

CONSERVATIVE MEMBERS OF ANGLO-GERMAN FELLOWSHIP, 1936–7

Sandeman Allen, J.	West Birkenhead
Agnew, Peter	Camborne
Astor, W. W.	East Fulham
Bird, Robert	West Wolverhampton
Bower, Robert	Cleveland
Gower, Robert	Gillingham
Guiness, Loel	Bath
Haslam, H. C.	Horncastle
Hulbert, Norman	Stockport
James, A. W. H.	Wellingborough
Knox, Alfred	Wycombe
Mason, G. K. M.	North Croydon
Moore, Thomas	Ayr Burghs
Pownall, Assheton	East Lewisham
Rayner, Ralph	Totnes
Russell, Alexander	Tynemouth
Russell, Stuart	Darwen
Sanderson, Frank	Ealing
Smith, Louis	Sheffield Hallam
Stourton, J. J.	South Salford
Sueter, Murray	Hertford
Wickham, Edward	Taunton

Lords

Barnby

Decies

Eltisley

McGowan

Mount Temple

Earls

Galloway

Glasgow

Harrowby

Malmesbury

Marquess of Londonderry

Viscounts

Massereene

Ferrard

SUPPORTERS OF FRANCO

Balfour, George	Hampstead
Cazalet, Victor[b]	Chippenham
Channon, Henry 'Chips'	Southend
Crossley, A. C.	Streford
Denville, Alfred[b]	Newcastle Central
Donner, Patrick	Basingstoke
Emmott, Charles	Surrey East
Grant-Ferris, R.	St Pancras North
Hannon, Patrick	Moseley
Dunglass, Alex[a]	Lanark
James, A. W. H.	Wellingborough
Kerr, Charles[a]	Montrose Burghs
Knox, Alfred	Wycombe
Lennox-Boyd, Alan	Mid-Bedfordshire

McEwen, John[a]	Harwick and Haddington
Page-Croft, Henry[b]	Bournemouth
Ramsay, Archibald[a]	Peebles
Stewart-Sandeman, Nairne[b]	Middleton and Prestwich
Wilson, Arnold	Hitchin
Wolmer, Viscount[a]	Aldershot

NOTE

a   Member of United Christian Front
b   Member of Committee of Friends of Nationalist Spain

APPENDIX II:
RELATIONS BETWEEN FOREIGN POLICY SCEPTICS AND LOCAL PARTIES AND THEIR VOTING RECORD

Table A.2 Relations between foreign policy sceptics and local parties and their voting

Sceptic	Problems with local party (1)	MP opposed (by vote or abstention) to 1938 votes on foreign policy						Member Readopted by local party for 1945 and outcome
		Eden Vote[a]	4 April[b]	Munich Opp[c]	Govt[d]	Anglo-Italian Ratification[e]	19 Dec. Vote of Confidence[f]	
EDENITES								
Adams, Vyvyan	**	*	*	*	*	*	*	*Dft
Amery, Leo	—	—	—	*	*	—	—	*Dft
Bower, Robert		—	—	*	*	—	—	*Dft
Cartland, Ronald	***	—	—	*	*	*	*	Died
Cranborne, Robert	**	*	—	*	*	*	*	HofL
Crossley, Anthony	**	—	—	*	*	—	*	Died
Duff Cooper, Alfred	***	—	—	*	*	—	*	Rtd
Duggan, Hubert		*	—	*	*	*	*	Died
Eden, Anthony	—	*	—	*	*	*	—	*Rtn
Emrys-Evans, Paul	**	*	—	*	*	*	—	*Dft
Gunston, Derek		—	—	*	*	—	—	*Dft
Herbert, Sidney		*	*	*	*	—	—	Died
Joel, Dudley		*	—	*	*	*	*	Died
Kerr, Hamilton		*	—	*	*	—	—	*Dft
Law, Richard	**	—	—	*	*	*	*	*Dft
Macnamara, J.R.J.	*	*	—	—	—	—	—	Died
Patrick, Mark	*	*	—	—	—	—	—	Died
Ropner, Leonard		*	—	*	*	*	*	*Rtn
Thomas, J.P.L.	**	*	*	*	*	*	*	*Rtn
Tree, Ronald	**	*	—	—	—	—	*	*Dft
CHURCHILL GROUPIES								
Atholl, duchess of	***	*	*	A	A	A	CH	DS, 1938
Boothby, Robert	*	—	*	—	*	*	—	*Rtn
Bracken, Brendan		*	—	*	*	*	*	*Dft
Churchill, Winston	***	*	*	*	*	*	*	*Rtn
Keyes, Roger		*	—	*	*	—	*	Rtd
Macmillan, Harold	—	*	—	*	*	*	*	*Dft
Sandys, Duncan	**	—	*	*	*	*	—	*Dft
Spears, Edward		*	—	*	*	*	*	*Dft
Wolmer, Viscount	***	—	—	*	*	—	—	HofL

Notes:

Col. (1) problems with local party: * = minor ** = moderate to serious *** = major —- = none blank = not known

*Dft – selected but defeated in election

*Rtn – selected and returned in election

HofL – elevated to House of Lords Rtd.– retired from politics d. Munich votes, government motion, 6 October 1938

Died – died in advance of election

DS – deselected

CH – applied to Chiltern Hundreds to resign seat and fight by-election

A – absent with leave from division

—- – supported government in division

* – abstained, or voted against, government in division

a. Opposition vote of censure, 22 February 1938 following Eden's resignation

b. Vote of confidence over foreign policy, 4 April 1938

c. Munich votes, Opposition motion, 6 October 1938

d. Munich votes, Government motion, 6 October 1938

e. Vote to ratify Anglo-Italian agreement, 2 November 1938

f. Vote of confidence over foreign policy, 19 December 1938

Notes

INTRODUCTION

1 *Hansard: House of Commons Debates*, vol. 350, col. 297, 3 Sept. 1939.
2 Chamberlain MSS: Neville to Hilda Chamberlain, 15 Oct. 1939, NC18/1/1125; diary, 10 Sept. 1939, NC2/26. The Chamberlain papers are cited with the permission of Dr B. S. Benedikz, Birmingham University Library. Neville to Archbishop of Canterbury, 5 Sept. 1939, cited K. Feiling, *The Life of Neville Chamberlain*, London, Macmillan, 1946, 419.
3 A Conservative is taken to mean an identifiable member of that political party, whether they are a member of a constituency association in the localities, a Member of Parliament sitting on the backbenches or a serving minister in the National government. During this period the party's official title was the Conservative and Unionist party, but for the purposes of simplicity and continuity the term Conservative shall be used throughout this work.
4 See D. C. Watt, 'The historiography of appeasement', in C. Cook and A. Sked (eds) *Crisis and Controversy: Essays in Honour of A. J. P. Taylor*, London, Macmillan, 1976, 110–29.
5 *Daily Telegraph*, 28 May 1992, for when Major signed an Anglo-Czech treaty nullifying the Munich agreement; B. Ingham, *Kill The Messenger*, London, Harper Collins, 1991, 271, for Thatcher's apology to the Czechs in 1990. Douglas Hurd, following the Iraqi seizure of Kuwait in 1990, echoed the populist belief that appeasing aggressors only encouraged further outrages: *Daily Telegraph*, 14 Jan. 1991, 'Why Iraq's challenge has to be crushed'.
6 Cato, *Guilty Men*, London, Gollancz, 1940.
7 W. N. Medlicott, *British Foreign Policy since Versailles, 1919–63*, London, Methuen, 1967, xix.
8 P. M. Kennedy, 'The tradition of appeasement in British foreign policy, 1895–1939', *British Journal of International Studies*, 2, 3 (1976), 195–215; P. W. Schroeder, 'Munich and the British tradition', *Historical Journal*, 19, 1 (1976), 223–43.
9 K. Robbins, *Appeasement*, Oxford, Blackwell, 1991, 8. See P. Kennedy,

The Realities Behind Diplomacy, London, Fontana pbk edn, 1981, chapters 5 and 6 *passim* for further expansion.

10 R. A. C. Parker, *Chamberlain and Appeasement: British Policy and the Coming of the Second World War*, London, Macmillan, 1993, 345.

11 H. Kissinger, *Diplomacy*, London, Simon and Schuster, 1994, 312.

12 N. Henderson, *Water Under The Bridges*, London, Hodder and Stoughton, 1945, 49.

13 Q. Hogg, *The Left Was Never Right*, London, Faber, 1945.

14 J. W. Wheeler-Bennett, *Munich, Prologue to Tragedy*, London, Macmillan, 1948; M. Gilbert and R. Gott, *The Appeasers*, London, Weidenfeld and Nicolson, 1962; Richard Lamb, *The Drift to War, 1922–39*, London, Bloomsbury, 1989.

15 For the revisionists, see for example W. N. Medlicott, *Britain and Germany: The Search for Agreement, 1933–7*, London, Athlone Press, 1969; D. C. Watt, *How War Came: The Immediate Origins of the Second World War*, London, Heinemann, 1989; K. Middlemas, *Diplomacy of Illusion: The British Government and Germany, 1937–9*, London, Weidenfeld and Nicolson, 1972.

16 For example I. Colvin, *The Chamberlain Cabinet*, London, Gollancz, 1971.

17 For example: J. Harvey (ed.) *The Diplomatic Diaries of Oliver Harvey, 1937–9*, London, Collins, 1970; R. R. James (ed.) *Chips: The Diaries of Sir Henry Channon*, London, Weidenfeld and Nicolson, 1967; K. Young (ed.) *The Diaries of Sir Robert Bruce Lockhart*, London, Macmillan, 1973; N. Nicolson (ed.) *The Diaries and Letters of Harold Nicolson*, London, Collins, 1966; Lord Birkenhead, *Halifax: The Life of Lord Halifax*, London, Hamish Hamilton, 1965; R. J. Minney (ed.) *The Private Papers of Hore-Belisha*, London, Collins, 1960.

18 G. C. Peden, *British Rearmament and the Treasury, 1932–9*, Edinburgh, Scottish Academic Press, 1984; R. P. Shay, *British Rearmament in the Thirties: Politics and Profits*, Princeton NJ, Princeton University Press, 1977; G. Post Jnr, *Dilemmas of Appeasement: British Deterrence and Defence, 1934–7*, Cornell, Cornell University Press, 1993; R. A. C. Parker, 'British rearmament, 1936–9: treasury, trade unions and skilled labour', *English Historical Review*, 96, 2 1981, 306–43; B. Bond, *British Military Policy between the Two World Wars*, Oxford, Clarendon Press, 1980; U. Bialer, *Shadow of the Bomber: The Fear of Air Attack and British Politics*, London, Royal Historical Society, 1980; M. Smith, *British Air Strategy Between the Wars*, Oxford, Clarendon Press, 1984; A. Adamthwaite, *France and the Coming of the Second World War*, London, Frank Cass, 1977; R. Young, *In Command of France: French Foreign Policy and Military Planning, 1933–40*, Cambridge MA, Harvard University Press, 1978; W. Wark, *The Ultimate Enemy: British Intelligence and Nazi Germany, 1933–9*, Oxford, Oxford University Press, 1986; S. Roskill, *Naval Policy Between the Wars, 1930–9*, vol. 2, London, Collins, 1976; C. Andrew, *The Secret Service: The Making of the British Intelligence Community*, London, Heinemann, 1986.

19 J. Charmley, *Chamberlain and the Lost Peace*, London, Hodder and Stoughton, 1989; Parker, *Chamberlain*; Eden: D. Carlton, *Anthony Eden: A Political Biography*, London, Allen Lane, 1981; R. R. James, *Anthony*

Eden, London, Weidenfeld and Nicolson, 1986; A. R. Peters, *Anthony Eden at the Foreign Office*, Aldershot, Gower, 1986; D. Dutton, *Anthony Eden: A Life and Reputation*, London, Arnold, 1996; Churchill: P. Addison, *Churchill on the Home Front*, London, Cape, 1992; J. Charmley, *Churchill: The End of Glory*, London, Hodder and Stoughton, 1993; C. Ponting, *Churchill*, London, Sinclair-Stevenson, 1994; M. Gilbert, *Churchill: A Life*, London, Heinemann, 1991; Halifax: A. Roberts, *The Holy Fox*, London, Weidenfeld and Nicolson, 1991; Simon: D. Dutton, *Simon: A Political Biography*, London, Aurum Press, 1992; N. Thompson, *The Anti-Appeasers: Conservative Opposition to Appeasement in the 1930s*, Oxford, Oxford University Press, 1971; M. Cowling, *The Impact of Hitler: British Politics and British Policy, 1933–40*, Cambridge, Cambridge University Press, 1975.

20 W. Churchill, *The Second World War: The Gathering Storm*, London, Cassell, 1948.

21 J. S. Rasmussen, 'Party discipline in war-time: the downfall of the Chamberlain government', *Journal of Politics*, 32, 2 1970, 379–406; K. Jeffreys, 'May 1940: the downfall of Neville Chamberlain', *Parliamentary History*, 10, 2 1991, 363–78.

22 P. Addison, *The Road to 1945: British Politics and the Second World War*, London, Cape, 1975.

23 B. Harrison, *Separate Spheres*, London, Croom Helm, 1978.

24 J. Ramsden, *The Making of Conservative Party Policy: The Conservative Research Department since 1929*, London, Longman, 1980, 3.

25 A detailed listing of the location of pre-1945 constituency records can be obtained from Stuart Ball, Department of History, University of Leicester.

26 J. Ramsden, *Balfour and Baldwin*, London, Longman, 1978. This volume was a contribution to the Longmans history of the Conservative party. In recent years, Ramsden has completed two volumes using the same methodological approach on the post-1940 period, taking the history up to 1975. J. Ramsden, *The Age of Churchilll and Eden*, London, Longman, 1995; J. Ramsden, *The Winds of Change: Macmillan to Heath*, London, Longman, 1996.

27 S. Ball, *Baldwin and the Conservative Party*, London, Yale University Press, 1988.

28 D. Tanner, *Political Change and the Labour Party, 1900–18*, Cambridge, Cambridge University Press, 1990.

29 For an excellent bibliography of writing on the party see S. Ball, 'The Conservative party since 1900: a bibliography', in A. Seldon and S. Ball (eds) *Conservative Century*, Oxford, Oxford University Press, 1994, 727–72.

30 For example: R. N. Kelly, *Conservative Party Conferences: The Hidden System*, Manchester, Manchester University Press, 1989; S. Ball, 'The 1922 committee: the formative years, 1922–45', *Parliamentary History*, 9, 1 1990, 129–57; P. Norton, 'Parliamentary party and party committees', and J. Barnes and R. Cockett, 'The making of party policy', in A. Seldon and S. Ball (eds) *Conservative Century*, Oxford, Oxford University Press, 1994, 97–145, 347–82; J. Ramsden, *Conservative Party Policy*; J. Fisher, 'Party finance' in P. Norton (ed.) *The Conservative Party*, London,

Prentice Hall/Harvester Wheatsheaf, 1996, 157–69; M. Pinto-Duschinsky, *British Political Finance, 1830–1980*, Washington, American Enterprise Institute, 1982; P. Norton, *Conservative Dissidents: Dissent within the Parliamentary Conservative Party, 1970–4*, London, Temple Smith, 1978; R. J. Jackson, *Rebels and Whips: Dissension and Cohesion in British Political Parties since 1945*, London, Macmillan, 1968; P. Whiteley, P. Seyd and J. Richardson, *True Blues: The Politics of Conservative Party Membership*, Oxford, Oxford University Press, 1994.

31 R. Williams, *Defending the Empire: The Conservative Party and British Defence Policy, 1899–1915*, London, Yale University Press, 1991; R. J. Q. Adams and P. Poirier, *The Conscription Controversy in Britain, 1900–1918*, London, Macmillan, 1987.

32 Ball, *Baldwin, passim*.

33 See S. Ball, 'Local Conservatism and the evolution of the party organisation', in A. Seldon and S. Ball, *Conservative Century*, Oxford, Oxford University Press, 1994, 261–311.

34 For further analysis of the party organisation see: R. T. McKenzie, *British Political Parties: The Distribution of Power within the Conservative and Labour Parties*, London, Heinemann, 1963, 21–60, 188–253; Ramsden, *Conservative Party Policy*; A. M. Potter, 'The English Conservative constituency association', *The Western Political Quarterly*, 9, 2 1956, 363–75.

35 McKenzie, *British Political Parties*.

36 J. Barnes and D. Nicholson (eds) *The Empire at Bay: The Leo Amery Diaries, 1929–45*, London, Hutchinson, 1988, 10 Nov., 15 Nov. 1937, 452; Cilcennin MSS: account of debate of [Conservative] foreign affairs committee (incomplete), n.d. [?March 1938], (Victor Raikes), Cilc. coll. 52.

37 P. Dennis, *Decision by Default: Peacetime Conscription and British Defence, 1919–39*, London, Routledge and Kegan Paul, 1972, 106; Headlam MSS: Lt Gen. John Dill to Cuthbert Headlam, 24 Mar. 1937, D/He/135/72.

38 Avon MSS: correspondence between Eden and Dawson, 16–20 June 1937, AP13/1/52–52H; Eden to Philip Dawson, 16 June 1937, AP13/1/52A.

39 For example, A. Crozier, *Appeasement and Germany's Last Bid for Colonies*, London, Macmillan, 1987, 225. Peters, *Anthony Eden*, 285–95, suggests the rift had emerged between August and September 1937 over Chamberlain's attempts to restart talks with the Italians.

40 Headlam MSS: diary, 7 Sept., 12 Sept. 1937, D/He/33; Avon MSS: Kenneth Chance to Eden, 5 Feb. 1937, AP13/1/51T.

41 See Amery's and Page-Croft's letters to *The Times*, 22 Dec. 1936, 18 Oct. 1937; C[onservative] P[arty] A[rchive], M[icro] F[iche] A[rchive], National Union, exec. 10 Mar. 1937, card 56.

42 *Documents on British Foreign Policy*, II, XVI, appendix 3: Plymouth Report, 9 June 1936, paras 46, 165.

43 Parker, *Chamberlain*, 74.

44 For historical analysis of Eden's resignation see N. Rose, 'The resignation of Anthony Eden', *Historical Journal*, 25, 4 1982, 911–31; R. Douglas, 'Chamberlain and Eden', *Journal of Contemporary History*, 13, 1 1978, 97–116; Parker, *Chamberlain*, 93–123; Peters, *Anthony Eden*, 321–57.

45 *Hansard*, vol. 333, cols 1399–1413, 24 Mar. 1938.
46 Parker, *Chamberlain*, 137.
47 *Documents on British Foreign Policy*, 3rd series, I 349, 26–7 May 1938, 403–12.
48 Caldecote MSS: Inskip diary, 8, 14 Sept. 1938; Winterton MSS: diary, 14 Sept. 1938, 1/43; Cab. 23/95, 38(38), 14 Sept. 1938.
49 Headlam MSS: diary, 11 Jan. 1939; For historical analysis of the visit see P. Stafford, 'The Chamberlain-Halifax visit to Rome: a reappraisal', *English Historical Review*, 158, 1 1983, 61–100.
50 See S. Newman, *March 1939: The British Guarantee to Poland*, Oxford, Clarendon Press, 1976; A. Prazmowska, *Britain, Poland and the Eastern Front, 1939*, Cambridge, Cambridge University Press, 1987.
51 Beamish MSS: autobiographical notes, 2 Sept. 1939, BEAM3/3.

CHAPTER 1

1 A. Duff Cooper, *Old Men Forget*, London, Hart Davis, 1953, 180–82; R. R. James (ed.) *Chips: The Diaries of Sir Henry Channon*, London, Weidenfeld and Nicolson, 1967, 4 Aug.–20 Sept. 1936, 105–13; S. de Chair, *Morning Glory: Memoirs from the Edge of History*, London, Cassell, 1954, 41–4; S[cottish] C[onservative Party] A[rchive], Scottish Junior Unionist League, central council, 20 Nov. 1937, 26 Mar. 1938, Acc. 10424/91.
2 Avon MSS, Kenneth Chance to Eden, 5 Feb. 1937, AP13/1/51T.
3 Altrincham MSS, Col. Fitzgerald to Edward Grigg, 25 Sept. 1938, MS/Film 1005, Reel #7.
4 J. Barnes and D. Nicholson (eds) *The Empire At Bay: The Leo Amery Diaries, 1928–45*, London, Hutchinson, 1988, 11 Apr. 1938, 501.
5 For example: J. B. C. Grundy, *The Second Brush Up Your German*, London, Dent, 1939.
6 Headlam MSS, diary, 5, 10, 12 Sept. 1937, D/He/33.
7 R. R. James, *Victor Cazalet: A Portrait*, London, Hamish Hamilton, 1976, 182–3.
8 Cazalet MSS, journal, 4 Aug. 1937, D/He/33.
9 Cazalet MSS, journal, 22 Apr. 1938, 18, 20 Mar., 29 Apr.–1 May 1939; Headlam MSS, diary, 3, 18 Feb., 24 Mar., 15 May 1939, D/He/35.
10 P. Meehan, *The Unnecessary War: Whitehall and the German Resistance to Hitler*, London, Sinclair-Stevenson, 1992, 3–7.
11 Avon MSS, Cranborne to Eden, 29 Oct. 1938, AP14/1/721; Heneage MSS, Heneage to J. M. Lill, 12 Oct. 1938, HNC1/L; Clitheroe C[onservative] A[ssocation], AGM 3 Mar. 1938, DDX800/1/3; *Birmingham Post*, 29 April 1938, Lennox-Boyd addressing Birmingham Conservative women; Lord Londonderry, *Ourselves and Germany*, London, Robert Hale, 1938, 168–9.
12 See G. T. Waddington, ' "An idyllic and unruffled atmosphere of complete Anglo-German misunderstanding": aspects of the operations of the Dienststelle Ribbentrop in Great Britain, 1934–8', *History* 82, 256 (1997), 44–72.
13 N. Smart (ed.) *The Diaries and Letters of Robert Bernays*, Lampeter,

Edwin Mellen Press, 1996, 19 May 1934, 138–9. In his memoirs Tree overlooks his audience with Hitler which is typical of these lively but selective reminiscences, R. Tree *When The Moon Was High: Memoirs of Peace and War*, London, Macmillan, 1975, 57–9.

14 G. C. Webber, 'Patterns of membership for the British Union of Fascists', *Journal of Contemporary History*, 19, 4 (1984), 575–606.

15 A. Wilson, *Walks and Talks Abroad: The Diary of a Member of Parliament in 1934–6*, London, Oxford University Press, 1936, 191–200; James, *Cazalet*, 182–3; Headlam MSS, diary, 7, 11 Sept. 1937, D/He/33.

16 J. Charmley, *Duff Cooper: The Authorized Biography*, London, Macmillan, 1986, 74–5; James, *Chips*, 4 Aug.–20 Sept. 1936, 105–13.

17 Wilson, *Walks and Talks Abroad*, 280–1.

18 C[onservative] P[arty] A[rchive], 1922 Committee, 24 Feb. 1936, CPA/1922CMMTEE.

19 Charmley, *Duff Cooper*, 74–6.

20 One example was Arnold Wilson, who despite his age of fifty-eight secured an active service duty with the RAF as a tail gunner only to be killled on 31 May 1940 during the Dunkirk evacuation.

21 For example, Ronald Tree following visit to Berlin in 1934, Tree, *Memoirs*, 56.

22 CPA, 1922 Committee, 24 June, 8 July 1935, 24 Feb., 27 Apr., 25 May, 27 July 1936, CPA/1922CMMTTE.

23 Waddington, 'Dienststelle Ribbentrop', 59; Tree, *Memoirs*, 56.

24 S. Haxey, *Tory MP*, London, Left Book Club/Gollancz, 1939, 209.

25 *Hansard: House of Commons Debates*, vol. 346, col. 356 (Mander), 19 Apr. 1939; col. 502 (Adams), 20 Apr. 1939; cols 787–8 (Adams), 24 Apr. 1939; vol. 346, col. 357 (Pownall), 19 Apr. 1939.

26 Ashley MSS, Anglo-German Fellowship files, 1935–8, BR81/1, BR81/9.

27 Ashley MSS, Nevile Henderson to Mount-Temple, 1937–9. Letter cited 9 Mar. 1938, BR72/6; *The Times*, 26 Feb. 1938.

28 For a list of Conservative members of the Anglo-German Fellowship see Appendix 1.

29 S. Ball, *Baldwin and the Conservative Party*, London, Yale University Press, 1988, 210, 224–5. *The Times* was the newspaper predominately read by the upper strata of British society which would include not only MPs but also the leading figures in constituency associations.

30 Winchester CA, exec. 26 May 1937, 73M86W/5.

31 R. Cockett, *Twilight of Truth: Chamberlain, Appeasement and the Manipulation of the Press*, London, Weidenfeld and Nicolson, 1989, 122.

32 F. R. Gannon, *The British Press and Germany, 1936–9*, Oxford, Clarendon Press, 1971, 36–7; For circulation figures of papers see Cockett, *Twilight of Truth*, 25; and for the social class and readership of the papers see S. Ball, *Baldwin*, 224–5.

33 Waddington, 'Dienststelle Ribbentrop', 54.

34 *The Times*, 12 Oct. 1938. In fact Mount-Temple had been warned to avoid associating with the Link by the secretary of the Anglo-German Fellowship on the grounds that it was indiscriminate and its members without standing and influence. Ashley MSS, T. Conwell-Evans to Mount-Temple, 18 Jan. 1938, BR81/9.

35 R. A. C. Parker, *Chamberlain and Appeasement*, London, Macmillan, 1993, 3.

36 I. McLaine, *Ministry of Morale: Home Front Morale and the Ministry of Information in World War Two*, London, Allen & Unwin, 1979, 156. For the anti-German culture movement of the 1914–18 war see S. Hynes, *A War Imagined: The First World War and English Culture*, London, Bodley Head, 1990, 67–78; also for more on Anglo-Germanic cultural links see J. Mander, *Our German Cousins: Anglo-German Relations in the 19th and 20th Centuries*, London, John Murray, 1974; and P. Kennedy, *The Rise of Anglo-German Antagonism, 1860–1914*, London, Allen and Unwin, 1980, 109–23, 389–400.

37 J. A. Ramsden, *The Age of Balfour and Baldwin*, London, Longman, 1978, x, notes a survey of Conservative MPs carried out in 1976 on reading matter: few admitted to being influenced by the books they read, although those that did agreed that it was history and biography (rather than philosophy) that guided their thinking.

38 Parker, *Chamberlain*, 8.

39 Chamberlain MSS, Neville to Ida, 11 Sept. 1938, NC18/1/1068.

40 S. H. Roberts, *The House That Hitler Built*, London, Methuen, 1937.

41 J. Harvey (ed.) *The Diplomatic Diaries of Oliver Harvey*, London, Collins, 1970, 31 Jan. 1938, 80–1; Avon, *The Eden Memoirs: Facing the Dictators*, London, Cassell, 1962, 570–1.

42 Chamberlain MSS, Neville to Hilda, 30 Jan. 1938, NC18/1/1037.

43 Headlam MSS, diary, 11 Feb. 1938, D/He/34.

44 Headlam MSS, diary, 1 Oct. 1938, D/He/34.

45 Cooper, *Old Men Forget*, 230; He developed this theme during his resignation speech to the House of Commons in Oct. 1938, *Hansard*, vol. 339, cols 29–40, 3 Oct. 1938.

46 James, *Chips*, 1 Aug., 8 Nov. 1936, 73, 78; Cazalet MSS, journal, Jan. 1939.

47 S. Hetherington, *Katharine Atholl, 1874–1960: Against the Tide*, Aberdeen, Aberdeen University Press, 1989, 169–70; S. Ball, 'The politics of appeasement: the fall of the Duchess of Atholl and the Kinross and West Perth by-election', *Scottish Historical Review*, 1990, vol. LXIX, 56.

48 Barnes and Nicholson, *Amery Diaries*, 14 May 1934, 380.

49 De Chair, *Morning Glory*, 41.

50 Brooks MSS, journal 25–6 Jan. 1936.

51 Chelmsford CA, AGM 20 Mar. 1939, D/Z96/4.

52 Ruggles-Brise MSS, *East Anglian Daily Times*, 27 Jan. 1939 – Ruggles-Brise: 'Germany was the disturber of the peace with her armed might in 1914, and today she was even more so'. Not all Conservatives accepted Germany's 'war guilt'. C. T. Culverwell during the Munich debate expressed his lack of belief in German 'war guilt', *Hansard*, vol. 339, cols 106–7, 3 Oct. 1938.

53 Birmingham CA, central council, 24 Mar. 1935, AQ329.94249CON f. 40.

54 Headlam MSS, diary, 16 Apr. 1939, D/He/35.

55 *The Scotsman*, 6 Oct. 1938, 'Viscount Traprain: views on European situation'.

56 *Hansard*, vol. 321, col. 634, 4 Mar. 1937.

57 South Oxfordshire CA, AGM 18 June 1938, S.Oxon.Con.I/3.

58 *Hansard*, vol. 305, col. 58 (Winterton), 22 Oct. 1935.
59 Smart, *Bernays Diaries*, 19 May 1934, 140; Tree, *Memoirs*, 57.
60 *Labour Party Conference Report*, 1936, 203.
61 For a summary of what each of the main newspapers reported about the *Anschluss* see Gannon, *British Press*, 149–65. Not all Conservatives felt able to accept the reports of German brutality immediately. The 'fraterniser' Lambert Ward questioned the authenticity of such reports in parliament. *Hansard*, vol. 333, cols 133–6, 14 Mar. 1938.
62 *Hansard*, vol. 333, col. 73, 14 Mar. 1938; Headlam MSS, diary, 24 Mar. 1938, D/He/34.
63 Makins MSS, diary, 28 Nov. 1938.
64 G. Alderman, *The Jewish Community in British Politics*, Oxford, Clarendon Press, 1983, 120.
65 Belisha's fall from power is considered in greater detail in Chapter 6.
66 James, *Chips*, 15 Sept., 15, 21 Nov. 1938, 166, 177–8.
67 Chamberlain MSS, Neville to Ida, 13 Nov. 1938, NC18/1/1076; Neville to Ida, 30 July 1939, NC18/1/1110.
68 Headlam MSS, diaries, 13, 14 Nov. 1938, 29 Apr., 30 July 1939, D/He/34–5.
69 *Hansard*, vol. 304, cols 953–7, 16 July 1935; vol. 314, col. 1629, 10 July 1936.
70 A. Wilson *Thoughts and Talks, 1935–7: The Diary of a Member of Parliament*, London, Longmans, 1938, 213.
71 Cazalet MSS, journal, 25 Nov. 1938; *The Times*, 6 May 1938.
72 *The Times*, 19 Nov. 1938.
73 Ashley MSS, R. C. Reginald Mills to Mount-Temple, 21 Nov. 1938, BR81/9.
74 Chelmsford CA, women's council, 22 Nov. 1938, D/Z96/13.
75 *The Times*, 15 Nov. 1938.
76 L. London, 'British reactions to the Jewish flight from Europe', in P. Catterall (ed.) *Britain and the Threat to Stability in Europe, 1918–45*, London, Leicester University Press, 1993, 57–73; L. London, 'British immigration control procedures and Jewish refugees, 1933–9', in W. E. Mosse (ed.) *Second Chance*, Tubingen, Leo Baeck Institute 48, 1991, 485–517; L. London, 'Jewish refugees, Anglo-Jewry and British government policy, 1937–40', in D. Cesarani (ed.) *The Making of Modern Anglo-Jewry*, Oxford, Blackwell, 1990, 163–90; London suggests that it was Chamberlain's personal intervention in the issue of alien entry restrictions in the aftermath of *Kristallnacht* that caused an easing of the restrictions.
77 *Hansard*, vol. 326, cols 1986–7, 20 July 1937.
78 *Hansard*, vol. 326, col. 1836, 19 July 1937.
79 CPA, M[icro] F[iche] A[rchive], National Union, exec. 14 Dec. 1938, card 59; Essex and Middlesex labour advisory cttee., AGM, 5 Feb. 1938, ARE8/1/1.
80 Makins MSS, diary, 20 Dec. 1938.
81 Adams MSS, H. Waite to Adams, July 1939, Dr C. G. Kay Sharp to Adams, 20 July 1938; Adams to Dr Waite, 15 July 1938, file 9, BLPES; Hailes MSS: Dr Knox-Thompson to Buchan-Hepburn, 25 July 1938; Buchan-Hepburn to Dr Knox-Thompson, 27 July 1938, HAIL1/2.

82 N. J. Crowson, 'The British Conservative party and the Jews during the late 1930s', *Patterns of Prejudice* 29 (1995), 27–9; For history of internment see P. and L. Gillman, *Collar the Lot: How Britain Interned and Expelled its Wartime Refugees*, London, Quartet, 1980.

83 These themes are considered further in Crowson, 'Conservative party and the Jews', 16–23.

84 Londonderry, *Germany*, 170–1.

85 J. R. J. Macnamara, *The Whistle Blows*, London, Eyre and Spottiswode, 1938, 210.

86 *Hansard*, vol. 341, col. 1457, 21 Nov. 1938.

87 J. M. McEwen, 'Conservative and Unionist MPs, 1919–39', PhD thesis, University of London, 1959, 36–7, 424. All but one-sixth of Conservative MPs Church of England; a further forty Catholics, twenty Wesleyan Methodists, eleven Jews, seven Presbytarians, three Unitarians, three Friends, two Congregationalists and one Baptist. The remainder was Church of Scotland.

88 Butler MSS, R. A. Butler to Lord Bradbourne, 1 Jan. 1938, RABG8 29.

89 A. Roberts, *Holy Fox: A Biography of Lord Halifax*, London, Weidenfeld and Nicolson, 1991, 70–4; Lord Halifax, *Fulness of Days*, London, Collins, 1957, 184–5, 191.

90 Cilcennin MSS, J. P. L. Thomas to anon., 12 Apr. 1938, Cilc.coll.40.

91 Ball, 'The politics of appeasement', 60–1.

92 A. Chandler, 'Munich and morality: the Bishops of the Church of England and appeasement', *Twentieth Century British History*, 5, 1 (1994), 84.

93 A. Wilkinson, *Dissent or Conform? War, Peace and the English Churches, 1900–45*, London, SCM Press, 1987; Chandler, 'Munich and morality', 77–99; T. Moloney, *Westminster, Whitehall and the Vatican: The Role of Cardinal Hinsley, 1935–43*, Tunbridge Wells, Burns and Oates, 1985; on the Conservatives and religion see P. Catterall, 'The party and religion', in A. Seldon and S. Ball (eds) *Conservative Century: The Conservative Party since 1900*, Oxford, Oxford University Press, 1994, 637–70.

94 Cilcennin MSS, transcript of speech, n.d. (Oct./Nov. 1938), Cilc.coll.54.

95 Derby CA, AGM, 23 Mar. 1939.

96 Emrys-Evans MSS, Evans to Eden, 17 Mar. 1940, AddMS.58242 ff. 25–32.

97 Avon MSS, Mark Patrick to Eden, 15 Mar. 1938, AP14/1/795.

98 Ruggles-Brise MSS, *Hertfordshire and Essex Observer*, 5 Nov. 1938; *East Anglian Daily Times*, 27 Jan. 1939; Halifax, *Fulness of Days*, section on visit to Hitler, 185.

99 B. Coleman, 'The Conservative party and the frustration of the extreme right', in A. Thorpe (ed.) *The Failure of Political Extremism in Inter-War Britain*, Exeter, Exeter University Press, 1989, 49–66.

100 Atholl MSS, James Paton to Duchess of Atholl, 9 June 1937, File 22/18; *The Scotsman*, 7 Sept. 1936, Ford to the editor.

101 *Hansard*, vol. 321, col. 624, 4 Mar. 1937.

102 R. Blake, *The Conservative Party from Peel to Thatcher*, London, Fontana, 1985, 225.

103 N. Nicolson, *Diaries and Letters of Harold Nicolson*, London, Collins, 1966, 20 Sept. 1936, 273. Nicolson is referring to 'Chips' Channon.

104 Brooks MSS, journal, 15 Oct. 1939.
105 Headlam MSS, diary, 7, 10, 11 Sept. 1937.
106 Roberts, *Holy Fox*, 70–4; Halifax, *Fulness of Days*, 184–5, 191.
107 Barnes and Nicholson, *Amery Diaries*, 13 Aug. 1935, 397.
108 L. S. Amery, *My Political Life: The Unforgiving Years*, London, Hutchinson, 1955, 130.
109 Cilcennin MSS, J. P. L. Thomas to anon., 12 Apr. 1938, Cilc.coll.40; a view supported by the Duchess of Atholl, 'I have regarded Mr Channon for the last eighteen months as one of the strongest pro-Nazis in our Party in the House'. Atholl MSS, Duchess to A. C. Alston, 16 Feb. 1938, File 22/5.
110 James, *Chips*, 6, 13 Aug. 1936, 106, 111.
111 South Oxfordshire CA, AGM 10 June 1939 (Sir Gifford Fox), S.Oxon.Con.I/3.
112 Headlam MSS, diary, 16 Apr., 15 May 1939, D/He/35.
113 James, *Chips*, 15 Mar. 1939, 186.
114 *Documents on British Foreign Policy*, 3, VI, Appendix 1(iv), 706.
115 Londonderry, *Germany*, 16–7.
116 Wilson, *Walks and Talks Abroad*, 96.
117 Macnamara, *The Whistle Blows*, 207.
118 Charmley, *Duff Cooper*, 76.
119 *The Scotsman*, 21 Nov. 1934.
120 Winterton MSS, diary, 9 Sept. 1935, 1/41.
121 Brooks MSS, journal, 21 Aug., 11 Dec. 1935.
122 J. Charmley, *Lord Lloyd and the Decline of the British Empire*, London, Weidenfeld and Nicolson, 1987, 214.
123 Brooks MSS, journal, 22 May 1939.
124 Headlam MSS, diary, 11 Jan. 1939, D/He/35.
125 Hailes MSS, anon. to Buchan-Hepburn, 25 Mar. 1936, Cameron Foster to B-H, 26 Mar. 1936, HAIL1/2; see also Smart, *Bernays Diaries*, 17 Mar. 1936, 247; Boyd MSS, Lady Massereene to Lennox-Boyd, 10 Mar. 1936, MSS.Eng.c.3459 f. 87.
126 Clitheroe CA, AGM 3 Mar. 1938, DDX800/1/3.
127 Selborne MSS, second Earl to Lord Wolmer, 28 Mar. 1938, MS.Eng.hist.d.443 ff. 108–11.
128 Clitheroe CA, AGM 3 Mar. 1938, DDX800/1/3.
129 *Hansard*, vol. 326, col. 1877, 19 July 1937; Even after the invasion of Prague, de Chair told parliament that he did 'not think Herr Hitler means to challenge the dominance of this country, and that is why I believe that the Anglo-German agreement, signed by Herr Hitler and the Prime Minister [at Munich], was perfectly true when it said that there is no fundamental cause of war between the two countries'. *Hansard*, vol. 345, col. 494, 15 Mar. 1939.
130 Glyn MSS, Glyn to mother, 13 Sept. 1938, D/EGlC9/9.
131 *Preston Guardian*, 24 Mar. 1939.
132 Stockton CA, women's AGM, 19 Mar. 1938, D/X322/11.
133 Avon MSS, Emrys-Evans to J. P. L. Thomas, 19 Mar. 1938, AP14/1/799.
134 Tree, *Memoirs*, 56.
135 Headlam MSS, diary, 7 Sept. 1937, D/He/33.
136 Avon MSS, Kenneth Chance to Eden, 5 Feb. 1937, AP13/1/51T.
137 For an historical analysis of colonial appeasement see A. R. J. Crozier,

Appeasement and Germany's Last Bid for Colonies, London, Macmillan, 1988.

138 Selborne MSS, Wolmer to second Earl, 30 Mar. 1938, MS.Selborne.adds.5.

139 Cazalet MSS, journal, 14 Apr. 1938.

140 North Wiltshire CA, *North West Wilts Critic*, July 1938, 'Member's monthly letter', 2436/69.

141 Cazalet MSS, journal, 19 Apr. 1938.

142 Cazalet MSS, journal, 22 Apr. 1938. Emphasis added.

143 Cilcennin MSS, J. P. L. Thomas to anon, 12 Apr. 1938, Cilc.coll.40.

144 Selborne MSS, second Earl to Lord Wolmer, 31 Mar. 1938, MS.Eng.hist.d.443 ff.114–5; Birchall MSS, Francis Fremantle to J. D. Birchall, 10 June 1939, Box 33, cited with permission of the Birchall family.

145 Wilson, *Walks and Talks Abroad*, 229; *Essex Chronicle*, 19 May 1939, (Ruggles-Brise); Avon MSS: Cranborne to Eden, 21 Feb. 1939, AP14/2/22.

146 *Hansard*, vol. 321, col. 573, 1 Mar. 1937.

147 Clitheroe CA, div. council, 18 Nov. 1937, DDX800/1/3.

148 *Hansard*, vol. 341, col. 363, 10 Nov. 1938.

149 Cilcennin MSS, David [Lindsay] to J. P. L. Thomas, 28 [Mar.] 1938, Cilc.coll.29.

150 *Hansard*, vol. 360, cols 1167–8 (Winterton), 7 May 1940.

151 Gannon, *The British Press*, 292–3.

152 Hailes MSS, Buchan-Hepburn to Mr Johnstone, 23 Mar. 1938, HAIL1/2.

153 Avon MSS, Cranborne to Eden, 21 Feb. 1939, AP14/2/22.

154 Headlam MSS, diary, 16 Nov. 1938, D/He/34.

155 Headlam MSS, diary, 6 June, 8 Aug. 1939, D/He/35.

CHAPTER 2

1 CAB 23/82 19 June 1935.

2 Astor MSS, Sir William Munday to Lady Astor, 15 Dec. 1937, MS1416/1/1/1522.

3 R. C. Self (ed.) *The Austen Chamberlain Diary Letters*, London, Royal Historical Society/Cambridge University Press, 1995, 487.

4 For a history of the League of Nations Union see D. S. Birn, *The League of Nations Union, 1918–45*, Oxford, Clarendon Press, 1981, and especially 143–54 for the Peace Ballot.

5 Ceadel calculates that 38.2 per cent of the total population over the age of 18 participated in the ballot: M. Ceadel, 'The first British referendum: the Peace Ballot, 1934–5', *English Historical Review*, 95 (1980), 810–39.

6 T. Jones, *A Diary With Letters*, London, Oxford University Press, 1954, 30 Mar. 1935, 144.

7 Birmingham C[onservative] A[ssociation], management cttee, 12 Oct. 1934, AQ329.94249CON f. 268; Northern Area CA, council, 22 Sept. 1934, NRO3303/1.

8 These were the secretary Dame Adelaide Livingstone and her lieutenant Major Gordon Dickson. Birn, *League of Nations*, 147.

9 Headlam MSS, diary, 22 Sept. 1934, D/He/30.
10 J. Barnes and D. Nicholson (eds) *The Empire at Bay: The Leo Amery Diaries*, London, Hutchinson, 1988, editorial, 322.
11 Birn, *League of Nations*, 145.
12 For example: Chichester CA, general purposes cttee, 26 Nov. 1934, CO/ICHaddmss12088; Glasgow CA, general cttee, 7 Jan. 1935, Acc10424/74; S[cottish] C[onservative] Party] A[rchive], Western div. council, 5 Sept. 1934, Acc10424/31 f. 140.
13 Birmingham CA, management cttee, 12 Oct., 9 Nov., 14 Dec. 1934, AQ329.94249CON ff. 268, 273–5, 287–8.
14 Barnes and Nicholson, *Amery Diaries*, editorial, 323.
15 SCA, eastern prov. area, exec. 12 Apr. 1935, 9 Nov. 1938, Acc10424/48–9; C[onservative] P[arty] A[rchive], M[icro] F[iche] A[chive], National Union, gen. purposes sub-cttee, 12 June 1935, card 52; Essex and Middlesex prov. area, council, 1 July 1936 ARE8/1/1; 1922 Committee, 1 Nov. 1937, CPA/1922CMMTEE.
16 Jones, *Diary*, 30 Mar. 1935, 144.
17 CAB 23/82 48(35) f. 297, 23 Oct. 1935.
18 Emrys-Evans MSS, Evans to Margesson, 13 July 1936, 58248 ff. 23–5.
19 CAB 23/82 35(35), 3 July 1935.
20 R. A. C. Parker, *Chamberlain and Appeasement*, London, Macmillan, 1993, 49.
21 CAB 23/82, 21 Aug. 1935.
22 *Manchester Guardian*, 27 Sept. 1935, letter to editor.
23 *Manchester Guardian*, 22 Oct. 1935, speech by Brig.-Gen. Nation.
24 *Manchester Guardian*, 27 Sept. 1935, speech by Churchill.
25 *Manchester Guardian*, 30 Aug. 1935, letter to editor.
26 *Manchester Guardian*, 17 Oct. 1935.
27 *Hansard: House of Commons Debates*, vol. 305, 22–4 October 1935.
28 Barnes and Nicholson, *Amery Diaries*, 11, 15 Oct. 1935, 401.
29 Brooks MSS, journal, 6 Oct. 1935, citing a conversation with Herbert Williams.
30 Beaverbrook MSS, Lennox-Boyd to Beaverbrook, 25 Oct. 1935, BBK.C.55.
31 Beaverbrook MSS, Leo Amery to Beaverbrook, 12 Nov. 1936, BBK.C.7.
32 N. Smart (ed.) *Diaries and Letters of Robert Bernays*, Lampeter, Edwin Mellen Press, 1996, 23 Aug. 1935, 220; J. Barnes and K. Middlemas, *Baldwin*, London, Weidenfeld and Nicolson, 1969, 849.
33 Cab 23/82 48(35), 23 Oct. 1935.
34 Stannage, *Baldwin*, 291.
35 Derby MSS, G. N. Carter (agent, Manchester CA) to Derby, 8 Nov. 1935, 920(DER)17 16/3.
36 The National government quota consisted of 388 Conservative, 35 Liberal National and 8 National Labour MPs.
37 Adapted from T. Stannage, *Baldwin Thwarts the Opposition: The British General Election of 1935*, London, Croom Helm, 1980, 291–2.
38 Barnes and Nicholson, *Amery Diaries*, 10 Dec. 1935, 404.
39 *Hansard*, vol. 307, cols 2007–17 (Hoare), 2030–1 (Baldwin), 19 Dec. 1935.
40 Headlam MSS, Cuthbert Headlam to wife, 17–19 Dec. 1935, D/He/284/13.

41 Bute and North Ayrshire CA, AGM, 20 Dec. 1935.
42 S. de Chair, *Morning Glory: Memoirs from the Edge of History*, London, Cassell, 1994, 125. Similarly the response of Victor Cazalet: Cazalet MSS, journal, 9 Dec. 1935.
43 *Notices of Motions*, 11 Dec. 1935.
44 See *Notices of Motions*, 1935–9.
45 J. A. Cross, *Sir Samuel Hoare: A Political Biography*, London, Cape, 1977, 250; and Parker, *Chamberlain*, 54.
46 Cited in J. Ramsden 'Note: 1931 to 1939' in C. Cook and J. Ramsden (eds) *By-elections in British Politics*, London, Macmillan, 1973, 116. Baldwin was referring to the change of heart over a weekend by MPs during the Abdication crisis.
47 Jones, *Diary*, 9 Feb. 1936, 171.
48 D. Waley, *British Public Opinion and the Abyssinian War*, London, Temple Smith, 1975, 65.
49 R. R. James (ed.) *Chips: The Diaries of Sir Henry Channon*, London, Weidenfeld and Nicolson, 1969, 17 Dec. 1935, 48–9; Jones, *Diary*, 14 Jan. 1936, 161; Waley, *Public Opinion*, 65.
50 Emrys-Evans MSS, Harold Nicolson to Evans, 13 Nov. 1935, Add.MS.58248 f. 41.
51 Barnes and Middlemas, *Baldwin*, 890.
52 *Notices of Motions*, 11, 12 Dec. 1935.
53 *Hansard*, vol. 307, col. 2052, 19 Dec. 1935.
54 Information derived from *Notices of Motions*; *The Times*; Barnes and Nicholson, *Amery Diaries*; Nicolson (ed.) *The Diaries and Letters of Harold Nicolson*, London, Collins, 1966; Waley, *Public Opinion*; James, *Chips*.
55 *The Times*, 18 Dec. 1935, Harold Macmillan to the editor.
56 Brooks MSS, journal, 11 Dec. 1935.
57 Winterton MSS, diary, 16 Dec. 1935, 1/41.
58 CAB 23 (90B) 56(35), 18 Dec. 1935.
59 Derby MSS, Derby to Beaverbrook, 21 Feb. 1936, 920DER(17)47/1; also I. Colvin, *Vansittart in Office*, London, Gollancz, 1965, 83.
60 Jones, *Diary*, 7 Jan. 1936, 160
61 Brooks MSS, journal, 10 Jan. 1936, views of Jimmy Thomas and Oliver Baldwin.
62 see Smart, *Bernays Diaries*, 9 May 1936, 260–1.
63 Crookshank MSS, diary, 8 Mar. 1936, MS.Eng.hist.d.359 f. 109.
64 Cazalet MSS, journal, 4–6 Mar. 1936.
65 Barnes and Nicholson, *Amery Diaries*, 7 Mar. 1936, 410.
66 N. Thompson, *The Anti-Appeasers: Conservative Opposition to Appeasement in the 1930s*, Oxford, Clarendon Press, 1971, 107.
67 *News Chronicle*, 17 Mar. 1936; Winterton MSS, diary, 17 Mar. 1936, 1/41.
68 Barnes and Nicholson, *Amery Diaries*, 10 Mar. 1936, 410.
69 Winterton MSS, diary, 12 Mar. 1936, 1/41.
70 PREM1/94.
71 Barnes and Nicolson, *Amery Diaries*, 17 Mar. 1936, 411.
72 *Hansard*, vol. 309, col. 2058, (Grigg) 10 Mar. 1936.
73 Winterton MSS, diary, 17 Mar. 1936, 1/41.
74 Hailes MSS, anon to Patrick Buchan-Hepburn, 25 Mar. 1936; Cameron

Foster to B-H, 26 Mar. 1936, HAIL1/2; Emrys-Evans MSS, Jock McEwen to Evans, 24 Mar. 1936, Add.MS. 58248 f. 17; see also Cazalet MSS, journal, 4–6 Mar. 1936.

75 PREM1/94.

76 PREM1/94.

77 *Hansard*, vol. 309, col. 1492, 23 Mar. 1936.

78 Nicolson, *Nicolson Diaries*, 17 Mar. 1936, 252; Barnes and Nicholson, *Amery Diaries*, 17 Mar. 1936, 411.

79 PREM1/94.

80 Cab 23/83 24(36) f. 378, 25 Mar. 1936.

81 Cab 23/83 18(36) ff. 291–2, 11 Mar. 1936. An interpretation confirmed by Smart, *Bernays Diaries*, 17 Mar. 1936, 247.

82 Cab 23/83 24(36), 25 Mar. 1936, ff. 380–1.

83 Avon MSS, Lumley to Eden, 23 Apr. 1936, AP14/1/598.

84 Barnes and Nicholson, *Amery Diaries*, 5 Mar. 1936, 409–10.

85 Boyd MSS, Charles Petrie to Boyd, 11 Apr. 1936, MSS.Eng.c.3459 ff. 91–2.

86 Sourced from: *Hansard*; *Notices of Motions*; Barnes and Nicholson, *Amery Diaries*; Cazalet MSS; 1922 Committee MSS; Nicolson, *Nicolson Diaries*.

87 Derby MSS, Derby to Beaverbrook, 4 Mar. 1936, 920DER(17)47/1.

88 Nicolson Diary, 14 May 1936, cited in Waley, *Public Opinion*, 79.

89 Barnes and Nicholson, *Amery Diaries*, 7, 14 May 1936, 416–17.

90 Winterton MSS, diary, 6 May 1936, 1/41.

91 Glasgow CA, general cttee 25 May 1936, Acc10424/74.

92 CAB23/83–4 39(36) ff. 212–21, 27 May 1936 – of those who spoke, Chamberlain, Simon, Halifax and Collins favoured abandoning sanctions, whilst Eden and Zetland argued for their maintenance.

93 CAB23/84 40(36), 29 May 1936 – this time Swinton, Hailsham, Inskip, Duff Cooper, MacDonald, Chamberlain and Baldwin spoke in favour of their removal; Elliot and Wood favoured their maintenance until some form of return had been secured.

94 Chamberlain MSS, diary, 17 June 1936 – cited K. Feiling, *Life of Neville Chamberlain*, London, Macmillan, 1946, 296.

95 R. R. James (ed.) *Memoirs of a Conservative: J. C. C. Davidson's Memoirs and Papers, 1910–37*, London, Weidenfeld and Nicolson, 1969, 411–12.

96 James, *Chips*, 18 June 1936, 66–7; Brooks MSS, journal, 9 July 1936, attending meeting of Conningsby Club.

97 Barnes and Nicholson, *Amery Diaries*, 15 June 1936, 421; Nicolson, *Nicolson Diaries*, 18 June 1936, 265.

98 CPA, 1922 Committee, 15 June 1936, CPA/1922CMMTEE.

99 Barnes and Nicholson, *Amery Diaries*, 15 June 1936, 421; CAB23/84 42(36) f. 295, 17 June 1936.

100 For example see the arguments employed by Erskine-Hill in *The Scotsman*, 22 June 1936, 'Edinburgh MP on sanctions'; and by Arthur Heneage: Heneage MSS, Heneage to Mr Yarker, 25 June 1936, HNC4/18; Heneage to Mr Gardiner, 26 June 1936, HNC4/18.

101 *Hansard*, vol. 309, col. 1652, 5 Mar. 1936.

102 Barnes and Nicholson, *Amery Diaries*, 23 June 1936, 422.

103 Stockton CA, special general meeting, 23 July 1936, D/X322/5.

104 Cazalet MSS, journal, 21 June 1936.
105 SCA, eastern div. council, 10 June 1936, Acc.10424/44; South Oxfordshire CA, AGM, 18 June 1938, S.Oxon.Con.I/3.
106 See Table 3.4.
107 Barnes and Nicholson, *Amery Diaries*, 8 July 1936, 423–4. Amery and co. used the Chamberlain Centenary rally to foster the colonial cause.
108 *Notices of Motions*, 10 Feb. 1936.
109 *Hansard*, vol. 308, col. 934 (Thomas), 12 Feb. 1936.
110 *Hansard*, vol. 310, col. 2415, 6 Apr. 1936.
111 Barnes and Nicholson, *Amery Diaries*, 19 May 1936, 417; L. Amery, *Unforgiving Years*, 248; CPA, MFA, National Union general purposes sub-cttee, 20 May 1936, card 54. The original motion had been passed by Bournemouth, 24 April, forwarded to the Wessex Area and carried unanimously by its AGM, 16 May, before going to the National Union.
112 CPA, MFA, National Union central council, 24 June 1936, card 131; see Barnes and Nicholson, *Amery Diaries*, for account of meeting, 24 June 1936, 422.
113 CPA, MFA, National Union executive, 16 July 1936, 'Report of the resolutions sub-committee on the deputation to the Prime Minister . . . ', card 54.
114 *Hansard*, vol. 315, col. 1132 (Eden), 27 July 1936.
115 CPA, 1922 Committee, 27 July 1936, CPA/1922CMTTEE.
116 Beaverbrook MSS, Amery to Beaverbrook, 12 Nov. 1936, BBK.C.7.
117 Barnes and Nicholson, *Amery Diaries*, 30 Jan. 1936, 407.
118 Norwood CA, AGM 7 Feb. 1936, IV/166/1/15.
119 Barnes and Nicholson, *Amery Diaries*, 3 Apr. 1936, 412–13.
120 Smart, *Bernays Diaries*, 9 Apr. 1936, 254.
121 Barnes and Nicholson, *Amery Diaries*, 27 Apr. 1936, 414–15.
122 Amery, *The Unforgiving Years*, 248.
123 *Notices of Motions*, 22 July 1936.
124 This is comparing the signatures with *Notices of Motions*, 22 July 1936, with the 82 MPs identified by J. M. McEwen, 'Conservative and Unionist MPs, 1914–39', University of London, PhD, 1959, 498–500, who opposed the India Bill.
125 Cited A. J. Crozier, *Appeasement and Germany's Last Bid for Colonies*, London, Macmillan, 1989, 169.
126 See G. Stone, 'Britain, France and the Spanish problem, 1936–9', in D. Richardson and G. Stone (eds) *Decisions and Diplomacy: Essays in Twentieth-Century International History*, London, Routledge, 1995, 129–52; K. W. Watkins, *Britain Divided: The Effect of the Spanish Civil War on British Political Opinion*, London, Nelson, 1963; T. Buchanan, ' "A far away country of which we know nothing"? Perceptions of Spain and its civil war in Britain', *Twentieth Century British History*, 4, 1 (1993), 1–24.
127 Winterton MSS, diary, 2 Aug. 1936, 1/42.
128 James, *Cazalet*, 191; K. Atholl, *Searchlight on Spain*, Harmondsworth, Penguin, 1938; Kinross and West Perth CA, minute books, 1936–8, *passim*.
129 Penryn and Falmouth CA, AGM 31 Oct. 1936, DDX551/10; *The Scotsman*, 7 Sept. 1936, Patrick Ford to the editor.

130 A. Wilson, *Thoughts and Talks, 1935–7: The Diary of a Member of Parliament*, London, Longmans, 1938, 373.
131 James, *Chips*, 29 Mar. 1938, 153.
132 cited in D. Little, 'Red scare, 1936: anti-bolshevism and the origins of British non-intervention in the Spanish civil war', *Journal of Contemporary History*, 23 (1988), 296.
133 Wilson, *Thoughts and Talks*, 371.
134 James, *Chips*, 14 Sept. 1936, 113.
135 See Appendix 1 for names of pro-Franco Conservatives.
136 R. R. James, *Churchill: A Study in Failure*, London, Weidenfeld and Nicolson, 1970, 405–9, quote from 407.
137 Chelmsford CA, exec. 15 Dec. 1936, D/Z 96/7.
138 Nicolson, *Nicolson Diaries*, 15 July 1937, 307; Wilson, *Thoughts and Talks*, 373.
139 *Notices of Motions*, 18 Dec. 1937, 14 signatures.
140 H. Page-Croft, *Spain: The Truth At Last*, cited in Parker, *Chamberlain*, 89.
141 Hoare's predecessor John Simon was very unpopular with Conservatives and was moved by Baldwin in June 1935 to the Home Office.
142 Beaverbrook MSS, Amery to Beaverbrook, 12 Nov. 1936, BBK.C.7.
143 Barnes and Nicolson, *Amery Diaries*, editorial, 489–90.
144 Chamberlain MSS, diary, 19 Jan. 1936, NC2/23A.
145 James, *Chips*, 24 June 1936, 67.

CHAPTER 3

1 Headlam MSS, diary, 31 Jan. 1938, D/He/34; emphasis added. See similar complaints in A. Wilson, *Thoughts and Talks, 1935–7: The Diary of a Member of Parliament*, London, Longmans, 1938, 73.
2 D. C. Watt, *How War Came: The Immediate Origins of the Second World War*, London, Heinemann, 1989; R. A. C. Parker, *Chamberlain and Appeasement*, London, Macmillan, 1993; J. Charmley, *Chamberlain and the Lost Peace*, London, Hodder and Stoughton, 1989; C. Hill, *Cabinet Decision-Making in Foreign Policy: The British Experience, October 1938–June 1941*, Cambridge, Cambridge University Press, 1991.
3 Lord Avon, *Facing the Dictators: The Eden Memoirs*, London, Cassell, 1962, 445; Lord Halifax, *Fulness of Days*, London, Collins, 1957, 193; Somervell MSS, journal, Apr. 1937; Headlam MSS, diary, 28 May, 8 Nov. 1937, D/He/33.
4 J. Barnes and D. Nicholson (eds) *The Empire At Bay: The Leo Amery Diaries*, London, Hutchinson, 1988, 10 Nov. 1937, 451–2; *Hansard: House of Commons Debates*, vol. 333, col. 1482, 24 Mar. 1938.
5 Clitheroe C[onservative] A[ssociation], div. council, 18 Nov. 1937 (Brass), DDX800/1/3.
6 Barnes and Nicholson, *Amery Diaries*, 15 Nov. 1937, 452; see also Headlam MSS, diary, 15 Nov. 1937, D/He/33.
7 Barnes and Nicholson, *Amery Diaries*, 15 Nov. 1937, Edward Grigg's opinion, 452.
8 Barnes and Nicholson, *Amery Diaries*, 17 Feb. 1938, 455; J. Harvey (ed.) *The Diplomatic Diaries of Oliver Harvey*, London, Collins, 1970, 17 Feb.

1938, 93; see also N. Nicolson (ed.) *Diaries and Letters of Harold Nicolson, 1930–39*, London, Collins, 1966, 17 Feb. 1938, 323; an incomplete set of minutes for this particular meeting can be found in Cilcennin MSS, Cilc.coll.52.

9 Winterton MSS, diary, 22 Feb. 1938, 1/43.

10 R. R. James, *Victor Cazalet: A Portrait*, London, Hamish Hamilton, 1976, 198.

11 *The Times*, 23 Feb. 1938. This amendment was supported by E. Spears, H. Nicolson, A. Crossley, G. Nicholson, Hills, E. Makins, J. R. J. Macnamara, R. Turton, R. Cary, Eckersley, R. A. Pilkington, D. Gunston, M. Patrick, B. Cruddas, Emrys-Evans, H. Macmillan, R. Cartland. See also Makins MSS, diary, 22 Feb. 1938.

12 See N. J. Crowson, 'Conservative parliamentary dissent over foreign policy during the premiership of Neville Chamberlain: myth or reality?' *Parliamentary History*, 14, 3 (1995), 322, fn. 27 for list of abstainers. For the hard data determining the abstentions see N. J. Crowson 'Facing the Führer: The Conservative party's attitudes and responses to Germany, 1937–40', Southampton University, PhD, 1994, 214.

13 Parker, *Chamberlain*, 122, citing the French ambassador to London.

14 Harvey, *Harvey Diaries*, 21–3 Feb 1938, 97–100. Harvey's emphasis.

15 Hailes MSS, Buchan-Hepburn to Lord Mayor of Liverpool, 22 Feb. 1938, HAIL1/2; Birchall MSS, 'Notes on Eden resignation', 25 Feb. 1938, Box 33; Stockton CA, men's branch AGM 10 Mar. 1938, D/X322/8.

16 *Hansard*, vol. 332, col. 142 (McCorquodale), 21 Feb. 1938; col. 274 (Anderson), 22 Feb. 1938.

17 D. Carlton, *Anthony Eden: A Biography*, London, Allen Lane, 1981, 129–30.

18 R. Cockett, *Twilight of Truth: Chamberlain and the Manipulation of the Press*, London, Weidenfeld and Nicolson, 1989, 49–52.

19 R. Churchill, *Rise and Fall of Sir Anthony Eden*, London, MacGibbon and Kee, 1954, 154, implied 'Eden group' existed before his resignation; J. Wheeler-Bennett, *Munich: Prologue to Tragedy*, London, Macmillan, 1948, 183, says after the resignation, whilst Eden vaguely suggests the summer of 1938: Lord Avon, *The Reckoning: The Eden Memoirs*, London, Cassell, 1964, 31. See Crowson, 'Conservative parliamentary dissent', 315–36 for a more realistic timescale and explanation.

20 For example: Middleton CA, finance and general purpose cttee 24 Feb. 1938, PLC 1/2; Chelmsford CA, exec. 3 Mar. 1938, D/Z96/7; Sowerby CA, exec. 23 Feb. 1938, CV2; West Leeds CA, exec. 28 Feb. 1938, no. 5 minute book; Kinross and West Perth CA, exec. 22 Apr. 1938; Makins MSS, diary, 25 Feb. 1938.

21 C[onservative] P[arty] A[rchive], correspondence between H. W. Bettle (North Staffordshire Political Union) and Percy Cohen, n.d. and 22 Mar. 1938, CCO1/2/269.

22 Hailes MSS, Buchan-Hepburn to Lord Mayor of Liverpool, 22 Feb. 1938, HAIL1/2.

23 Headlam MSS, diary, 20, 22 Feb. 1938, D/He/34.

24 Atholl MSS, James Paton to Duchess, 10 Mar. 1938, File22/18; Duchess to members of Kinross association (published pamphlet), 6 May 1938,

File22/1; Kinross and West Perth CA, exec. 22 Apr. 1938 and addendum to meeting authorised 13 May 1938.

25 N. Nicolson, *People and Parliament*, London, Weidenfeld and Nicolson, 1958, 59.

26 Leeds West CA, exec. 28 Feb. 1938, no. 5; Chelmsford CA, exec. 3 Mar. 1938, D/Z96/7.

27 L. D. Epstein, 'British MPs and their local parties: the Suez cases', *American Political Science Review*, 2, June 1960, 374.

28 Nicolson, *Nicolson Diaries*, Nicolson to wife, 25 Feb. 1938, diary, 7 Apr. 1938, 326–7, 333; Emrys-Evans MSS, Evans to Doncaster, 1 Mar. 1938, n.d. [after 12 Apr. 1938], Add.MS.58249; Barnes and Nicholson, *Amery Diaries*, 24 Feb. 1938, 458. J. Charmley, *The End of Glory: Churchill*, London, Hodder and Stoughton, 1993, 338, has confused the accounts of the meeting of the Foreign Affairs Committee for 24 Feb. and 7 Apr. and portrayed them as occurring only during the 7 Apr. meeting.

29 R. R. James (ed.) *Chips: The Diaries of Sir Henry Channon*, London, Weidenfeld and Nicolson, 1967, 4 May 1939, 197.

30 Emrys-Evans MSS, Eden to Evans, 28 Apr. 1938, Add.MS.58242.

31 Cilcennin MSS, J. P. L. Thomas to anon, 12 Apr. 1938, Cilc.coll.40.

32 Headlam MSS, diary, 17 Feb., 12 Mar., 7 May 1938, D/He/34.

33 Stockton CA, women's AGM 19 Mar. 1938 (Macmillan), D/X322/11; See also *Hansard*, vol. 333, col. 73 (Page-Croft), 14 Mar. 1938; Also, Headlam MSS, diary, 22, 24 Mar., 7 May 1938, D/He/34.

34 Cazalet MSS, journal, Mar. 1937, *passim*, 4 Aug. 1937, 10 Mar. 1938.

35 City of London CA, AGM 17 May 1938, 487/31.

36 Winterton MSS, diary, 14 Mar. 1938, 1/43; *Hansard*, vol. 333, cols 64 (Boothby), 120–3 (Atholl), 150–1 (Adams), 14 Mar. 1938.

37 *Hansard*, vol. 333, col. 50, 14 Mar. 1938.

38 Cilcennin MSS, Ronald Cartland to J. P. L. Thomas, 22 Mar. 1938, Cilc.coll.44; Winterton MSS, diary, 16 Mar. 1938, 1/43.

39 Barnes and Nicholson, *Amery Diaries*, 20–21 Mar. 1938, 498–9; Headlam MSS, diary, 12 Mar. 1938, D/He/34; Butler MSS, Michael Beaumont to Butler, 16 Mar. 1938, RABG9 ff.5–6; James, *Chips*, 20 Mar. 1938, 152; Avon MSS, Mark Patrick to Eden, 22 Mar. 1938, AP14/1/796; Stirling CA, *Stirling Journal and Advertiser*, 12 May 1938.

40 *The Times*, 19 Mar. 1938.

41 Emrys-Evans MSS, Evans to Chamberlain, 20 Mar. 1938, Add.MS.58248 f.48; *Hansard*, vol. 333, col. 955–6, 21 Mar. 1938.

42 *Hansard*, vol. 333, cols 953–5, 959, 21 Mar. 1938.

43 For a more detailed analysis of the government's deliberations over a guarantee see Parker, *Chamberlain*, 134–9 and Charmley, *Chamberlain*, 64–8. Parker argues that Chamberlain and Halifax were both anxious to avoid a guarantee and that the Chiefs of Staff assessment that Czechoslovakia was indefensible provided the justification and not the explanation for the 24 Mar. declaration by Chamberlain.

44 J. Charmley, *Duff Cooper: The Authorised Biography*, London, Macmillan PaperMac, 1986, 110.

45 Avon MSS, Mark Patrick to Eden, 22 Mar. 1938, AP14/1/796.

46 *Hansard*, vol. 333, cols 1463, 24 Mar. 1938.

47 Cazalet MSS, journal, 24 Mar. 1938.

48 Barnes and Nicholson, *Amery Diaries*, 24 Mar. 1938, 499.
49 Avon MSS, Mark Patrick to Eden, 25 Mar. 1938, AP14/1/797.
50 *Skyrack Express*, 1 Apr. 1938.
51 Vote of confidence, 4 April 1938: 'Certain abstainers' V. Adams, Duchess of Atholl, W. S. Churchill, S. Herbert, D. Sandys, J. P. L. Thomas, R. Boothby; 'Probables' R. Perkins, J. J. Withers; 'Possibles' A. Chorlton.
52 Chamberlain MSS, G. W. Rickards to Chamberlain, 30 Mar. 1938, NC7/11/31/226; Murray F. Sueter to Chamberlain, 31 Mar. 1938, NC7/11/31/258; Tynemouth CA, exec. 25 Mar. 1938, TWAS 1633/2; Pembroke CA, AGM 26 Mar. 1938, HDSO/51/1; CPA, M[icro]F[iche] A[rchive], National Union, exec. 6 Apr. 1938, card 58 approved and forwarded to the PM a number of motions of approval from East Leicester CA, Bosworth CA, Finchley CA, and Kingston-upon-Thames CA.
53 Brooks MSS, journal, 4 May 1938.
54 Mass Observation Archive, A7 West Fulham by-election report, March 1938.
55 Avon MSS, J. P. L. Thomas to Eden, 9 April 1938, AP14/1/823.
56 CPA, 'List of suggested key constituencies' memo by D. K. Clarke, 7 July 1937, CRD1/7/35.
57 Brooks MSS, journal, 4 May 1938.
58 North Wiltshire CA, *North West Wilts Critic*, July 1938, 'Lessons of the by-elections: three victors tell how they won', 2436/69.
59 CPA, 'By-election results' memo by H. G. Hanrott, 13 June 1938, CRD1/7/35.
60 From J. Ramdsen and C. Cook (eds) *By-elections in British Politics*, London, Macmillan, 1973, 371.
61 Headlam MSS, diary, 15 Aug. 1938, D/He/35; for Halifax's assessment of success see Charmley, *Chamberlain*, 90.
62 Adams MSS, C. H. Thickbroom to Fred Owen, 7 Aug. 1938, File 7.
63 North Wiltshire CA, *North West Wilts Critic*, 'Member's monthly letter', July 1938, (Cazalet) 2436/69.
64 Caldecote MSS, diary, 30 Aug. 1938, INKP1/1.
65 Avon MSS, Cranborne to J. P. L. Thomas, 15 Aug. 1938, AP14/1/826A.
66 Winterton MSS, diary, 15 Aug. 1938, 1/43.
67 Glyn MSS, Ralph Glyn to mother, 13 Sept. 1938, D/EGlC9/9.
68 Winterton MSS, diary, 13 Sept. 1938, 1/43.
69 Headlam MSS, diary, 10 Sept. 1938, D/He/34.
70 'Hitler and the outbreak of World War Two', HiDES, Hossbach Memorandum: minutes of meeting at Reichs Chancellery, 5 Nov. 1937; *Documents on German Foreign Policy*, D, 2, 221, 357–8, Directive for Operation Green.
71 Headlam MSS, diary, 14 Sept. 1938; Crookshank MSS, diary, 15 Sept. 1938, MS.Eng.hist.d.359 f.214.
72 Headlam MSS, diary, 15 Sept. 1938; Crookshank MSS, diary, 15 Sept. 1938, MS.Eng.hist.d.359 f.214.
73 Headlam MSS, diary, 17, 19, 25, 26 Sept. 1938, D/He/34. Winterton also confirms this in his diary. He felt that the 'crisis varies from day to day. One day hopeful, the next most gloomy like variations in the health of a sick patient'. Winterton MSS, diary, 5 Sept. 1938, 1/43. For the reactions

of an 'ordinary' civilian living in Streatham see Samuel Rich MSS, diary, Sept. 1938, AJ217/34.

74 Headlam MSS, diary, 26 Sept. 1938, D/He/34.
75 James, *Chips*, 28 Sept. 1938, 170.
76 Barnes and Nicholson, *Amery Diaries*, 28 Sept. 1938, 520.
77 Headlam MSS, Leslie Lonie to Headlam, 28 Sept. 1938, D/He/135/136.
78 Atholl MSS, Duke of Atholl to James Paton, 2 Nov. 1938, File 22/13.
79 Rab Butler to Lord Halifax, 30 July 1938, FO800/328.
80 Crookshank MSS, diary, 4, 6 Oct. 1938, MS.Eng.hist.d.359 f.218; Chamberlain MSS, Neville to Ida, 9 Oct. 1936, NC18/1/1071; N. Smart (ed.) *The Diaries and Letters of Robert Bernays, 1932–9*, Lampeter, Edwin Mellen Press, 1996, 8 Oct. 1938, 372.
81 For further analysis of censure of dissidents and the features of rebellion see Crowson, 'Conservative parliamentary dissent'; N. Thompson, *Anti-Appeasers: Conservative Opposition to Appeasement in the 1930s*, Oxford, Oxford University Press, 1971; and M. Cowling, *The Impact of Hitler: British Politics and Policy*, Cambridge, Cambridge University Press, 1975.
82 Winchester CA, AGM 25 Mar. 1939, 73M86W/5; *Hampshire Advertiser*, 1 Apr. 1939.
83 Harvey, *Harvey Diaries*, 12 Oct. 1938, 213.
84 Chamberlain MSS, Ida to Neville, 9 Oct. 1938, NC18/2/1096; Hilda to Neville, 13 Oct. 1938, NC1/15/3/159.
85 Somerset de Chair to author, 2 Sept 1992.
86 Avon MSS, Roger Lumley to Eden, 2 Oct. 1938, AP13/1/66P.
87 Heneage MSS, Heneage to J. M. Lill, 12 Oct. 1938, HNC 1/L; Heneage to J. R. Jennings, 16 Nov. 1938, HNC 1/J.
88 *Staffordshire Chronicle*, 11 Mar. 1939.
89 Makins MSS, diary, 6 Oct. 1938.
90 Almond MSS, Fylde by-election address, DDX1202/1/24.
91 Almond MSS, J. R. Almond to Lord Derby, 5 Nov. 1938, DDX1202/1/47.
92 One such association that bought the leaflet was Sowerby, who thought it 'good propaganda' and distributed 18,500 copies at a cost of £32. 16*s*. 9*d*. Sowerby CA, finance cttee, 2 Nov. 1938, CV3.
93 S[cottish] C[onservative Party] A[rchive], western div. council, 2 Nov. 1938, Acc 10424.
94 The details of the dissidents' meetings during September 1938 are explained in the editorial analysis of the Barnes and Nicholson, *Amery Diaries*, 483–90.
95 Chamberlain MSS, Leo Amery to Chamberlain, 6 Oct. 1938, NC7/2/82; A. Roberts, *Holy Fox: A Biography of Lord Halifax*, London, Weidenfeld and Nicolson, 1991, 125.
96 See Crowson, 'Conservative parliamentary dissent', 327, fn. 48, for names of abstainers. For data on abstentions see Crowson, 'Facing the Führer', 217.
97 Avon MSS, R. Tree to Eden, 7 Oct. 1938, AP14/1/836; Tree, *Memoirs*, 82.
98 Cilcennin MSS, J. P. L. Thomas, transcript of speech n.d. [Oct./Nov. 1938], Cilc.coll.54; J. P. L. Thomas to G. C. Irving, 20 Oct. 1938, Cilc.coll.37; Selborne MSS, Wolmer to Sir Godfrey Fell, 7 Oct. 1938, MS.Eng.hist.c.1014 ff.51–8; Emrys-Evans MSS, Emrys-Evans to

Doncaster, 7 Oct. 1938, Add.MS.58249; Atholl MSS, 'The Munich conference and after', Duchess of Atholl, 7 Nov. 1938, file 22/2; *Hansard*, vol. 339, cols 110–14 (Richard Law), 3 Oct. 1938; H. Macmillan, *The Price of Peace*, London, Heron, 1938.

99   Makins MSS, diary, 21 Feb., 21 June, 17 Dec. 1938.

100   See S. Ball, 'The politics of appeasement: the fall of the Duchess of Atholl and the Kinross and West Perth by-election, December 1938', *Scottish Historical Review*, LXIX, 1 (1990), 49–83.

101   Headlam was amused by Cooper's resignation for he had once told him that there were three golden rules in politics: 'never ask for anything, never refuse anything, never resign'. Headlam MSS, diary, 1 Oct. 1938, D/He/34.

102   Winterton MSS, diary, 30 Sept. 1938, 1/43.

103   Stone CA, newspaper clippings, Nov. 1938, D1289/5/2.

104   Newbury CA, exec 12 Nov. 1938, letter from Mr Cathorine-Hardy, D/EX409/3; Headlam MSS, diary, 10 Oct. 1938, D/He/34.

105   Avon MSS, Hugh Molson to Eden, 20 Sept. 1938, AP 14/1/781.

106   Emrys-Evans MSS, Evans to Doncaster, n.d. [after 12 Apr. 1938] Add.MS.58249.

107   Emrys-Evans MSS, Doncaster to Evans, 12 Oct. 1938, Add.MS.58249.

108   Emrys-Evans MSS, Doncaster to Harriss, 18 Nov. 1938, Add.MS.58249 ff.43–4.

109   *Nottingham Evening Post*, 4 Nov. 1938.

110   York CA, exec. 17 Nov. 1938; West Leeds CA, exec. 5 Dec. 1938; Avon MSS, Arthur Mann to Forbes Adam, 30 Nov. 1938, AP14/1/777A.

111   Chelmsford CA, exec. 3 Mar. 1938, D/Z96/7; West Leeds CA, exec. 28 Feb. 1938; Aldershot CA, central council, 22 Oct. 1938, exec. 14 Dec. 1938, 114M84/2.

112   Compare Aldershot CA, central council, 22 Oct. 1938, exec. 14 Dec. 1938; Selborne MSS, correspondence between Sir Godfrey Fell and Wolmer, Oct. 1938, MS.Eng.hist.c.1014; with Kinross and West Perth CA, exec. 2 June 1937, 22 Apr. 1938, special general meeting 13 May 1938, exec. 27 May, 31 Oct. 1938; Atholl MSS, 'Résumé of proceedings of exec. . . . 27 May 1938' by Will Hally, file 22/6; 'Table of events in regard to Kinross and West Perth exec.' by Duchess, n.d. [1938] file 22/6; Duke of Atholl to Paton, 2 Nov. 1938, file 22/13.

113   M. Gilbert, *Winston S. Churchill: V: 1922–39*, London, Heinemann, 1976, 1012, 1014–15; R. R. James, *Boothby: A Portrait*, London, Curtis and Hodder, 1991, 186–8; Avon MSS, correspondence between Eden and Spenser Flowers, 4 Oct. 1938, AP13/1/66I-J.

114   Kinross CA, exec. 30 June 1937.

115   Winchester CA, exec. 27 May 1937, 73M86W/5.

116   Emrys-Evans MSS, Doncaster to Evans, 12 Apr 1938, Add.MS.58249.

117   Stockton CA, financial cttee, 23 Nov. 1938, exec. 27 Feb. 1939, D/X 322/5.

118   Kinross CA, addendum to exec. 13 May 1938.

119   e.g. Sowerby CA, exec. 24 Nov. 1937, CV2; Chelmsford CA, 'honorary treasurer's report' year ending Dec. 1936, D/Z96/3; Headlam MSS, diary, 21 Jan. 1937, D/He/33; J. Ramsden, *The Age of Balfour and Baldwin*, 359–60.

120 *Hansard*, vol. 339, col. 243, 4 Oct. 1938.

121 Harvey, *Harvey Diaries*, 8 Oct. 1938, 210.

122 Brooks MSS, journal, 5 Oct. 1938.

123 West Leeds CA, exec 24 Feb. 1938, no. 5 minute book; Emrys-Evans MSS, Doncaster to Evans, 12 Oct. 1938, Add.MS.58249.

124 Brooks MSS, journal, 17, 18, 19 Oct 1938.

125 Newbury CA, constituency council 12 Nov. 1938, D/EX409/3.

126 Brooks MSS, journal, 5 Oct. 1938, referring to conversation with Hacking.

127 CPA, 'by-elections results Nov. 1935–Nov. 1938', D. F. Clarke, 14 Nov. 1938; 'by-election results', D. F. Clarke to J. Ball, 28 Nov. 1938, CRD1/7/35.

128 *News Chronicle*, 28 Nov. 1938.

129 Chamberlain MSS, Neville to Hilda, 11 Dec. 1938, NC18/1/1079.

130 Headlam MSS, diary, 13 Nov. 1938, D/He/34; Chelmsford CA, women's council 22 Nov. 1938, D/Z96/13.

131 *News Chronicle*, 28 Nov. 1938: A British Institute of Public Opinion survey asked the sample 'Do you think the persecution of the Jews in Germany is an obstacle to good understanding between Britain and Germany?' Yes 73 per cent, No 15 per cent, No Opinion 12 per cent.

132 Harborough CA, constituency council 19 Nov. 1938, DE 1170/4; Chelmsford CA, exec. 4 Nov. 1938; Headlam MSS, diary, 10 Oct. 1938, D/He/34; Inverness CA, exec. and AGM 20 Oct. 1938.

133 South Oxfordshire CA, AGM 18 June 1938, exec. 9 Nov. 1938, S.Oxon.Con.I/3.

134 Birchall MSS, Sir Robert Brooke-Popham to J. D. Birchall, 14 Oct. 1938, Box 33.

135 CPA, MFA, National Union, exec. 14 Dec. 1938, card 58; Maidstone CA, exec. 21 Feb. 1939, A3/1/2; Heneage MSS, *Home and Empire*, (Louth edn) 28 Nov. 1938, HNC 2/48; Stockton CA, AGM 10 Mar. 1939, D/X322/5.

136 *The Times*, 15 Nov. 1938; *Financial Times*, 15 Nov. 1938; *Notices of Motions*, 14 Nov. 1938.

137 Cilcennin MSS, Robert Boothby to Lt-Col. Duff, 2 Dec. 1938, Cilc.coll.42.

138 Avon MSS, Emrys-Evans to Eden, 4 Nov. 1938, AP14/1/742.

139 Ruggles-Brise MSS, *Essex County Telegraph*, 17 Dec. 1938.

140 CPA, MFA, National Union, exec. 14 Dec. 1938, card 59.

141 Avon MSS, Eden to Timothy Eden, 9 Nov. 1938, AP14/1/737C.

142 James, *Boothby*, 187.

143 CPA, H. G. Hanrott, 'Munich by-elections', 25 Nov. 1938, CRD1/7/35. For analysis of Oxford, Bridgwater and Kinross see I. McLean, 'Oxford and Bridgwater' in Ramsden and Cook, *By-Elections in British Politics*, 140–65; Ball, 'Politics of appeasement'.

144 Brooks MSS, journal, 16 Feb. 1939 citing Hacking.

145 Glyn MSS, Ralph Glyn to mother, 30 Jan. 1939, D/EGlC9/10.

146 Avon MSS, Cranborne to Eden, n.d. [before 3 Feb. 1939 since this is date of Eden's reply], AP14/2/20.

147 SCA, western div. council, 1 Feb. 1939, Acc10424.

148 Barnes and Nicholson, *Amery Diaries*, 16 Mar. 1939, 549.

149 Headlam MSS, diary, 15 Mar. 1939, D/He/35.
150 *Hansard*, vol. 345, col. 466, 15 Mar. 1939.
151 *Hansard*, vol. 345, col. 470, 15 Mar. 1939.
152 *Hansard*, vol. 345, col. 523, 15 Mar. 1939. Other Conservatives who defended Chamberlain in the debate were: cols 477–80 (Somerville), 489–94 (de Chair), 501–5 (Donner).
153 James, *Chips*, 15 Mar. 1939, 186.
154 York MSS, diary, 15 Mar. 1939.
155 Barnes and Nicholson, *Amery Diaries*, 16 Mar. 1939, 548.
156 Northern Counties Area, AGM 18 Mar. 1939, NRO3303/1.
157 Derby CA, AGM 23 Mar. 1939; Maidstone CA, AGM 27 Mar. 1939, A3/1/2; SCA, Scottish Junior League, central council 25 Mar. 1939, Acc10424/91.
158 Harborough CA, AGM, 29 Apr. 1939, DE 11170/4; CPA, MFA, National Union, exec. 14 June 1939, card 60.
159 James, *Chips*, 3 Apr. 1939, 192; Also, the sceptic Ronald Tree expressed his approval to his association, Harborough CA, AGM 29 Apr. 1939, DE1170/4; *Hansard*, vol. 345, cols 2496–505 (Churchill), 2511–15 (Eden), 2524–9 (Nicolson), 3 Apr. 1939.
160 York MSS, diary, 31 Mar. 1939.
161 Headlam MSS, diary, 31 Mar. 1939, D/He/35.
162 L. Amery, *My Political Life*, London, Hutchinson, 1955, 315.
163 Hitler on 28 Apr. had made a speech accusing Britain of trying to encircle Germany.
164 City of London CA, AGM 16 June 1939, 487/31.
165 Sowerby CA, AGM 11 May 1939 (McCorquodale), CV3.
166 *Hansard*, vol. 333, cols 93–100, 14 Mar. 1938; cols 1444–55, 24 Mar. 1938; vol. 346, cols 29–38, 13 Apr. 1939.
167 W. S. Churchill, *Arms and the Covenant*, London, Cassell, 1938, 451.
168 Selborne MSS, 'The relative situation in Sept. 1938 and Sept. 1939', MS.Eng.hist.c.1015 ff.13–27; Paul Emrys-Evans to Wolmer, 21 Nov. 1939, MS.Eng.hist.c.1014 ff.221–24.
169 Ruggles-Brise MSS, *Hertfordshire and Essex Observer*, 5 Nov. 1938; *Halstead Gazette*, 2 Dec. 1938; *East Anglian Daily Times*, 27 Jan. 1939. This theme of anti-communism is developed further in Chapter 2.
170 Barnes and Nicholson, *Amery Diaries*, 26, 27 Sept. 1938, 516–20.
171 Headlam MSS, diary, 28 May 1939, D/He/35.
172 Barnes and Nicholson, *Amery Diaries*, 19 May 1939, 553; James, *Chips*, 13 Apr., 5 May 1939, 193, 197.
173 Avon MSS, Eden to Cranborne, 12 July 1939, AP14/2/28.
174 Avon MSS, Eden to Cranborne, 12 July 1939, AP14/2/28.
175 Chamberlain MSS, Neville to Ida, 10 June 1939, NC18/1/1102.
176 Glyn MSS, Glyn to mother, 2 July 1939, D/EGlC9/10.
177 Hailes MSS, Buchan-Hepburn to Chas Adamson, 30 July 1939, HAIL 1/2.
178 *Hansard*, vol. 350, col. 2495, 2 Aug. 1939. After this attack, Chamberlain sought to have Cartland deselected. Chamberlain MSS, Neville to Ida, 5 Aug. 1939, NC18/1/1111, R. H. Edwards to Chamberlain, 4 Aug. 1939, NC7/11/32/38, T. B. Pritchett to R. Cartland, 4 Aug. 1939, NC7/11/32/39. See also B. Cartland, *Ronald Cartland*, London, Collins, 1942, 219–29.

179 Avon MSS, Cranborne to Eden, 17 Aug. 1939, AP14/2/32A.
180 Headlam MSS, diary, 1, 17 Aug. 1939, D/He/35.
181 James, *Chips*, 22 Aug. 1939, 208.
182 Elliot MSS, Walter Elliot to wife, 27 Aug. 1939, Box7F1.

CHAPTER 4

1 Tynemouth C[onservative] A[ssociation], exec[utive] 4 May 1934, 1633/1; Northern Area Council, 22 Sept. 1934, NRO 3303/1; Chichester CA, exec. 22 Oct. 1934, CO/ICHAddMSS 12089; S[cottish] C[onservative Party] A[rchive], Scottish annual conference, 23 Nov. 1934, Acc 10424/64; See also P. Kyba, *Covenants Without The Sword*, Waterloo, Ontario, Wilfrid Laurier University Press, 1983, 54–7, 61–4, 91–8, 103–11, 122–8 for 1933 and 1934 Conservative attitudes to disarmament and rearmament.
2 C[onservative] P[arty] A[rchive], M[icro] F[iche] A[rchive], National Union general purposes sub-cttee, 12 June 1935, card 52, series II.
3 Winchester CA, selection cttee, 11 Mar. 1935 (Gerald Palmer) 73M86W/4.
4 Derby MSS, Midleton to Derby, 27 Mar. 1935, Derby to Midleton, 28 Mar. 1935, 920DER(17)47/3.
5 *The Times*, 10 Nov. 1933.
6 *The True Facts*, London, Conservative Central Office, Mar. 1935.
7 Chichester CA, general purposes cttee, 25 Mar. 1935, CO/ICHaddmss12088; CPA, MFA, National Union, general purposes sub-cttee, 12 June 1935, card 52; Birmingham CA, management cttee, 14 June 1935, AQ329.94249CON f. 77.
8 J. Barnes and K. Middlemas, *Baldwin*, London, Weidenfeld and Nicolson, 1969, 859.
9 J. Ramsden, *The Age of Balfour and Baldwin*, London, Longman, 1979, 344.
10 Kyba, *Covenants*, 168–9.
11 cited K. Feiling, *The Life of Neville Chamberlain*, London, Macmillan, 1946, 314.
12 See U. Bailer, *Shadow of the Bomber: The Fear of Air Attack and British Politics*, London, Royal Historical Society, 1980, *passim*; M. S. Smith, 'Rearmament and deterrence in Britain in the 1930s', *Journal of Strategic Studies*, 1978, vol. 1, 313–37.
13 *Hansard: House of Commons Debates*, vol. 270, col. 632, 10 Nov. 1932; For the reaction of backbenchers and the House of Commons see S. Ball (ed.) *The Headlam Diaries*, London, Historians' Press, 1992, 10 Nov. 1932, 250; and N. Smart (ed.) *The Diaries and Letters of Robert Bernays, 1932–9*, Lampeter, Edwin Mellen Press, 1996, 11 Nov., 193–214.
14 For arguments over British defence policy and priorities during the 1930s see B. Bond, *British Military Policy Between Two World Wars*, Oxford, Clarendon Press, 1980, especially chs. 7–9; Dennis, *Decision By Default*, London, Routledge and Kegan Paul, 1972, especially chs. 3–5; M. Smith, *British Air Strategy Between The Wars*, Oxford, Clarendon Press, 1984, chs. 5–7.
15 See N. H. Gibbs, *History of the Second World War: I: Grand Strategy: Rearmament Policy*, London, HMSO, 1976, 187–226.

16 For example, see CPA, MFA, National Union general purposes sub-committee, 11 Mar. 1936, 20 May 1936, card 54; Birmingham CA, AGM, 20 Mar. 1936, AQ329.94249CON ff. 158–9.

17 In 1935 the speakers were Professor Lindeman (air defence) in Feb.; Admiral Sir Herbert Richmond (naval defence) in Apr.; and Field Marshal Lord Milne (Commmittee on Imperial Defence) in May; During 1936 Major-General Sir John Davidson (defence organisation) in Mar.; Field Marshal Sir Philip Chetwode (imperial defence) also in Mar.; Thomas Inskip (supply and coordination of defence) in May; and Churchill (air defence) in Dec.. CPA, 1922 Committee, 1936–7 *passim*, CPA/1922CMMTEE. Interestingly, those who spoke during 1937 and 1938 on defence matters were politicians, with the exception of Liddell-Hart in Dec. 1937.

18 Brooks MSS, journal, 18 Mar. 1936. Rothermere did so 'because he desires evidence that these inept dullards were warned, and have no excuse for neglecting British rearmament'.

19 *Hansard*, vol. 317, cols 1098–1118 (Churchill), 12 Nov. 1936; Winterton MSS, diary, 12 Nov. 1936, 1/42; CPA, 1922 committee, 7 Dec. 1936, CPA/1922CMMTEE.

20 Churchill tabled an amendment to the address on 4 Nov. 1936 regretting the weakness of air defence. He only secured the support of five other MPs (*Notices of Motions*, 4 Nov. 1936).

21 G. Peden, *British Rearmament and the Treasury*, Edinburgh, Scottish Academic Press, 1979, 64–5; R. P. Shay, *British Rearmament in the Thirties: Politics and Profits*, Princeton N.J., Princeton University Press, 1977, 145–7; Gibbs, *Rearmament Policy*, 275–95.

22 Peden, *Treasury*, *passim*; Shay, *British Rearmament*, 35–46, 77–8, 84–5, 142–4.

23 West Devon CA, exec. 8 Dec. 1933, D399/3/1

24 *Hansard*, vol. 311, cols 183–8, 251–5, 22 Apr. 1936.

25 *Hansard*, vol. 311, cols 200–7, 22 Apr. 1936.

26 *Hansard*, vol. 311, cols 188–94 (Davison), 226–31 (Hills), 22 Apr. 1936.

27 *Hansard*, vol. 311, cols 326–39, 23 Apr. 1936.

28 *Hansard*, vol. 313, cols 255–6, 10 June 1936.

29 For the Treasury decision making process with the tax see R. P. Shay, 'Chamberlain's folly: the National Defence Contribution of 1937', *Albion*, 1975, vol. 7, 317–21.

30 Chamberlain MSS, Neville to Hilda, 25 Apr. 1937, NC18/1/1005.

31 *Hansard*, vol. 322, col. 1601, 20 Apr. 1937.

32 *Hansard*, vol. 322, cols 1615–20, 20 Apr. 1937.

33 *Hansard*, vol. 322, cols 1619–20, 20 Apr. 1937.

34 B. E. V. Sabine, *British Budgets in War and Peace, 1932–45*, London, Allen and Unwin, 1970, 103.

35 *Hansard*, vol. 322, col.1873–81, 21 Apr. 1937; Sabine, *Budgets*, 107.

36 By the time the of the second reading of the bill two critical EDMs (in names of Stourton and Mellor) had been tabled by Conservatives. They secured the support of thirty-three MPs. *Notices of Motions*, 31 May 1937.

37 Winterton MSS, diary, 21 Apr. 1937, 1/42.

38 J. Barnes and D. Nicholson (eds) *The Empire At Bay: The Leo Amery*

Diaries, 1929–45, London, Hutchinson, 1984, 20 Apr., 27 May 1937, 440; see also Winterton MSS, diary, 21 Apr. 1937, 1 June 1937, 1/42.

39 Cazalet MSS, journal, 1 June 1937.
40 Barnes and Nicholson, *Amery Diaries*, 27 May 1937, 340.
41 This figure was Joseph Ball, director of the CRD, usually a staunch ally of Chamberlain. This appears to be the one instance when he betrayed his political master: see J. Ramsden, *The Making of Conservative Party Policy*, London, Longman, 1980, 87–8; for an example of industry lobbying see Hannon MSS, Chamberlain to Hannon (as president of National Union of Manufacturers), 23 Apr. 1937, Box 87, File 1.
42 Winchester CA, exec. 27 May 1937, 73M86W/5; Heneage MSS, Mr Greenfield to Arthur Heneage, 22 Apr. 1938, HNC 1/G; Mr Charlesworth to Heneage, 13 May 1937, HNC 1/C; Mr Goulton to Heneage, 25 May 1937, HNC 1/G; Atholl MSS, James Paton to Duchess of Atholl, 1 May 1937, File 22/18. See also SCA, Western division propaganda cttee, 26 May 1937, Acc10424/32 f.71.
43 Furthermore, it is calculated that in 1939 181 Conservative MPs held directorships in a variety of transport, distribution and manufacturing enterprises. S. Newton, *Profits of Peace: The Political Economy of Anglo-German Appeasement*, Oxford, Clarendon Press, 1996, 26.
44 Chamberlain MSS, Neville to Hilda, 25 Apr. 1937, NC18/1/1003; Headlam MSS, diary, 22 Apr. 1937, D/He/33; R. R. James (ed.) *Chips: The Diaries of Sir Henry Channon*, London, Weidenfeld and Nicolson, 1967, 1 June 1937, 130. Simon's amendments had first been suggested by Beverley Baxter during the report stage of the budget in late April. *Hansard*, vol. 323, cols 292–4, 27 Apr. 1937.
45 Heneage MSS, Mr Charlesworth to Heneage, 13 May 1937, HNC1/C.
46 Peden, *Treasury*, 105.
47 *Hansard*, vol. 321, col. 53 (Williams), 55 (Lewis), 1 Mar. 1937; vol. 322, cols 1629–32 (Wardlaw-Milne), 20 Apr. 1937; vol. 323, col. 288 (Boothby), 27 Apr. 1937.
48 Peden, *Treasury*, 89; *Hansard*, vol. 322, cols 1613–16, 1621–2, 20 Apr. 1937.
49 Peden, *Treasury*, 89; Shay, *British Rearmament*, 159.
50 Sowerby CA, AGM 12 Apr. 1937, CV2.
51 For example: CPA, Wessex Provincial Area, exec. 1 May 1937, ARE10/1/2 adopted the resolution 'that this meeting realising that a strong and united British Empire is the best guarantee of world peace, assures the National government of its full support in the steps being taken to strengthen the defence forces'.
52 North Wiltshire CA, *North West Wilts Critic*, 'Member's monthly letter', Apr. 1937, (Cazalet), 2–3, 2436/69; Rushcliffe CA, AGM 20 Feb. 1937, (Assheton), DD.PP.1/1; Ipswich CA, exec. 26 Mar. 1937, (Ganzoni), GK 401/1/1.
53 Atholl MSS, Peter Comrie to Duchess of Atholl, 9 June 1938, file 95/2.
54 I. Macleod, *Neville Chamberlain*, London, Muller, 1961, 184; Stannage, *Baldwin*, 135–6; S. Haxey, *Tory MP*, London, Left Book Club, 1939, ch. 2, points to the links that Conservatives had with the defence industry.
55 Stannage, *Baldwin*, 161.

56 CPA, 1922 Cttee, 25 Jan. 1937, CPA/1922CMMTEE; *Notices of Motion*, 25 Jan. 1937 EDM in name of A.A. Somerville.

57 Penryn and Falmouth CA, AGM 31 Oct. 1936 (Petherick), DDX551/10; *Darwen News*, 31 July 1937, (Russell); *Hansard*, vol. 320, cols 2219–26 (Chamberlain), 25 Feb. 1937, vol. 321, col. 679 (Chamberlain), 4 Mar. 1937.

58 CPA, MFA, National Union exec. 16 July 1936, card 54.

59 Northern Counties Area CA, AGM 27 Feb. 1937, NRO 3303/1. This resolution was forwarded to the National Union executive and on their recommendation forwarded to the Minister of Air, CPA, MFA, National Union, exec. 10 Mar. 1937, card 56. Also Norwich CA, AGM 23 Apr. 1937, SO122/4.678x9; Chelmsford CA, AGM 24 Mar. 1937, D/Z96/4.

60 CPA, MFA, National Union exec. 10 Mar. 1937, card 56.

61 Selborne MSS, memo by Churchill, 'Points for consideration', May 1936, Ms.Eng.hist.d.450 ff. 52–4.

62 CPA, 1922 Committee, 18 May 1936 (Inskip), CPA/1922CMMTEE; Glyn MSS, Glyn to mother, 30 Jan. 1939, D/EGlC9/10.

63 Winterton MSS, diary 15 Mar. 1936, 1/41.

64 *Hansard*, vol. 326, col. 2940–3, 27 July 1937.

65 *Hansard*, vol. 326, cols 2966–70, quote col. 2970, 27 July 1937.

66 Peden, *Treasury*, 41, argues it was the Treasury's 'rationing' ceiling that led to the Inskip review.

67 For further analysis see Shay, *British Rearmament*, 173–83; G. C. Peden, 'A matter of timing: the economic background to British foreign policy', *History*, 1984, vol. 69, 15–28.

68 The deputation consisted of Salisbury, Churchill, Austin Chamberlain, Grigg, Fitzalan, Winterton, Guest, Trenchard, Wolmer, Milner, Home, Amery and Keyes. Between July and Nov. 1936, this deputation had three meetings with Baldwin. Winterton MSS, diary, 28 Aug. 1936, 1/42.

69 CPA, 1922 Committee, 1 Feb. 1937, CPA/1922CMMTEE.

70 *Hansard*, vol. 321, cols 1926 (Winterton), 1934–42 (Amery), 1946–7 (Knox), 1970–1 (Anstruther-Gray), 1975, 1979 (Grigg), 16 Mar. 1937.

71 CPA, 1922 Committee, 21 June 1937; see also Barnes and Nicholson, *Amery Diaries*, 2 July 1937 445–6.

72 Although this is not reflected in a comparison of actual parliamentary debate time devoted to the army estimates between 1937 and 1938. In 1937, 16 and 18 Mar. 12 hrs 10 mins compared 1938 10 and 22 Mar. 12 hrs 51 mins. The estimates in 1938 for air secured 14 hrs 29 mins and the navy, 10 hrs 45 mins.

73 *Hansard*, vol. 332, col. 1558, 7 Mar. 1938.

74 Makins MSS, diary, 10 Mar. 1938; Barnes and Nicholson, *Amery Diaries*, 10 Mar. 1938, 460; *Hansard*, vol. 332, col. 2174 (Knox), 10 Mar. 1938.

75 *Hansard*, vol. 332, col. 2136, 10 Mar. 1938.

76 Barnes and Nicholson, *Amery Diaries*, 7 Mar. 1938, 459.

77 Barnes and Nicholson, *Amery Diaries*, 12 Mar. 1938, 496.

78 *Hansard*, vol. 333, col. 290 (Assheton), 15 Mar. 1938.

79 Sowerby CA, AGM 16 Mar. 1938, (McCorquodale), CV3.

80 CPA, Wessex Prov. Area, exec. 7 May 1938, ARE10/1/2; CPA, MFA, National Union, exec. 6 Apr. 1938, approving resolution from East Leicester CA, card 58; Heneage MSS, Arthur Heneage, 'Home and

Empire' (Louth edn), 24 Mar. 1938; Clitheroe CA, AGM 3 Mar. 1938, (Brass), DDX 800/1/3.

81 Rushcliffe CA, AGM 5 Mar. 1938, DD.PP1/1; Cilcennin MSS, Gerald [Creasy] to J. P. L. Thomas, 23 Mar. 1938, Cilc.coll.45.

82 Cilcennin MSS, David [Lindsay] to J. P. L. Thomas, 28 [Mar.] 1938, Cilc.coll.29.

83 Cilcennin MSS, unsigned carbon of letter, 13 Apr. 1938, Cilc.coll.39.

84 J. Harvey (ed.) *The Diplomatic Diaries of Oliver Harvey*, London, Collins, 1970, 13 Apr. 1938, 127.

85 *Hansard*, vol. 333, cols 1052–3, 22 Mar. 1938.

86 *Hansard*, vol. 333, cols 1062–4, 22 Mar. 1938.

87 *Hansard*, vol. 333, col. 1074, 22 Mar. 1938.

88 *Hansard*, vol. 333, cols 1091–2, 22 Mar. 1938.

89 *Hansard*, vol. 333, col. 1410, 24 Mar. 1938.

90 Cilcennin MSS, J. P. L. Thomas to anon., 12 Apr. 1938, Cilc.coll.40.

91 *Hansard*, vol. 333, cols 1471–3, 24 Mar. 1938.

92 Cazalet MSS, journal, 24 Mar., 10 Apr. 1938.

93 *Hansard*, vol. 335, cols 1758–90, 12 May 1938. During his speech, Winterton was repeatedly interrupted, especially by Churchill and Sandys. Winterton MSS, diary, 12 May 1938, 1/43.

94 Barnes and Nicholson, *Amery Diaries*, 18 May 1938, 505. Indeed Winterton agreed with this assessment, Winterton MSS, diary, 12 May 1938, 1/43.

95 James, *Chips*, 13 May 1938, 155.

96 Makins MSS, diary 9, 12 May 1938; Barnes and Nicholson, *Amery Diaries*, 9 May 1938, 503.

97 *Notices of Motions*, 12 May 1938; N. Nicolson (ed.) *The Diaries and Letters of Harold Nicolson, 1930–9*, London, Collins, 1966, Nicolson to wife, 17 May 1938, 341; Chamberlain made the Labour motion a vote of confidence and comfortably survived the division. Only Churchill and Robert Perkins were prepared to abstain. Thomas Moore, supported by 120 other Conservatives, tabled a counter-EDM which rejected the need for an enquiry, *Notices of Motions*, 16 May 1938; see also Smith, *British Air Strategy*, 210–11.

98 Avon MSS, Eden to Arthur Mann, 27 May 1938, AP14/1/772A.

99 *Hansard*, vol. 321, col. 2620, 22 Mar. 1937.

100 Shay, *British Rearmament*, 220.

101 Winterton MSS, diary, 16 May 1938, 1/43. Winterton 'felt very crushed at this tragic curbing of two months strenuous but happy work'.

102 U. Bialer, 'Elite opinion and defence policy', *British Journal of International Studies*, 1979–80, vol. 5–6, 32, 40–3.

103 P. R. C. Groves, *Behind the Smoke Screen*, London, Faber and Faber, 1934.

104 *Hansard*, vol. 275, col. 1822, 14 Mar. 1933.

105 *Documents on British Rearmament*, Southampton University Library, Committee of Imperial Defence, sub-committee on defence policy and requirements, minutes 14, 16 Jan. 1936. Cab 16/123. (Xerox of original from PRO).

106 W. Wark, *The Ultimate Enemy: British Intelligence and Nazi Germany*, Oxford, Oxford University Press, 1986, chs 2–3.

107 Bialer, *Shadow of the Bomber*, *passim*; Smith, *British Air Strategy*, chs 5–7.

108 *Hansard*, vol. 321, cols 1703–4 (Moore-Brabazon), 1768–9 (Balfour), 1776–7 (Simmonds), 15 Mar. 1937; vol. 321, cols 2599 (Sueter), 2610 (Churchill), 22 Mar. 1937; Balfour was not the only Conservative who expressed exasperation with Churchill's attacks on the government's air policies: Austin Hopkinson wrote to Winterton complaining that he did not 'like Winston's calm assumption that he alone has any regard for the country. He talks and talks while some of us work – and I doubt whether his talk does anything except hinder us'. Winterton MSS, Austin Hopkinson to Winterton, 27 May 1938, 2/66.

109 *Hansard*, vol. 333, cols 65 (Boothby), 281 (Moore-Brabazon), 14 Mar. 1938; vol. 335, cols 1827–9 (Wright), 12 May 1938.

110 North Wiltshire CA, *North West Wilts Critic*, Dec. 1938.

111 Elliot MSS, Walter Elliot to wife, 26 Oct. 1938, Acc 6721 Box 7F1.

112 Emrys-Evans MSS, Evans to Doncaster, 7 Oct. 1938, Add.MS.58249.

113 Glyn MSS, D/EGl 093; Heneage MSS, HNC2/ , Memo: 'A.A. defence, London'.

114 B. Bond (ed.) *Chief of Staff: The Diaries of Lieutenant-General Sir Henry Pownall, I, 1933–40*, London, Leo Cooper, 1972, 10 Oct. 1938, 165.

115 *Hansard*, vol. 340, cols 521–30, esp. 527–8, 3 Nov. 1938; Barnes and Nicholson, *Amery Diaries*, 3 Nov. 1938, 534. Patrick Hannon had been 'profoundly disturbed' by the methods Spears had employed and he forwarded a copy of the memo to both Chamberlain and Hore-Belisha: Hannon MSS, Hannon to Chamberlain, 14 Nov. 1938, Box 17 File 1; Hore-Belisha to Hannon, 15 Nov. 1938, Box 90.

116 Barnes and Nicholson, *Amery Diaries*, 24 Nov. 1938, 537.

117 Inverness CA, 'Annual report, 1938', 20 Oct. 1938; Winchester CA, exec. 29 Nov. 1938, 73M86W/5; *Hansard*, vol. 339, col. 245, 4 Oct. 1938.

118 *Essex County Telegraph*, 17 Dec 1938; similarly argued Inverness CA, 'Annual report' 20 Oct. 1938.

119 Selborne MSS, Wolmer to Godfrey Fell, 7 Oct. 1938, MS.Eng.hist.c.1014.

120 Selborne MSS, Wolmer to Godfrey Fell, 7 Oct. 1938, MS.Eng.hist.c.1014.

121 West Essex (now Epping) CA, special central council, 4 Nov. 1938, D/Z120A6853; For a historical analysis of Churchill and rearmament see D. C. Watt, 'Churchill and appeasement', in R. Louis and R. Blake (eds) *Churchill*, Oxford, Oxford University Press, 1993, 202–4.

122 C. Thornton-Kemsley, *Through Winds and Tides*, Montrose, Standard Press, 1974, 86–9.

123 Q. Hogg, *The Left Was Never Right*, London, Faber and Faber, 1945 especially 207–9.

124 Somerset de Chair to author, 2 Sept. 1992.

125 Butler MSS, Cuthbert Alport to Butler, 14 Sept. 1938, RABG934.

126 *Hansard*, vol. 339, cols 397–8, 5 Oct. 1938.

127 *Hansard*, vol. 339, col. 119, 3 Oct. 1938.

128 James, *Chips*, 15 June 1939, 203.

129 Chamberlain announced his intention to review the rearmament

programme in his closing speech during the Munich debate: *Hansard*, vol. 339, cols 551–2, 6 Oct. 1938.

130 *Hansard*, vol. 339, col. 407 (Sandeman Allen), 5 Oct. 1938; Inverness CA, 'Annual report, Oct. 1938'; CPA, women's advisory cttee, 24 Nov. 1938, ARE3/11/2; *Essex County Telegraph*, 17 Dec. 1938 (Ruggles-Brise and Oswald Lewis); Bute and North Ayrshire CA, AGM 23 Dec. 1938.

131 CPA, North West Area, quarterly council, 5 Nov. 1938, ARE3/1/2; Women's advisory cttee, 24 Nov. 1938 ARE3/11/2; *Hansard*, vol. 339, col. 398 (Wardlaw-Milne), 5 Oct. 1938, col. 536–7 (Grigg), 6 Oct. 1938; vol. 341, cols 58–9 (Macquisten), 8 Nov. 1938, cols 364 (Milner), 401 (Keyes), 10 Nov. 1938.

132 Almond MSS, Lancaster's by-election address, DDX1202/1/24.

133 Almond MSS, Almond to Lord Derby, 5 Nov. 1938, DDX1202/1/47.

134 *Staffordshire Chronicle*, 11 Mar. 1939, (Thorneycroft).

135 Heneage MSS, Heneage to J. M. Lill, 12 Oct. 1938, HNC1/L.

136 Bute CA, AGM 23 Dec. 1938.

137 Avon MSS, Evans to Eden, 4 Nov. 1938, AP 14/1/742, Eden to Evans, 8 Nov. 1938, AP 14/1/742A.

138 Avon MSS, Eden to Mr Meville, 15 Nov. 1938, AP14/1/779A.

139 *Hansard*, vol. 341, col. 47, 8 Nov 1938.

140 Barnes and Nicholson, *Amery Diaries*, 5, 12 Dec. 1938, 539, 540; CPA, 1922 Committee, 5 and 12 December 1938, CPA/1922CMMTEE.

141 Harvey, *Harvey Diaries*, 13 Dec. 1938, 227. The malcontents were Robert Hudson, Under-Secretary for Trade; Lord Strathcona, Under-Secretary for War; Marquess of Dufferin and Ava, Under-Secretary for the Colonies; Kenneth Lindsay, Parliamentary Secretary to the Board of Education; and Harry Crookshank, the rebellious Minister for Mines who had already threatened resignation over Eden's departure and the Munich agreement.

142 Barnes and Nicholson, *Amery Diaries*, 19 Dec. 1938, 540.

143 Harvey, *Harvey Diaries*, 13 Dec. 1938, 227.

144 Chamberlain MSS, Neville to Ida, 17 Dec. 1938, NC18/1/1080.

145 Glyn MSS, Glyn to mother, 30 Jan. 1939, D/EGlC9/10.

146 Chamberlain MSS, Neville to Hilda, 11 Dec. 1938, NC18/1/1079.

CHAPTER 5

1 This chapter is derived from my article 'The Conservative party and the call for national service, 1937–9: compulsion versus voluntarism', *Contemporary Record*, 9, 3 (1995), 507–28.

2 Keyes MSS, 'Ashridge Lecture', 29 Aug. 1937, AddMS 12/7.

3 *Hansard: House of Commons Debates*, vol. 310, col. 1992 (Baldwin), 1 Apr. 1936; vol. 331, col. 2057 (Chamberlain), 17 Feb. 1938; vol. 336, col. 1792 (Inskip), 30 May 1938; vol. 345, cols 2029–51 (Chamberlain), 29 Mar. 1939.

4 Before the First World War, the ostensibly non-political National Service League had widespread grassroots Conservative support. They claimed after the 1910 election to have 177 sitting MPs as members, in reality this

was more likely around eighty. No similar organisation existed in the 1930s, although there was the Army League (Citizens' Service League from January 1939) which did draw some support from late 1938. For National Service League see R. J. Q. Adams and P. P. Poirier, *The Conscription Controversy in Great Britain*, London, Macmillan, 1987, 23; J. Osborne, *The Voluntary Recruiting Movement in Britain, 1914–16*, London, Garland, 1982, 17–18; R. Williams, *Defending the Empire: The Conservative Party and British Defence Policy, 1899–1915*, London, Yale University Press, 1991, 57–8, 143–8, 150–4, 171, 185–92, 201, 220, 222.

5 Williams, *Defending the Empire*, 57.
6 C[onservative] P[arty] A[rchive], 1922 Committee, 16 May 1938, CPA/1922CMMTEE; *Hansard: House of Commons Debates*, vol. 339, cols 536–7, 6 Oct. 1938.
7 L. S. Amery, 'National service', *National Review*, vol. CXI, Dec. 1938, 725–35; *Hansard*, vol. 332, cols 2225–7 (Beamish), 10 Mar. 1938; *Glasgow Herald*, 22 Oct. 1938 (Richard Ropner prospective candidate for West Stirlingshire).
8 Osborne, *Voluntary Recruiting*, *passim*, especially 21–4; K. Grieves, *The Politics of Manpower, 1914–18*, Manchester, Manchester University Press, 1988, argues that a total war effort should include the ability to make effective use of mobilised resources and the existence of a coordinating manpower authority which he believes did not arise until the last year of the First World War, 207–9.
9 P. Dennis, *Decision By Default: Peacetime Conscription and British Defence, 1919–39*, London, Routledge and Kegan Paul, 1972.
10 CPA, 1922 Committee, 16 May 1938, CPA/1922CMMTEE.
11 For a history of the Territorial Army see P. Dennis, *The Territorial Army*, Woodbridge, Royal Historical Society, 1987.
12 For historical scrutiny of the 'fourth arm of defence', see G. Peden, *British Rearmament and the Treasury, 1932–9*, Edinburgh, Scottish Academic Press, 1979; R. P. Shay, *British Rearmament in the Thirties*, Princeton NJ, Princeton University Press, 1977; R. A. C. Parker, 'Economics, rearmament and foreign policy', *Journal of Contemporary History*, 10, 4 (1975), 637–48; R. A. C. Parker, 'British rearmament, 1936–9' *English Historical Review*, 96, 2 (1981), 306–43; Gustav Schmidt, *The Politics and Economics of Appeasement*, trans. Jackie Bennet-Ruete, Leamington, Berg, 1986.
13 *Hansard*, vol. 332, cols 1600–7 (Churchill), 7 Mar. 1938; vol. 332, cols 1620–6 (Grigg), 7 Mar. 1938; vol. 332, cols 2225–7 (Beamish), 10 Mar. 1938.
14 Atholl MSS, James Paton to Duchess of Atholl, 17 Mar. 1938, file 22/18.
15 Winchester CA, AGM 26 Mar. 1938, 73M86W/5. The motion was then forwarded to the National Union exec. which decided to allow it to 'lay on the table'. CPA, M[icro] F[iche] A[rchive], National Union, exec[utive] 16 June 1938, card 58.
16 North Wiltshire CA, AGM 1 Apr. 1938, 2436/1; Altrincham MSS, Col. Fitzgerald to Edward Grigg, 25 Sept. 1938, MS/Film1005 Reel#7. For further examples see: Kennington CA, 29 Apr. 1938; Altrincham MSS, Mabel S. Lomax to Edward Grigg, 12 Apr. 1938, MS/Film1005 Reel#7.

17 Chelmsford CA, AGM 29 Mar. 1938, D/Z 96/4; exec. 6, 27 May 1938, D/Z 96/7.
18 Williams, *Defending the Empire*, 188–9, 217.
19 Adams MSS, Frederick Walker to Vyvyan Adams, 13 Oct. 1938, file 10.
20 Compare Williams, *Defending the Empire*, 147, with L. S. Amery, *My Political Life: The Unforgiving Years*, London, Hutchinson, 1955, 299 fn. 1. By 1938 Salisbury was a member of the Army League.
21 For instance, Sir Thomas Inskip, Minister for the Coordination of Defence, foresaw a situation whereby the unions 'would make conditions: for example, they might demand the Government undertake the use of arms in support of Czecho-Slovakia, or insist on the question being dealt with by the League of Nations'. Cited in Peden, *Treasury*, 82; For analysis of the unions' attitudes to national service and conscription see H. Clegg, *A History of British Trade Unions since 1889: Volume III: 1934–51*, Oxford, Clarendon Press, 1994, 140–3.
22 Cilcennin MSS, 13 Apr. 1938, copy of unsigned letter – pencilled note at top: 'J. P. L. Thomas to Lord Baldwin', Cilc.coll.39. Tory peer Lord Tyrrell approached TUC leaders during Apr. 1938. J. Harvey (ed.) *The Diplomatic Diaries of Oliver Harvey*, London, Collins, 1970, 13 Apr. 1938, 122; Leo Amery and Sir Edward Grigg approached Labour leaders during the Czech crisis in an attempt to secure their support for national service: J. Barnes and D. Nicholson (eds) *The Empire At Bay: The Leo Amery Diaries*, London, Hutchinson, 1988, 490–1; Altrincham MSS, Edward Grigg to Lord Camrose, n.d., MS/Film1005 Reel#7.
23 CPA, 1922 Committee, 27 June 1938, CPA/1922CMMTEE.
24 Altrincham MSS, 'Deputation to the Prime Minister', 31 May 1938, MS/Film1012 Reel#14; Makins MSS, diary, 31 May 1938.
25 Altrincham MSS, Edward Grigg to Neville Chamberlain, 26 July 1938; Grigg to Geoffrey Dawson, 29 July 1938; Ralph Glyn to Grigg, 23 Sept. 1938, MS/Film1005 Reel#7. Signatories for the motion included Hugh O'Neill, chairman of the 1922 Executive Committee; John Anderson, shortly to be appointed Lord Privy Seal with responsibility for civil defence; and Ralph Glyn, PPS to Inskip.
26 CPA, 1922 Committee, 2 Nov. 1938, CPA/1922CMMTEE.
27 Keyes MSS, Letter to *Daily Telegraph*, 18 Aug. 1938, AddMS 12/7.
28 C.P. 177(37), Cab 24/270 cited Dennis, *Decision By Default*, 105.
29 *Hansard*, vol. 339, cols 398 (Wardlaw-Milne), 514 (Gilmour), 536–7 (Grigg), 5–6 Oct. 1938.
30 *Hansard*, vol. 342, col. 1065, 6 Dec. 1938.
31 Barnes and Nicholson, *Amery Diaries*, 27 Mar. 1939, 549.
32 Winchester CA, AGM, 26 Mar. 1938, central exec. council 29 Nov. 1938, AGM 28 Mar. 1938, 73M86W/5; *Hampshire Advertiser*, 1 Apr. 1939.
33 Altrincham MSS: Leo Amery to Edward Grigg, 12 Oct. 1938, MS/Film1005 Reel#7.
34 *The Times*, 1 July 1938.
35 CPA, MFA, National Union, exec. 9 Nov. 1938, card 58. In fact the resolutions sub-committee had already forwarded the South East area resolution 7 Sept. 1938 but without their endorsement.
36 Adams MSS, Frederick Walker to Vyvyan Adams, 13 Oct. 1938, file 10.
37 For example: Altrincham MSS, C. H. Fuller to Edward Grigg, 12 Oct.

1938, MS/Film1005 Reel#7; Chelmsford CA, exec. 4, 21 Nov. 1938, D/Z
96/7; CPA, women's advisory cttee 24 Nov. 1938, ARE 3/11/2; North
West Prov. Area, quarterly council, 5 Nov. 1938, ARE 3/1/2; S[cottish]
C[onservative Party] A[rchive], annual conference 17 Nov. 1938, Acc.
10424/64. The issue had also been discussed in the previous phase by the
CPA, South Eastern Prov. Area Council 20 July 1938, ARE 9/24/1.

38 *Daily Mail*, 26 Oct. 1938: readers were asked whether they favoured
compulsory or voluntary national service. They defined national service
as including 'not only military service, but ARP duties, work on munition, and in special industries, distribution of food, and other national
defence activities'. The result was 50.184 per cent for voluntary; 49.816
per cent for compulsory. Cited Dennis, *Decision By Default*, 149, fn. 4.

39 CPA, 1922 Committee, 2 Nov. and 12 Dec. 1938, CPA/1922CMMTEE.

40 Hailes MSS, Patrick Buchan-Hepburn to Mr A. R. Hughes, 15 Nov.
1938, HAIL 1/2; also Avon MSS, Sir Cecil Weir to Eden, 14 Nov. 1938,
AP 14/1/842.

41 *Hansard*, vol. 342, cols 597–604, 1 Dec. 1938; quote Anderson, 6 Dec.
1938, vol. 342, cols 1038–9.

42 Six backbench Conservative MPs spoke during the debate, four of whom
requested compulsion; a fifth admitted he had begun the debate
favouring a compulsory register but had been convinced by Anderson's
arguments for a voluntary system. See *Hansard*, vol. 342, cols 1023–140,
6 Dec. 1938.

43 Barnes and Nicholson, *Amery Diaries*, 6 Dec. 1938, 539.

44 N. J. Crowson, 'Citizen defence: the Conservative party and its attitude to
national service, 1937–57', in A. Beech and R. Weight (eds) *The Right to
Belong: Citizenship and National Identity in Britain, 1920–60*, London, I.
B. Tauris, forthcoming.

45 See Chelmsford CA, 1938, *passim*; CPA, MFA, National Union, women's
advisory committee, 24 Nov. 1938, card 58.

46 Avon MSS, J. P. L. Thomas to Eden, 25 Nov. 1938, AP14/1/829.

47 Barnes and Nicholson, *Amery Diaries*, 22 Sept. 1938, 512; Avon MSS,
Eden to Amery, 24 Oct. 1938, AP14/1/673A.

48 Barnes and Nicholson, *Amery Diaries*, 21 Mar. 1939, 549.

49 Compare Grigg's arguments in his book, E. Grigg, *Britain Looks At
Germany*, London, Nicolson and Watson, 1938, with Amery's memoirs,
My Political Life, 296–9; also Amery's article 'National service'.

50 See Grigg's justification of the necessity of appeasement: *Britain Looks
At Germany*, 20–1, 49–53, 73, 155.

51 Amery, *My Political Life*, 176, 239–42, 244, 259–95.

52 J. Turner (ed.) *The Larger Idea: Lord Lothian and the Problem of National
Sovereignty*, London, Historians' Press, 1988, 4; for Milner on compulsory service see Williams, *Defending the Empire*, 55–6, 147, 153, 155, 182.

53 Amery, 'National service'; Grigg, *Britain Looks At Germany*; Barnes and
Nicholson, *Amery Diaries*, editorial, 491–2; Keyes MSS, letters to *Daily
Telegraph*, 18 Aug. 1938, 11 Apr. 1939.

54 *Hansard*, vol. 342, cols 1096–9, quote, col. 1096 (Turton), 6 Dec. 1938;
Penryn and Falmouth CA, AGM 3 Dec. 1938 (Petherick), DDX 551/10;
The Times, 1 July 1938, 20 Apr. 1939.

55 Headlam MSS, diary, 2 Dec. 1938, D/He/34.

56 Hailes MSS, correspondence between Patrick Buchan-Hepburn and A. R. Hughes, Oct.–Nov. 1938, HAIL 1/2; Altrincham MSS, G. F. Panton to Sir Patrick Donner, 6 Dec. 1938 (copy sent by Donner to Grigg); Grigg to Donner, 9 Dec. 1938, quoting Altrincham agent's report from the constituency that 'opinion is very definitely that if we are to have a register at all it should be compulsory'. MS/Film1005 Reel#7.

57 Crookshank MSS, diary, 1 Dec. 1938, MSS.Eng.hist.d.360 f.322.

58 Dennis, *Territorial Army*, 236.

59 Mass-Observation Archive: FR, A16: 'Home or foreign?' April 1939 FR, A24: 'ARP survey in Fulham', Apr.–July 1939.

60 *Hansard*, vol. 344, cols 2161–82, 8 Mar. 1939.

61 *Hansard*, vol. 344, cols 2216 (Knox), 2223–4 (Macnamara), 2266 (Ponsonby), 2289 (Adams), 8 Mar. 1939.

62 B. Bond (ed.) *Chiefs of Staff: The Diaries of Lieutenant-General Sir Henry Pownall*, I, London, Leo Cooper, 1972, 27 Mar. 1939, 195.

63 *Hansard*, vol. 345, cols 446–7, 15 Mar. 1939.

64 Chelmsford CA, AGM 20 Mar. 1939, D/Z96/4.

65 CPA, 1922 Committee, 20 and 27 March 1939, CPA/1922CMMTEE; quote from Barnes and Nicholson, *Amery Diaries*, 21 Mar. 1939, 549.

66 R. J. Minney (ed.) *The Private Papers of Hore-Belisha*, London, Collins, 1960, 185–8, for an account of the decision making process behind this decision.

67 Headlam MSS, diary, 30 Mar. 1939, D/He/35.

68 *Notices of Motions*, 28 March 1939.

69 Barnes and Nicholson, *Amery Diaries*, 27 Mar. 1939, 549–50.

70 *Notices of Motions*, 29 March 1939.

71 *Notices of Motions*, 18 April 1939. It did provoke an amendment proclaiming the benefits of voluntarism and arguing conscription could not be introduced without an electoral mandate, but it only secured seven signatures.

72 From the cabinet: Halifax, Simon and Hore-Belisha; see Minney, *Papers of Hore-Belisha*, 187, 195, and B. Bond, *British Military Policy between the Two World Wars*, Oxford, Clarendon Press, 1980, 309–10. From parliamentarians: *The Times*, letters to editor 21, 23 Mar. 1939; Chamberlain MSS, Leo Amery to Neville Chamberlain, 24 Mar. 1939, NC7/2/89; Selborne MSS, Wolmer, Grigg and Amery tabled the motion on 18 Apr.. It secured sixty-five Tory signatures (Amery in memoirs claims nearly seventy: *My Political Life*, 311). *Amery Diaries*, 13, 18 Apr. 1939, 551; *Notices of Motions*, 18 Apr. 1939. For constituency demands: North Wiltshire CA, AGM 21 Apr. 1939, 2436/1; City of Leeds CA, AGM 21 Apr. 1939, 1. AGM minute book, 1937–56; Aldershot CA, central council, 15 Apr. 1939, 114M84/2; Horncastle CA, AGM 17 Apr. 1939, Misc.Dep.268/1.

73 *Hansard*, vol. 346, cols 1343–1464, 26 Apr. 1939; For the party reaction to its introduction see: North Hampshire CA, AGM 5 May 1939, NHCA/1/7; Sowerby CA, AGM 11 May 1939, CV3; Harborough CA, AGM 29 Apr. 1939, DE1170/4; SCA: eastern div., central exec. 3 May 1939, Acc.10424/49; Oxford University CA, 'A statement of the principles of new Conservatism', 1 June 1939, MS.Eng.hist.d.2042/1;

Winterton MSS, diary, 26 Apr. 1939, 1/44. For a military perspective see Bond, *Pownall Diaries*, 24 Apr. 1939, 201.

CHAPTER 6

1 The phrase 'phoney war' was American and it only came into British circulation later. At the time in Britain the period was known as the 'bore war' or 'strange war'. A. Calder, *The People's War: Britain, 1939–45*, London, Cape, 1969, 57.

2 Headlam MSS, diary, 26 Oct. 1939, D/He/35; C[onservative] P[arty] A[rchive], Douglas Hacking, 12 Sept. 1939, cited in 1940 annual report, North West Area council, 15 June 1940, ARE3/1/2; to a level these fears were not without justification. In spring 1940 there were fifty-one resolutions on the agenda of the Labour party conference calling for a termination of the by-election truce. Cited Addision, *Road to 1945: British Politics and the Second World War*, London, Cape, 1975, 58.

3 Derby MSS, Sir E. Ramsden to all CA chairmen, 23 Sept. 1939, 920DER(17)16/3.

4 I. McLaine, *Ministry of Morale: Home Front Morale and the Ministry of Information in World War Two*, London, Allen and Unwin, 1979, 46.

5 Northwich C[onservative] A[ssociation], chairman's advisory cttee 22 Sept. 1939, LOP1/1/4; Ayr Burghs CA, exec[utive] and finance cttee 21 Sept. 1939; Ealing CA, exec. 30 Sept. 1939, 1338/2; Barkston Ash CA, AGM 23 Apr. 1940.

6 Edinburgh North CA, women's exec., 2 Oct. 1939.

7 Hailes MSS, E. Deane (East Toxteth CA) to Buchan-Hepburn, 18 June 1940, HAIL1/4.

8 Addision, *Road to 1945*, 69.

9 B. Cartland, *Ronald Cartland*, London, Collins, 1942, 231; York MSS, diary, 31 Aug. 1939; Goodhart, *The 1922: The Story of the Conservative Backbenchers' Parliamentary Committee*, 93.

10 R. R. James, *Victor Cazalet: A Portrait*, London, Hamish Hamilton, 1976, 218–9; Birchall MSS, Frank Fremantle to J. D. Birchall, 15 July 1940, Box 33.

11 Hailes MSS, E. Deane to Buchan-Hepburn, 18 June 1940, HAIL1/4; Cartland, *Ronald*, 232, 238.

12 R. Tree, *When The Moon was High: Memoirs of Peace and War*, London, Macmillan, 1975, 92.

13 A. Duff Cooper, *Old Men Forget*, London, Hart-Davis, 1953, 262–76.

14 Emrys-Evans MSS, Richard Law to Evans, 30 Dec. 1939, Add.MS.58239 ff. 4–6; both these men would be called to government office when Churchill became PM.

15 Birchall MSS, Frank Fremantle to J. D. Birchall, 9 Feb., 15 July 1940, Box 33.

16 R. R. James (ed.) *Chips: The Diaries of Sir Henry Channon*, London, Weidenfeld and Nicolson, 1967, 4 Sept., 20 Sept. 1939, 217, 221.

17 Beamish MSS, autobiographical notes, 2 Sept. 1939, BEAM3/3; Headlam MSS, diary, 1–3 Sept. 1939, D/He/35.

18 Rich MSS, diary, 3–5 Sept. 1939, AJ217/35 for the reactions of civilians

to the declaration of war and the first air raids on London. Cazalet MSS, journal, 6 Sept. 1939, referring to 3 Sept..

19 The navy was involved in skirmishes, the most famous of which being the sinking of the *Graf Spee* in Dec. 1939, whilst the RAF confined themselves to dropping leaflets over Germany and the occasional bombing raid.

20 Birchall MSS, T. Inskip to J. D. Birchall, 27 Sept. 1939, Box 33.

21 Selborne MSS, Wolmer to Churchill, 6 Sept. 1939, MS.Eng.hist.d.450 f. 62.

22 Cilcennin MSS, Cranborne to J. P. L. Thomas, 29 Sept. 1939, Cilc.coll.27.

23 *Hansard: House of Commons Debates*, vol. 360, cols 1167–8, 7 May 1940.

24 Mass-Observation Archive, TB: file5/H, 'Somerset de Chair questionnaire and responses, Nov. 1939'.

25 Cartland, *Ronald*, 234, 250; Barkston Ash CA, AGM 2 Apr. 1940; Headlam MSS, diary, 14 Jan. 1940, D/He/36.

26 Mass-Observation Archive, FR: 125, 'Morale: summary of M-O reports submitted to Home Intelligence (Feb.–May 1940) and M-O morale reports dating back to Munich.

27 Mass-Observation Archive, TB: file5/H, 'Somerset de Chair questionnaire and responses, Nov. 1939', Shipdham branch.

28 Headlam MSS, diary, 10 Sept. 1939, D/He/35. The government announced on 8 Sept. that this was the timetable on which they were planning the war effort.

29 Selborne MSS, Wolmer to Churchill, 6 Sept. 1939, MS.Eng.hist.d.450 f. 62.

30 A. Roberts, *Eminent Churchillians*, London, Weidenfeld and Nicolson, 1994, 139.

31 J. Barnes and D. Nicholson (eds) *The Empire at Bay: The Leo Amery Diaries 1929–45*, London, Hutchinson, 1988, 27 Sept., 14 Nov. 1939, 573, 575; Chamberlain MSS, Clement Davies to Chamberlain, 14 Dec. 1939, NC7/11/32/62.

32 Barnes and Nicholson, *Amery Diaries*, 14 Nov. 1939, 11 Jan., 13 Mar., 4 Apr. 1940; surprisingly Boothby's biographer makes little reference to this, merely mentioning in passing the existence of the group and a little later citing a retrospective interview Boothby gave which explains Clement Davies' role in Chamberlain's fall, R. R. James, *Boothby: A Portrait*, London, Curtis and Hodder, 1991, 232, 236, 245.

33 Barnes and Nicholson, *Amery Diaries*, editorial, 562. It was this committee that proposed making Amery Minister for Economics.

34 Emrys-Evans MSS, Lord Salisbury to Evans, 31 Mar. 1940, Add.MS.58245.

35 Emrys-Evans MSS, Evans to Amery, 1 July 1954, Add.MS.58247 f.22.

36 Selborne MSS, Salisbury to Wolmer, 1 May 1940, MS.Eng.hist.d.451 f.111.

37 Barnes and Nicholson, *Amery Diaries*, 16 Apr. 1940, 587.

38 Barnes and Nicholson, *Amery Diaries*, editorial, 567.

39 For historical analysis of the British declaration of war see R. A. C. Parker, 'The British government and the coming of war with Germany', in M. D. R. Foot (ed.) *War and Society*, London, Paul Elek, 1973, 1–16; C. Hill, *Cabinet Decisions in Foreign Policy: The British Experience*

October 1938–June 1941, Cambridge, Cambridge University Press, 1991, 85–99.

40 Headlam MSS, diary, 2 Sept. 1939, D/He/35.

41 For an analysis of the decision making process taking place during the rejection of these terms see Hill, *Cabinet Decisions*, ch. 5, 100–45. For Chamberlain's parliamentary rejection see *Hansard*, vol. 352, cols 563–8, 12 Oct. 1939.

42 M. Gilbert, *Finest Hour: Winston S. Churchill: VI: 1939–41*, London, Heinemann, 1983, 27–8. See also L. Field, *Bendor: The Golden Duke of Westminster*, London, Weidenfeld and Nicolson, 1983, 260–4. The issue of Westminster's pro-German sentiments is virtually ignored in Ridley's account, occupying only one page out of two hundred: G. Ridley, *Bend'Or: Duke of Westminster: A Personal Memoir*, London, Robin Clark, 1985, 144. The cabinet was being briefed on these meetings by Hankey with information from Lord Mottistone, S. Roskill, *Hankey: Man of Secrets*, vol. 3, London, Collins, 1974, 431.

43 John Colville, *The Fringes of Power: The Downing Street Diaries, 1939–55*, London, Hodder and Stoughton, 1985, 9 Feb. 1940, 94–5; Brocket was arguing in a similar manner: see Addison, *Road to 1945*, 71; For Buccleuch's pre-war 'enthusiasm' see Butler MSS, Buccleuch to Rab Butler, 24 Apr. 1939, RABG10 f.3.

44 For an recent study of the persistence of the 'peace' lobby and its links with the City and big business, see S. Newton, *Profits of Peace: The Political Economy of Anglo-German Appeasement*, Oxford, Clarendon Press, 1996, especially 151–7.

45 Brooks MSS, 'draft letter', Rothermere to Chamberlain, 25 Sept. 1939 – never sent. The letter had been drafted by Collin Brooks and he recorded his 'great relief' that the letter was not sent.

46 Bower MSS, Leo Amery to Robert Bower, 7 Oct. 1939, 1/4.

47 Goodhart, *The 1922*, 94.

48 Barnes and Nicholson, *Amery Diaries*, 4 Oct. 1939, 575; CPA, 1922 Committee, 4 Oct. 1939, CPA/1922CMMTEE.

49 *Hansard*, vol. 339, col. 107, 3 Oct. 1938; *Bristol Evening Post*, 7 Nov. 1938.

50 Bristol West CA, special exec. 15 Dec. 1939 – these resolutions were confirmed by the AGM 6 May 1940, 38036/BW/2(b).

51 Bristol West CA, special exec. 22 May 1944, 38036/BW/1(b); Culverwell to Down-Shaw, 6 June 1944, 38036/BCA/1(a).

52 S[cottish] C[onservative Party] A[rchive], western association, div. council 15 Dec. 1939, Acc.10424.

53 Barkston Ash CA, AGM 2 Apr. 1940.

54 Maidstone CA, AGM 9 Mar. 1940, A3/1/2.

55 For the reactions of Ramsay's Peebles Conservative Association, see: *Peeblesshire Advertiser*, 16, 17 Mar. 1940; *The Times*, 24 May 1940, 25 Mar., 4 Aug. 1941; *Hardwick Express*, 29 Sept. 1944, chairman of CA: 'so far as we are concerned, Captain Ramsay has no longer anything to do with us'.

56 For further details of the Tyler Kent affair, see: R. Thurlow, *Fascism in Britain: A History, 1918–85*, Oxford, Blackwell, 1987, 194–5; R. Bearse and A. Read, *Conspirator: Untold Story of Churchill, Roosevelt and Tyler*

Kent, London, Macmillan, 1992.

57 A. W. H. Ramsay, *The Nameless War*, Devon, Britons Publishing, 1952, 93–111, quotes 104–5. These MPs were Harold Mitchell, Charles Kerr and Albert Edmondson. See Newton, *Profits of Peace*, 153.

58 J. S. Wiggan, 'The link', St Andrews, MA dissertation, 1985.

59 R. Griffiths, *Fellow Travellers of the Right: Enthusiasts for Nazi Germany, 1933–9*, London, Constable, 1980, 371–2. He suggests that internment only removed the eccentrics and that the real sympathisers (mainly from the aristocracy) remained free for the duration of the war.

60 Headlam MSS, diary, 14 Jan. 1940, D/He/36.

61 McLaine, *Ministry of Morale*, 34–5.

62 Bower MSS, Leo Amery to Robert Bower, 7 Oct. 1939, 1/4.; CPA, 1922 Committee, 20 Sept. (Spears), 4 Oct. 1939 (Loftus and Spens), CPA/1922CMMTEE; Glyn MSS, 'Notes on general British military position', Nov. 1939, D/Egl 0127/3.

63 CPA, 1922 Committee, 11 Oct. 1939, CPA/1922CMMTEE.

64 Mass-Observation Archive, TB: file 5/H, 'Somerset de Chair questionnaire and responses, Nov. 1939'.

65 Barnes and Nicholson, *Amery Diaries*, 4 Sept. 1939, 571.

66 Crookshank MSS, diary, 3 Sept. 1939, Ms.Eng.hist.d.360 f.30; Wallace MSS, diary, 3 Sept. 1939, MS.Eng.hist.c.495; Emrys-Evans MSS, Evans to James Stuart, 12 Feb. 1940, Add.MS.58248 f. 74; Richard Law to Evans, 13 Sept. 1939, Add.MS.58239 ff. 2–3.

67 Barnes and Nicholson, *Amery Diaries*, 4 Apr. 1940, 585.

68 Emrys-Evans MSS, Amery to Evans, 10 Apr. 1940, Add.MS.58245; R. Cockett, *The Twilight of Truth: Chamberlain and the Manipulation of the Press*, London, Weidenfeld and Nicolson, 1989, 150.

69 *The Times*, 12 Apr. 1940.

70 Headlam MSS, diary, 5 Dec. 1939, D/He/35.

71 Mass-Observation Archive, TB: file5/H, 'Somerset de Chair questionnaire and responses, Nov. 1939', Swaffham, Nordelph; York CA, exec. 20 Oct. 1939, Acc156/22.

72 James, *Cazalet*, 218–9.

73 Ronald Cartland to Lady Colefax, cited Cartland, *Ronald*, 244.

74 C. Thornton-Kemsley, *Through Winds and Tides*, Montrose, Standard Press, 1974, 116–19.

75 Cartland, *Ronald*, 243.

76 Cilcennin MSS, Cranborne to J. P. L. Thomas, 29 Sept. 1939, Cilc.coll.27.

77 McLaine, *Ministry of Morale*, 45.

78 Mass-Observation Archive, TB: file 5/H, 'Somerset de Chair questionnaire and responses, Nov. 1939', Dewer.

79 Barnes and Nicholson, *Amery Diaries*, 22 Nov. 1939, 576.

80 Addision, *Road to 1945*, 65–6, citing Nancy Astor to Lord Lothian, 23 Nov. 1939.

81 Wallace MSS, diary, 26 Sept. 1939, MS.Eng.hist.c.495.

82 Mass-Observation Archive, TB: file 5/H, 'Somerset de Chair questionnaire and responses, Nov. 1939'.

83 For an analysis of the press demands over 'war aims', and how either the editors or proprietors of some papers suppressed criticisms of the government, see Cockett, *Twilight of Truth*, 152–9.

84   Headlam MSS, diary, 24 Sept. 1939, D/He/35.
85   Selborne MSS, Wolmer to Editor, *Aldershot News*, 16 Oct. 1939, MS.Eng.hist.c.1014 ff. 157–60.
86   Lord Lloyd, *The British Case*, London, Eyre and Spottiswode, 1939, quotes 13, 44. Includes an introduction by Lord Halifax.
87   CPA, 1922 Committee, 25 Oct. 1939, CPA/1922CMMTEE.
88   Ayr Burghs CA, central council, Sept. 1939.
89   Selborne MSS, Wolmer to Editor, *Aldershot News*, 16 Oct. 1939, MS.Eng.hist.c.1074 ff. 157–60.
90   Barkston Ash CA, AGM 2 Apr. 1940 – emphasis added.
91   Gilbert, *Churchill, 1939–41*, 50, 81.
92   D. J. Wendan, 'Churchill, radio and cinema', in R. Blake and R. Wm Louis (eds) *Churchill*, Oxford, Oxford University Press, 1993, 222; Colville, *Diaries*, 12, 13 Nov. 1939, 56.
93   *Hansard*, vol. 360, col. 1168, 7 May 1940.
94   McLaine, *Ministry of Morale*, 142.
95   D. Dilks (ed.) *The Diaries of Sir Alexander Cadogan*, London, Cassell, 1973, 23 Sept. 1939, 219.
96   A. Roberts, *Holy Fox: A Biography of Lord Halifax*, London, Weidenfeld and Nicolson, 1991, 185.
97   Wallace MSS, diary, 18 Mar. 1940, MS.Eng.hist.c.496.
98   Northern Counties Area, AGM 6 Apr. 1940, NRO3303/1; City of Leeds CA, AGM 6 May 1940; Barkston Ash CA, AGM 2 Apr. 1940; Mass-Observation Archive, TB: file5/H, 'Somerset de Chair questionnaire and responses, Nov. 1939'.
99   Chamberlain MSS, Neville to Ida, 23 Apr. 1939, NC18/1/1095.
100 Cazalet MSS, journal, 11 Oct. 1939.
101 *Us: Mass-Observation's Weekly Intelligence Service*, 6, 9 Mar. 1940, 44. The original questionnaire is to be found in Mass-Observation Archive, TB: file5/H, 'Somerset de Chair questionnaire and responses, Nov. 1939'. In addition, Eden 36 per cent, Halifax 32 per cent, Kingsley Wood 18 per cent, Morrison and Hore-Belisha 10 per cent each, Chatfield, Simon and Neville Henderson 3 per cent each. Rather surprisingly a number of the responses included the name of the former ambassador to Berlin, Nevile Henderson!
102 Cockett, *Twilight of Truth*, 158.
103 Headlam MSS, diaries, 1 Oct. 1939, 20 Jan. 1940, D/He/35–6; Wallace MSS, diary, 24 Oct. 1939, MS.Eng.hist.c.495.
104 Makins MSS, diary, 14 Apr. 1940.
105 Gilbert, *Churchill, 1939–41*, 51.
106 Wallace MSS, diary, 11 Oct. 1939, MS.Eng.hist.c.495; an assumption shared by Cazalet, who felt the broadcast and House of Commons speech were a 'tremendous success', Cazalet MSS, journal, 11 Oct. 1939; also Cartland, *Ronald*, 232.
107 Brooks MSS, journal, 11 Apr. 1940.
108 Cockett, *Twilight of Truth*, 151–2.
109 Birchall MSS, Frank Fremantle to J. D. Birchall, 1 Mar. 1940, Box 33; the secretary of Shipdham Conservatives considered Greenwood and Herbert had adopted a 'reasonable and helpful' approach to the war. See Mass-Observation Archive, TB: file 5/H, 'Somerset de Chair question-

naire and responses, Nov. 1939'. De Chair's seat was a safe Conservative constituency. Branch secretaries were asked if any increase in Labour support was perceived: 28 per cent said less, 3 per cent more, and 60 per cent politics forgotten/no change. They were also asked if they favoured a coalition government: 57 per cent said no, 14 per cent yes, 23 per cent indifferent. For analysis of Labour's activities during the phoney war period see S. Brooke, *Labour's War: The Labour Party during the Second World War*, Oxford, Clarendon Press, 1992, 34–51; for the Conservative party's response to social reform during the war see H. Kopsch, 'The approach of the Conservative party to social policy during World War Two', London University, PhD, 1970.

110 See Ralph Glyn's comments cited Addision, *Road to 1945*, 68.
111 Wallace MSS, diary, 12 Nov. 1939, MS.Eng.hist.c.495.
112 Chamberlain MSS, Neville to Ida, 17 Dec. 1938, NC18/1/1080.
113 Emrys-Evans MSS, Cranborne to Evans, 7 May 1940, Add.MS.58240 ff. 32–4. In fact, this view had been articulated by a leader in *The Times*, 16 Apr. 1940, which angered Chamberlain. See James, *Chips*, 16 Apr. 1940, 241.
114 Colville, *Diaries*, 9, 14, 17 Nov., 28 Dec. 1939, 56–8, 67.
115 For further historical analysis of this episode, see A. J. Trythall, 'The downfall of Leslie Hore-Belisha', *Journal of Contemporary History*, 16, 3 (1981), 391–411.
116 Colville, *Diaries*, 4 Jan. 1940, 75.
117 Rich MSS, diary, 16 Jan. 1940, AJ217/36.
118 Colville, *Diaries*, 16 Jan. 1940, 80; Cazalet MSS, journal, 6, 9 Jan. 1940.
119 Headlam MSS, diary, 12 Nov. 1937, D/He/33.
120 Headlam MSS, diary, 3 Feb. 1940, D/He/36.
121 Headlam MSS, John Dill to Headlam, 27 Jan. 1940, D/He/135/74.
122 *Truth*, 30 June 1937, 12, 19 Jan. 1940. Cockett, *Twilight of Truth*, who uncovered much of this rather sordid episode, refers to the 12 Jan. 1940 article 11 but has misdated it as 4 Jan. See also A. J. Kushner, 'Clubland, cricket tests and alien internment, 1939–40', *Immigrants and Minorities*, 11, 3 (1992), 80–2. For attacks on Churchill and Eden see *Truth*, 27 Oct. 1939, 8 Mar. 1940.
123 Cockett, *Twilight of Truth*, 169.
124 Makins MSS, diary, 19 May 1938.
125 James, *Chips*, 8 Jan. 1940, 229; B. Bond (ed.) *Chief of Staff: The Diaries of Lieutenant-General Sir Henry Pownall*, London, Leo Cooper, 1972, 11 Jan. 1940, 275.
126 Cazalet MSS, journal, 5 Jan. 1940.
127 Headlam MSS, diary, 6 Jan. 1940, D/He/36.
128 Emrys-Evans MSS, Evans to Eden, 7 Jan. 1940, Add.MS.58242 f. 20.
129 James, *Chips*, 6 Jan. 1940, 228.
130 Birchall MSS, Frank Fremantle to J. D. Birchall, 9 Feb. 1940, Box 33.
131 Crookshank MSS, diary, 13 Feb. 1940, MS.Eng.hist.d.360 f.52; Colville, *Diaries*, 19 Mar. 1940, 99.
132 Wallace MSS, diary, 19 Mar. 1940, MS.Eng.hist.c.946.
133 Crookshank MSS, diary, 4 Apr. 1940, MS.Eng.hist.d.360 f.55; Wallace MSS, diary, 3 Apr. 1940, MS.Eng.hist.c.496.

134 Selborne MSS, letter to *Aldershot Times*, 13 May 1940 – minute on draft, MS.Eng.hist.c.1015 ff.46–9.
135 Chamberlain MSS, Neville to Ida, 30 Mar. 1940, NC18/1/1148.
136 Emrys-Evans MSS, diary, 2 May 1940, Add.MS.58246 ff.123–9.
137 City of Leeds CA, AGM 6 May 1940.
138 Northern Counties Area, AGM 6 Apr. 1940, NRO33033/1; Headlam MSS, diaries, Sept. 1939–May 1940 *passim*, D/He/35–6.
139 Mass-Observation Archive, FR: 125, 'Morale: summary of M-O reports submitted to Home Intelligence', Feb.–May 1940; FR: 95, 'Norway crisis, 3 May 1940' noted 'two marked tendencies: 1. a steady and rapid increase in pessimism, 2. a soaring distrust of news channels'.
140 Emrys-Evans MSS, diary, 7 May 1940, Add.MS.58246 ff. 123–9.
141 Chamberlain MSS, Neville to Hilda, 4 May 1940, NC18/1/1153.
142 *Hansard,* vol. 360, col. 1106, 7 May 1940; Wallace MSS, diary, 7 May 1940, MS.Eng.hist.c.946.
143 *Hansard*, vol. 360, cols 1140–50, quotes, cols 1141, 1146, 1150, 7 May 1940.
144 *Hansard*, vol. 360, cols 1178–91, 7 May 1940.
145 Crookshank MSS, diary, 7 May 1940, MS.Eng.hist.d.360; Wallace MSS, diary, 7 May 1940, MS.Eng.hist.c.496.
146 *Hansard*, vol. 360, cols 1106–16, (Page-Croft), 1151–60, (Southby), 7 May 1940.
147 Wallace MSS, diary, 7 May 1940, MS.Eng.hist.c.496.
148 James, *Cazalet*, 226.
149 James, *Cazalet*, 226; Addison, *The Road to 1945*, 98, fn. 75.
150 Emrys-Evans MSS, diary, 8 May 1940, Add.MS.58246.
151 Emrys-Evans MSS, Evans to James Stuart, 12 Feb. 1940, Add.MS.58248 f. 74.
152 Emrys-Evans MSS, Evans to Eden, 17 March 1940, Add.MS.58242 ff. 25–32.
153 *The Times*, 15 May 1940.
154 James, *Cazalet*, 226.
155 James, *Chips*, 8 May 1940, 246.
156 Cazalet MSS, journal, 9 May 1940.
157 *Hansard*, vol. 360, cols 1265–96, 8 May 1940.
158 James, *Chips*, 8 May 1940, 246. Tate withdrew the bet.
159 *Hansard*, vol. 360, col. 1266, 8 May 1940.
160 *Hansard*, vol. 360, col. 1301, 8 May 1940.
161 James, *Chips*, 8 May 1940, 246–7.
162 Waterhouse diary, 9 May 1940, cited Roberts, *Eminent Churchillians*, 145.
163 K. Feiling, *Life of Neville Chamberlain*, London, Macmillan, 1946, 303.
164 A. Howard, *Rab: The Life of R. A. Butler*, London, Cape, 1987, 94.
165 Tree, *Memoirs*, 114. Most probably Archibald Southby, a member of the RYS and a whip 1935–7.
166 James, *Chips*, 13 May 1940, 252.
167 Selborne MSS, Richard Law to Wolmer, 22 June 1940, MS.Eng.hist.c.1015 f.53.
168 Northwich CA, exec. 23 May 1940, LOP1/1/4; Northern Area Union, joint meeting, 5 Oct. 1940, NRO3303/1.
169 Selborne MSS, *Aldershot Times*, 31 May 1940, MS.Eng.hist.c.1015 f.52.

170 Chamberlain MSS, memo. from General Director, Robert Topping, to Chairman (Central Office), 26 June 1940, 3, NC8/21/19.
171 Birchall MSS, Frank Fremantle to J. D. Birchall, 15 July 1940, Box 33. This view is not shared by Roberts, *Eminent Churchillians*, 137–210; Roberts argues that Churchill's position was not secure amongst Conservatives until May 1941. The account often fails to distinguish between critics who were Conservatives and others who were coalition supporters. In addition it freely labels MPs as 'Chamberlainites' when a number certainly were not, e.g. Makins.
172 Duff Cooper, *Old Men Forget*, 188. James Stuart, at this time deputy whip, describes in his memoirs an incident in which a number of MPs were summoned to the Smoking Room to await the PM's visit and the awkwardness of the situation as the backbenchers sought to conduct a conversation on fly-fishing – Chamberlain's passion. Viscount Stuart, *Within the Fringe*, London, Bodley Head, 1967, 83.

CONCLUSION

1 R. T. McKenzie, *British Political Parties: The Distribution of Power within the Conservative and Labour Parties*, London, Heinemann, 1963.
2 S. Ball, *Baldwin and the Conservative Party*, London, Yale University Press, 1988, xv–xvi.
3 Ball, *Baldwin, passim*.
4 *The Times*, 1 June 1937.
5 R. J. Minney (ed.) *The Private Papers of Hore-Belisha*, diary, 25 May 1937, 16.
6 Chamberlain MSS, Neville to Hilda, 27 Mar. 1938, NC18/1/1043.
7 N. Nicolson (ed.) *The Diaries and Letters of Harold Nicolson*, London, Collins, 1966, 11 Apr. 1939 (Harold Macmillan), 397; A. J. P. Taylor (ed.) *Off the Record: W. P. Crozier: Political Interviews, 1933–44*, London, Macmillan, 1973, 156, interview with Bracken, 29 Mar. 1940.
8 C[onservative] P[arty] A[rchive], D. Clark to J. Ball, 28 Nov. 1938, CRD1/7/35.
9 *Hansard: House of Commons Debates*, vol. 360, col. 1317 (Courthorpe), 8 May 1940.
10 Chamberlain MSS, Neville to Ida, 25 May 1940, NC18/1/1158.

BIBLIOGRAPHY
PRIMARY MATERIAL

N.B. for secondary sources consulted please refer to the notes.

Archives

Conservative Leadership

Avon [Anthony Eden] MSS *Birmingham University Library*
R. A. Butler MSS *Trinity College, Cambridge*
Caldecote [Thomas Inskip] MSS *Churchill College, Cambridge*
Neville Chamberlain MSS *Birmingham University Library*
Harry Crookshank MSS *Bodleian Library, Oxford*
Walter Elliot MSS *National Library of Scotland*
David Margesson MSS *Churchill College, Cambridge*
Donald Somervell MSS *Bodleian Library, Oxford*
Euan Wallace MSS *Bodleian Library, Oxford*
Edward Winterton MSS *Bodleian Library, Oxford*

Conservative MPs, candidates and Peers

Vyvyan Adams MSS *BLPES*
Altrincham [Edward Grigg] MSS *Bodleian Library, Oxford*
Ashley [Mount-Temple] MSS *Southampton University*
Lord and Lady Astor MSS *Reading University Library*
Duke and Duchess of Atholl MSS *Blair Atholl Castle*
T. P. H. Beamish MSS *Churchill College, Cambridge*
Lord Beaverbrook MSS *House of Lords Record Office*
John Birchall MSS *Courtesy of Birchall family*
Robert Bower MSS *Churchill College, Cambridge*
Victor Cazalet MSS *Courtesy Sir Edward Cazalet*
Cilcennin [J. P. L. Thomas] MSS *Dyfed Record Office, Carmarthen*
17th Earl of Derby MSS *Liverpool Record Office*
Paul Emrys-Evans MSS *British Library*
Ralph Glyn MSS *Berkshire Record Office*
Hailes [Patrick Buchan-Hepburn] MSS *Churchill College, Cambridge*

Patrick Hannon MSS *House of Lords Record Office*
Cuthbert Headlam MSS *Durham Record Office*
Arthur Heneage MSS *Lincolnshire Archives*
Roger Keyes MSS *British Library*
Ernest Makins MSS *Courtesy of Lord Sherfield*
Edward Ruggles-Brise MSS *Courtesy of Sir John Ruggles-Brise*
2nd Earl of Selborne MSS *Bodleian Library, Oxford*
3rd Earl of Selborne [Lord Wolmer] MSS *Bodleian Library, Oxford*

Conservative Party Officials

J. R. Almond MSS *Lancashire Record Office*

Party organisation

National:
Conservative Party Archive (CPA) *Bodleian Library, Oxford*
Scottish Conservative Archive (SCA) *National Library of Scotland*

Regional (Bodleian Library, Oxford, unless stated otherwise)

Cornwall Provincial Area
Eastern Scotland *National Library of Scotland*
Essex and Middlesex Provincial Area
Northern Area *Northumberland Record Office*
North Western Area
South Eastern Provincial Area
Wessex
Western
Western Scotland *National Library of Scotland*

Local Associations (by regional area)

Metropolitan (London) Area

Clapham (Wandsworth) *BLPES*
Kennington (Lambeth) *BLPES*
London, *City of Westminster Public Library*
Norwood, *Lambeth Archives*
St George's Hanover, *Westminster Public Library*

Wessex Area

Aldershot, *Hampshire Record Office*
Dorset, *West Dorset Record Office*
Newbury, *Berkshire Record Office*

North Hampshire, *Bodleian Library, Oxford*
North Wiltshire (Chippenham), *Wiltshire Record Office*
Salisbury, *Wiltshire Record Office*
South Oxfordshire, *Oxfordshire Archives*
Winchester, *Hampshire Record Office*

West Midlands Area

Bewdley, *Worcester Record Office, St Helens Branch*
Birmingham, City of *Birmingham Central Library*
Edgbaston, *Birmingham Central Library*
Ladywood, *Birmingham Central Library*
Stafford, *Staffordshire Record Office*
Stone, *Staffordshire Record Office*
Warwick and Leamington, *Warwickshire Record Office*
Worcester, *Worcester Record Office*

Wales

Cardiff Central, *National Library of Wales*
Cardiff South, *National Library of Wales*
Llandaff and Barry, *National Library of Wales*
Monmouth, *National Library of Wales*
Pembrokeshire, *Pembroke Record Office*
Wrexham, *National Library of Wales*

East Midlands Area

Bosworth, *Leicestershire Record Office*
Derby, *Derbyshire Record Office*
Harborough, *Leicestershire Record Office*
Horncastle, *Lincoln Archives*
Rushcliffe, *Nottinghamshire Record Office*
South Nottingham, *Nottinghamshire Record Office*
West Derbyshire, *Derbyshire Record Office*

North Western Area

Accrington, *Manchester University Library*
Blackpool, *Lancashire Record Office*
Clitheroe, *Lancashire Record Office*
Darwen, *Lancashire Record Office*
Fylde (as part of Almond MSS), *Lancashire Record Office*
Middleton, Prestwich and Chadderton, *Lancashire Record Office*
Northwich, *Chester Record Office*
Waterloo, *Lancashire Record Office*

Essex and Middlesex Area

Chelmsford, *Essex Record Office*
Ealing Greater, *London Record Office*
West Essex (Epping), *Essex Record Office*

South Eastern Area

Chichester, *West Sussex Record Office*
Guildford, *Surrey Record Office*
Maidstone, *Kent Record Office*
Gravesend, *Kent Record Office*
Reigate, *Surrey Record Office*

Northern Area

Stockton and Thornaby, *Durham Record Office*
Tynemouth, *Tyne and Wear Archives*
West Newcastle, *Tyne and Wear Archives*

Yorkshire Area

Barkston Ash, *West Yorks Archives, Leeds*
Bradford Nat. Lib. Assoc., *West Yorks Archives, Bradford*
Bradford, City of *West Yorks Archives, Bradford*
Eccleshall, *Sheffield Archives*
Hallam, *Sheffield Archives*
Leeds, City of, *West Yorks Archives, Leeds*
Sheffield, City of *Sheffield Archives*
Sowerby, *Calderdale District Archives, Halifax*
West Leeds, *West Yorks Archives, Leeds*
York, *York Archives*

Western Area

Bristol, *Bristol Record Office*
North Cornwall, *Cornwall Record Office*
Penryn and Falmouth, *Cornwall Record Office*
Plymouth Sutton, *West Devon Record Office*
South East Cornwall, *Cornwall Record Office*
West Bristol, *Bristol Record Office*

Eastern Area

Ipswich, *Suffolk Record Office*
Bury St Edmunds (branch), *Suffolk Record Office*
Norwich, *Norfolk Record Office*

Universities

Oxford University, *Bodleian Library, Oxford*

Scotland

Ayr Burghs, *Ayr Conservative Association*
Bute and North Ayrshire, *Ayr Conservative Association*
Edinburgh North, *Edinburgh City Archives*
Glasgow, City of, *National Library of Scotland*
Inverness, *Inverness Conservative Association*
Kinross and West Perth, *North Tayside Conservative Association*
Stirling, *Stirling Conservative Association*

Conservative Agent's Organisations (Bodleian Library, Oxford unless stated otherwise)

National Association of Conservative and Unionist Women Organisers
National Society of Conservative Agents, *Westminster Public Library*
Metropolitan Conservative Agents Association *BLPES*
Wessex Area Agents Society
Wales and Monmouthshire Conservative and Unionist Women's Organisers
West Midlands Area Conservative and Unionist Women's Organisers
East Midlands Agents Association, *Derby Record Office*
Scottish Agents Association, *Ayr Conservative Association*

Miscellaneous Archival Material

Collin Brooks MSS *Courtesy of the Brooks family*
Samuel Rich MSS *Southampton University Archive*
Mass-Observation MSS *Sussex University Library*
'Documents on Rearmament' *Southampton University Library* (copies of originals from Public Record Office)

Index

ÃÃÃÃÃÃÃÃÃ

ÃÃÃÃÃÃ.